THE ESSENTIAL

# KERNER
# COMMISSION
# REPORT

# THE ESSENTIAL
# KERNER COMMISSION REPORT

---

EDITED AND INTRODUCED BY

## Jelani Cobb

with Matthew Guariglia

LIVERIGHT PUBLISHING CORPORATION
A Division of W. W. Norton & Company
*Independent Publishers Since 1923*

For information about permission to reproduce selections from this book,
write to Permissions, Liveright Publishing Corporation, a division of
W. W. Norton & Company, Inc., 500 Fifth Avenue, New York, NY 10110

For information about special discounts for bulk purchases, please contact
W. W. Norton Special Sales at specialsales@wwnorton.com or 800-233-4830

Manufacturing by LSC Communications, Harrisonburg
Production manager: Anna Oler

Library of Congress Cataloging-in-Publication Data

Names: United States. National Advisory Commission on Civil Disorders, author. |
Cobb, William Jelani, editor, author of introduction. | Guariglia, Matthew, editor.
Title: The essential Kerner Commission report / edited and introduced by Jelani Cobb,
with Matthew Guariglia.
Other titles: Report of the National Advisory Commission on Civil Disorders. |
Kerner Commission report
Description: First edition. | New York : Liveright Publishing Corporation, [2021] |
Includes bibliographical references and index.
Identifiers: LCCN 2021021164 | ISBN 9781631498923 (paperback) |
ISBN 9781631498930 (epub)
Subjects: LCSH: Race riots—United States—History—20th century. |
Police brutality—United States—Case studies. | Urban poor—United States. |
African Americans—Social conditions—20th century. | African Americans—
Economic conditions—20th century. | United States—Race relations.
Classification: LCC HV6477 .U54 2021 | DDC 363.32/30973—dc23
LC record available at https://lccn.loc.gov/2021021164

Liveright Publishing Corporation, 500 Fifth Avenue, New York, N.Y. 10110
www.wwnorton.com

W. W. Norton & Company Ltd., 15 Carlisle Street, London W1D 3BS

1 2 3 4 5 6 7 8 9 0

*For Lenox, my bright star in the night sky.*

# CONTENTS

Introduction by Jelani Cobb      ix

## THE ESSENTIAL KERNER COMMISSION REPORT

*The following table of contents is a redacted
version of the original contents page of
The Kerner Commission Report*

*Summary*      7
*Preface*      29

### Part I. What Happened?

CHAPTER 1    Profiles of Disorder      37
CHAPTER 2    Patterns of Disorder      87

### Part II. Why Did It Happen?

CHAPTER 4    The Basic Causes      137
CHAPTER 6    The Formation of the Racial Ghettos      141
CHAPTER 7    Unemployment, Family Structure and Social
Disorganization      156
CHAPTER 8    Conditions of Life in the Racial Ghetto      169

### Part III. What Can Be Done?

CHAPTER 11    Police and the Community      187
CHAPTER 12    Control of Disorder      218

CHAPTER 15    The News Media and the Disorders                235
CHAPTER 17    Recommendations for National Action             264

*Conclusion*                                                  275

Appendix: Frequently Asked Questions                         277
Additional Reading                                           285

# INTRODUCTION

---

## 1.

The findings of the Kerner Commission exist alongside those of the Warren and 9/11 Commissions among the handful of governmental reports whose historic import has outlived the moment in which they were issued. The *Warren Report*, intended to be the last word on the assassination of President John F. Kennedy, has been anything but, launching more inquiry and debate, not to mention conspiracy theories, in its wake than existed prior to its publication. The *9/11 Commission Report*, issued in the summer of 2004, traced the origins of the terrorist attacks that destroyed the World Trade Center, which had killed 2,753 people three years earlier. In so doing it became an essential guide to understanding the (ongoing) era of American politics that is defined by and continues to operate in response to the events of that indelible September morning.

The *Kerner Commission Report*, however, is different. The *Warren* and *9/11* reports are concerned with singular events, tragedies that have remained unique in either scale or kind since they were examined. They function as primary sources in history. The Kerner Commission, more formally known as The National Advisory Commission on Civil Disorders, details an extant problem, one that is defined by its redundancy. This was apparent even at the outset of the report's existence. When President Lyndon B. Johnson created the commission in July 1967 it was tasked with understanding what had happened up to that moment. Nearly two dozen uprisings or, in the antiseptic language of the report, "civil disorders," had occurred between 1964 and 1967, with the largest and most destructive taking place in the Watts neighborhood in Los Angeles over the course of five days in August 1965. The commission could not have known when it released its findings in March 1968 that it was issuing a preface, not a postscript. Martin Luther King Jr. was assassinated the following month, and more than one hundred American cities exploded into just the type of violence that the Kerner Commission had sought to understand if not prevent.

The proximity of the two events—the report's release and Martin Luther King's death—allowed for people to, over time, conflate them. It is not uncommon for people to believe that the Kerner Commission examined the unrest of *the entire sixties* rather than just the first installment of them. But the timing is important if only because the *Kerner Report* was fated, from the moment it reached shelves, to operate more crucially as a forecast than a review. We hear George Santayana's dictum that "those who fail to learn from history are doomed to repeat it" quoted with eye-rolling frequency. But Kerner establishes that it is possible for us to be entirely cognizant of history and repeat it anyway. Never was this more apparent than in the spring of 2020 when the half-century-old report reemerged as part of the stilted national dialogue on race, policing, and inequality.

Around 8:00 p.m. on the spring evening of May 25, 2020, four Minneapolis police officers arrested George Perry Floyd, a forty-six-year-old Black man, for allegedly passing a counterfeit twenty-dollar bill at a local convenience store. In the course of the arrest the part-time bouncer was handcuffed and beaten while inside a patrol car. The police assault culminated in Mr. Floyd lying on the pavement next to the car, still handcuffed, while a forty-four-year-old white officer, Derek Chauvin, cavalierly kneeled on his neck for at least eight minutes and forty-six seconds. Chauvin kept his knee in place despite the pleas of nearby observers who cried out that Floyd needed medical attention, despite Floyd's repeated assertions "I can't breathe" and "They'll kill me," while crying out to his deceased mother for help.[1] When Chauvin at long last relented, George Floyd was unconscious. He was taken by ambulance to a nearby hospital where he was pronounced dead.

The official police report on the matter made no mention of the methodical asphyxiation and falsely accused the deceased of having resisted arrest. This was immediately contradicted by a video of the incident taken by Darnella Frazier, a Black seventeen-year-old passerby, who happened upon the scene as she was walking her young cousin to the store.[2] The footage revealed a brutal, collaborative effort to extinguish George Floyd's life. At various points multiple officers were involved in compressing the victim's chest and airway.

The reaction to Floyd's death was immediate. The following day protesters began gathering on the 3700 block of Chicago Avenue South where Floyd had been killed. In a Facebook post the following morning, Jacob Frey, the mayor of Minneapolis, observed that "being black in America should not be a death sentence." He continued:

> For five minutes, we watched a white officer press his knee into a Black man's neck. Five minutes. When you hear someone calling for help, you're supposed to help. This officer failed in the most basic, human sense. What happened on Chicago and 38th last night is awful. It was traumatic. It serves as a reminder of how far we have to go.[3]

Later that day Minneapolis police chief Medaria Arradondo summarily fired all four officers, an action Frey described as "the right call." The following day he called for criminal charges.[4] The hasty bureaucratic reaction could not, however, stave off a tempest of outrage that was building even as the officers were being removed from the police force. By evening hundreds of protesters with signs saying "Stop Killing Black People" had swarmed into the streets of Minneapolis, gathering at the site of Floyd's death and at the Third Precinct, where the police officers who killed him had worked. The sustained protests turned sporadically violent with looting and arson in the area surrounding the site of Floyd's death, which would turn into a shrine shortly thereafter. On May 28, a multiracial crowd of demonstrators returned to the Third Precinct and, after police posted there abandoned the building, proceeded to burn it to the ground. Simultaneously, the video of Floyd's death circulated around the Internet, reaching a public that had been largely locked down due to the emergence of a coronavirus pandemic. The quarantine guaranteed that there would be few distractions to mitigate the horror of what transpired in Minneapolis. The video ricocheted around on social media, its gruesome content sparking new infernos of outrage wherever it landed. By May 2020 there were enough recordings of civilian deaths at the hands of police to nearly constitute a genre of video. A disproportionate number of those images depicted the deaths of African Americans. And as with any repetitive horror, there was growing concern on the part of activists and advocates that the public was becoming inured to the brutality being captured (largely on cell phones) with terrible redundancy. The images of George Floyd's death landed differently in part because of the excruciating length of the video—he was asphyxiated over the course of nearly nine minutes, an act that required profound and abhorrent levels of sadism from the police who committed it. This was one reason that the Floyd protests, some of them checkered with arson and looting, spread from an insulated locale on the south side of Minneapolis to Los Angeles, Atlanta, Washington, DC, New York, Salt Lake City, Chicago, Anchorage, and dozens of other American cities within days.

By the following week protests in some form had been reported in 350 cities in the United States, and the National Guard had been deployed to maintain the peace in twenty-three states.[5] In an inflammatory and flip reaction President Donald Trump tweeted in response to the spreading outrage, "When the looting starts the shooting starts"—the line was cribbed from Walter Headley, the notoriously racist Miami police chief who used it during hearings about crime in 1967. Trump also threatened to use the United States military to put down the demonstrations—which he later did in Portland (Oregon), Detroit, Cleveland, and Milwaukee. In another instance, federal agents, at the behest of the administration, were deployed to remove peaceful protesters from Lafayette Park, across the street from the White House. The agents fired tear gas and deployed a military helicopter to fly just above the heads of the crowd as an intimidation tactic. The footage was shocking—observers noted that the melee took place just ahead of the anniversary of the Tiananmen Square protests in China where, in 1989, the authoritarian government crushed prodemocracy demonstrations.[6] The vista of military force being used to suppress the First Amendment rights of American citizens was not only disturbing in the United States but around the world, where George Floyd's death was already being protested in more than sixty countries.

Some nine thousand Americans were arrested over the course of the two weeks that followed Floyd's death; hundreds of millions of dollars in arson damage and looting was sustained, and at least six people were killed. How, media, lawmakers, and the public seemed to wonder aloud, had the nation come to this point? The snap analyses pointed to the immediate context of George Floyd's death. In 2015, a Minneapolis police officer fatally shot Jamar Clark, an unarmed twenty-four-year-old African American who, eyewitnesses said, was handcuffed at the time of the shooting, though police disputed that claim. No charges were brought against the officers involved, resulting in an eighteen-day series of protests outside the city's Fifth Police Precinct. Then, in 2016, Philando Castile, an African American motorist, was pulled over by police in Falcon Heights, a suburb of Minneapolis. After Castile informed Officer Jeronimo Yanez that he was legally licensed to carry a firearm that was located in the car, Yanez panicked and shot Castile five times in front of his girlfriend and her four-year-old daughter. Yanez was later acquitted of manslaughter charges. The following year, Justine Damond, an unarmed woman, was shot and killed by an MPD officer named Mohamed Noor, an incident resulting in his firing and subsequent conviction on murder and manslaughter charges. Damond was the only white victim of the three incidents; Noor was the only Black officer and the only one convicted for a shooting.

In 2019 Bob Kroll, the president of the Police Officers Federation of Minneapolis, spoke at a rally for President Donald Trump, thanking him for putting an end to the "handcuffing and oppression of the police" and "letting the cops do their jobs." In the wake of Floyd's death Kroll noted that the incident "does look and sound horrible" and conceded that Chauvin should have been fired. The succinct explanation of what transpired on May 25 held that Floyd's death was the product of police departments in the Minneapolis area that had a troubled history with the use of deadly force. It was potentially aggravated by local police leadership. Kroll's comment suggested that rogue police felt emboldened by a president seemingly sympathetic to their way of operating.[7]

Yet here is where the fifty-two-year-old insights of Kerner remain most applicable. "Police are not merely the spark," the report tells us. They are part of the broader set of institutional relationships that enforce and re-create racial inequality. The problem is never simply the incident but the facts and factors that made such an incident possible, even predictable. Minneapolis, for instance, ranked in 2019 among the best places to live according to *US News & World Report*. But it was also among the cities with the worst socioeconomic disparities between Black residents and white residents, with a shocking, even for the United States, $47,000 gap separating the median household income of the two groups. Seventy-six percent of whites in the area owned their homes, only a quarter of Black residents did. The disparity is part of the long legacy of restrictive housing covenants—contracts prohibiting home sales to specific racial groups. In Minneapolis the practice began as early as 1910. In an op-ed published in the wake of the eruption in the streets, Betsy Hodges, the former mayor of Minneapolis, pointed to racial hypocrisy as a cause of the crisis.

> White liberals, despite believing we are saying and doing the right things, have resisted the systemic changes our cities have needed for decades. We have mostly settled for illusions of change, like testing pilot programs and funding volunteer opportunities. These efforts make us feel better about racism, but fundamentally change little for the communities of color whose disadvantages often come from the hoarding of advantage by mostly white neighborhoods.

Implicit within the *US News* ranking was the caveat that the Twin Cities area was among the best places *for white people* to live. Here again, *Kerner* is instructive. "Our Nation," it warned in 1968, "is moving toward two societies, one black, one white—separate and unequal." There were two realities in the Twin Cities, neatly calibrated by race.[8]

How did we get to this point, the nation asked? The *Kerner Commission Report* suggests that the more apt question should be how far the nation, in fact, has ever really diverged from such combustible moments. The most recent reports of state violence, the fiery reckonings in American streets, the often half-hearted scramble to attempt to understand the systemic failures and institutional rot that served as kindling for the latest conflagrations all seem like part of a grim recurrence of a chronic national predicament.

# 2.

*Kerner* has endured not simply for its prescience but also for the breadth of its analysis of the moment when it was conceived. The National Advisory Commission on Civil Disorders, which became more commonly known as the Kerner Commission—a reference to then-governor of Illinois Otto Kerner, who served as its chairman—was created by President Lyndon B. Johnson's Executive Order 11365 on July 28, 1967. The order was issued as entire stretches of the city of Detroit lay smoldering. The similarities to the Minneapolis protests are striking. On July 23, 1967, a police raid on an after-hours bar in Detroit sparked an explosion in which residents hurled rocks and bottles at police and culminated in a nearly week-long uprising marked by arson, looting, and forty-three deaths. Just eleven days earlier, the city of Newark had detonated following the assault on John Smith, a Black cab driver, by white police officers. The reactions in the community were immediate and incendiary. In the chaos of social retribution that ensued, twenty-six people were killed and hundreds more injured, while the city sustained an estimated ten million dollars in damage. The poet and activist Leroi Jones, later known as Amiri Baraka, a Newark native, was pulled over while driving and beaten beyond recognition by police amid the bedlam. He later captured the enraged chaos of the moment in the poem "Black People," which contained the memorable lines

> All the stores will open if you say the magic words
> The magic words are: Up against the wall motherfucker,
>     this is a stick up!

Charged with weapons possession, the poem was read by Judge Leon Kapp as evidence of Baraka's incorrigibility as he sentenced him to three years in prison, a conviction that was later overturned. Newark and Detroit were just the most notable of more than two dozen American cities that ignited in revolts in that summer of 1967.[9]

It appeared as though a valve of the city reservoir had been opened. An apocalyptic fury, the response to decades of discriminatory policy and centuries of racial exploitation, suddenly spewed out in American cities. President Johnson was more than a little familiar with this scenario. In March 1965, in response to the campaign for voting rights that had been orchestrated in Selma, Alabama, and the Bloody Sunday attacks upon marchers on the Edmund Pettus Bridge, Johnson declared his support for landmark legislation protecting the right of African Americans to vote. Having marshaled an almost historically unprecedented amount of political capital needed to see the bill through Congress—and in full awareness that protecting Black voting rights would fundamentally reorient American politics—Johnson signed the Voting Rights Act into law on August 6, 1965. Five days later police in Watts pulled over Marquette Frye, an African American driver, for reckless driving. In the argument that ensued police struck Frye several times, prompting residents to begin hurling objects at the officers. In what came to be known as the Watts riots, six days of civil unrest ensued, leaving in their wake thirty-four people dead and miles of Los Angeles pockmarked by charred ruins. The lessons were painfully obvious: even the iron-willed might of the president and his hugely Democratic Congress that had been required to pass the Civil Rights Act of 1964 and the Voting Rights Act in 1965 came a day late and a dollar short for Black residents, particularly those living in big cities, who had seethed for decades at the toll that racism took on their lives.

By 1967 Johnson had cause to worry that the anger vented in the streets of Watts had solidified into a zeitgeist that might find expression anywhere else in the country where the same conditions prevailed, and those conditions proliferated in many, many places throughout the United States. Creating the Kerner Commission can be viewed alongside the signing of the Civil Rights and Voting Rights acts and the initiation of the War on Poverty as cornerstones of Johnson's racial liberalism. Having grown up in Texas and seen firsthand the impact of the New Deal upon the lives of disadvantaged whites, his administration came to the recognition that Black America's fortunes had been vastly impacted by ways in which the welfare state had failed to include them. The willingness to both recognize this fact and act upon it made Johnson a renegade among his southern Democratic brethren, a point only further entrenched by his creation of the commission.

Johnson then charged the eleven-member Kerner panel with answering three questions: "What happened? Why did it happen? What can be done to prevent it from happening again and again?" These were Johnson's precise words. Addressing these questions, however, would mean answering dozens of subsidiary questions the roots of which lay deeply tangled in American history and public policy. The members themselves represented a cross section, albeit not a representative one, of domestic interests. Chaired by Kerner, the second-term Democratic governor of Illinois, the commission included two of his fellow Democratic elected officials, Congressman James Corman, the fourth-term representative of California's twenty-second district, and freshman senator Fred R. Harris of Oklahoma. They were joined by three Republicans, New York City mayor John V. Lindsay, Rep. William M. McCulloch of Ohio's fourth district, and Edward Brooke, the freshman Massachusetts lawmaker and the sole African American serving in the United States Senate at the time. By current standards the commission was overwhelmingly white (nine of the eleven members) and male (ten of eleven). Katherine Peden, the commerce secretary of Kentucky, was the sole female commission member. Roy Wilkins, the political moderate and executive director of the NAACP, joined Brooke as the only Black people at the table. In addition, I. W. Abel, president of the United Steelworkers of America, represented labor in the proceedings, and Herbert Jenkins, the police chief of Atlanta, Georgia, represented law enforcement. Charles Thornton, the CEO of Litton Industries, spoke for the manufacturing sector. Curiously, given the amount of detail the report devotes to analysis of the ways in which journalists covered the uprisings, there was no representative of print or broadcast media involved with the commission.

The charge given to them by Johnson involved a major reinvention of a wheel. While Johnson sought answers to immediate concerns, he was hardly the first politician to press for information on such matters. In 1919, the Chicago Race Riot—one of dozens that took place during the so-deemed Red Summer that year—spawned a commission that also sought to trace its origins and causes. In 1935 a riot broke out in Harlem, New York, following an allegation that police had killed a Puerto Rican teenager, and in its aftermath a commission explored the catalysts, finding them deeply rooted in segregation and inequality.

Similar incidents took place in Detroit and Harlem in 1943 and in Watts and Harlem again in 1965. Even as the Kerner team began its work, an analytic autopsy of the Newark riots that came to be known as the Lilly Report was already underway. Most of these reports struck similar themes. What differentiated the Kerner Commission from the outset was the historical scope of the investigations: the members were not seeking to understand a singular incident of disorder, but the phenomenon of rioting itself. Despite the heterogeneity of interests, if not the bipartisan backgrounds, of the members, the concluding report spoke with a strikingly unified voice about the problems that the various committee participants sought to understand. And that voice was an unabashedly integrationist one.

Their most immediate and salient observation was that, even though the police had been involved in these most volatile incidents, American cities were not simply facing a crisis of policing. Rather, police were simply the spear's tip of much broader systemic and institutional failures. As with Gunnar Myrdal's *An American Dilemma*, the landmark and exhaustive examination of "the Negro problem and modern democracy," that had been issued twenty-three years before, the *Kerner Report* noted that the "problem" had been, first and foremost, inaccurately diagnosed. The so-called Negro problem was, in fact, a *white* problem. Or, as the report noted in one of the oft-quoted sections of the summary, "What white Americans have never fully understood— but what the Negro can never forget—is that white society is deeply implicated in the ghetto. White institutions created it, white institutions maintain it, and white society condones it." The framing was significant, though not novel—W. E. B. Du Bois, who had died just five years earlier, E. Franklin Frazier, Abram Harris Jr., Horace Cayton Jr., and St. Clair Drake, among many other Black social scientists, had been making this point since the turn of the twentieth century. Yet here were people—white ones by and large—who had the ear of the most powerful policy makers in the nation cosigning this assessment. Myrdal's indictment helped frame the liberalism of the postwar United States; it's impossible to read *Kerner*, and particularly the expansive set of proposals throughout the text, and not suspect that a similar ambition was at play. The condition of the Negro was the truest barometer of American democracy and the test of the national creed. In a best-case scenario, *Kerner* would have become a kind of guidebook for the War on Poverty policies then being enacted by the Johnson administration.

In more practical terms, the commission recommended new community-based guidelines covering how police needed to interact with citizens of "the ghetto," as Black communities were dubiously classified in the report. It devoted an entire chapter to the ways in which justice should be administered in the course of riots; it suggested a national network of neighborhood task forces, local institutions that could bypass the bureaucracy and red tape of city administration and head off problems before they erupted into crises. It suggested "neighborhood service centers" to connect residents of these communities with job placement and other forms of assistance and proposed expanded municipal employment as a means of diminishing chronically high unemployment in these areas. Perceptively, its members suggested that the monochromatically white news media that reported on these uprisings was also a symptom of the bigger problem. That social upheaval that had been created by overwhelmingly white institutions and maintained by said white institutions was then investigated and reported upon by yet another overwhelmingly white institution constituted, in their assessment, a racial conflict of interest. They closed with a raft of specific recommendations for housing, employment, welfare, and education.

The validity of much, though not all, of this analysis has endured. The analysis of the plight of Black families (included in the full version of the report), for instance, was shot through with presumptions that would now be dismissed as patriarchal, carrying a strong whiff of the inherent condescension of Daniel P. Moynihan's widely derided 1965 study "The Black Family: A Case for National Action." Another glaring comment in the *Kerner Report*, this one tucked into the footnotes of the unabridged report in the chapter on "Control of Disorder," praised Deputy Chief Daryl F. Gates, who had been one of the field commanders during the Watts uprising, for his insights into policing. Gates went on to preside as chief during one of the most brutal periods in LAPD history, in which officers routinely used excessive force on Black residents. Those tactics hardly ended in the 1960s or even the 1980s, and became contributing factors to the Rodney King riots, larger and more devastating than those that had scarred Watts seventeen years before. If anything, Gates's so-called talents did more to foment many of the most egregious social disturbances of the era than prevent them from occurring in the first place.

Other portions of the report, particularly the chapter on "The Future of American Cities," were eerily prescient. This is not a good thing and becomes an important factor in why this work, written at a seemingly distant time in 1968, requires a close reading by twenty-first-century generations. In many ways American society did exactly what the report warned against and, as the serial disturbances of recent years suggest, reaped the consequences it predicted. The *Kerner Report*, having come out at the zenith of liberalism's influence in the twentieth century, becomes nothing less than a time capsule of the era, reflecting the intellectual thinking of an entire bygone generation. It makes a case for a decidedly liberal course of action regarding a national crisis with the presumption that this political mode, which had been more or less ascendant since the end of World War II, would remain regnant. The warnings issued in the report then were meant to alert the public to what would happen if the nation did not adopt a deeper, more committed, and truer form of liberalism that would enfranchise Black people as stakeholders. Yet it could not discern that so much of the American public had not the slightest appetite for such a form of liberalism. As would become quickly clear, they, the growing ranks of the "silent majority," wanted, in fact, much less liberalism in their lives and their government. This wave was just coming into view as the *Kerner Report* hit bookshelves in March 1968, but would come crashing ashore with a tidal force in the presidential election held only eight months later. In eight short but crucial months, the American political scene had changed ineradicably. Even then, there were signs that labor unions, a dominant force in American life, were weakening. A feeling was now coursing through white America that liberalism was no longer the creed of the future.

## 3.

The anarchic rage of protest produced one reaction within the liberal establishment and an equal but opposite one among conservatives. The violent disruptions at the Chicago Democratic Convention of 1968, creating some of the worst mayhem that had ever beset an urban political convention, handed former vice president Richard Nixon a political windfall. How could Democrats run the country, the campaign suggested, if they could not even run their own convention? Moreover, the reorientation of the axes of American politics that Johnson predicted as he signed the Voting Rights Act had begun to take effect. Having been trounced by Kennedy in Mississippi in 1960, the Republican Nixon now crushed the Democratic nominee Humphrey there eight years later. For decades the liberal wing of the Democratic Party had struggled to find equilibrium with its racially and socially conservative southern wing. The increasing southernization of the GOP meant that the voices of backlash had found a new avenue for expression. Moreover, the accelerating changes in the American economy—the first winds of deindustrialization, in particular—not only meant that it would be difficult to bring Black workers up to parity with their white counterparts, but presaged that whites would increasingly have a hard time keeping parity with their own economic expectations. This in turn further exacerbated white racial resentment. Implicit within the "law and order" appeals of the Nixon campaign was a rebuke to the uprisings of the era and to Democratic leadership that had presided over the cities where they occurred. (This criticism had so much potency that it would continue to be lobbed at Democratic politicians for decades, most notably in the spring of 2020 when the Trump administration assailed the mostly Democratic mayors of cities where rioting took place.)[10] As the historian Elizabeth Hinton has argued, the Johnson administration's "war on crime" had already laid the firmament for the shift that Nixon accelerated. In fact, when Bob Dylan, the most famous bard of the decade, sang that "The Times They Are A-Changin'," he might have been guilty of understatement. While *Kerner* had held that the riots were a result of the absence of true liberalism, the emerging consensus held that they were the product of too much of it. Nowhere was this more apparent than in Nixon's own administration.[11]

George Romney, the former governor of Michigan, would serve as secretary of housing and urban development in the new administration. The department, as Romney knew, was equipped with a powerful new tool: the 1968 Fair Housing Act, the third piece of landmark civil rights legislation of the era, passed by Congress in the wake of Martin Luther King's assassination. Romney, who as governor had coordinated the response to the 1967 Detroit riots, notably remarked that "force alone will not eliminate riots. We must eliminate the problems from which they stem."[12] But Romney's vigorous enforcement of the FHA during his tenure as HUD secretary created a backlash among Republicans and isolated him, a seemingly more liberal Republican, from Nixon. His departure from the post in 1972 marked another turn in the GOP's politics away from the concerns of antidiscrimination.[13]

The commission noted the unfairness of the criminal-justice system, but in the decade to come the system was more likely to be attacked for leniency. Rhetoric about "revolving door justice" and repeat offenders supplanted more nuanced discussions of which problems law enforcement should and should not address. In policy circles the indictment that racism had created many of the troubles within Black America was supplanted by "culture of poverty" arguments that accepted the premise that racism was but a residue compared with earlier eras and that Black poverty was the product of a morass of bad choices, weak values, and the lack of motivation. Having exonerated itself from any culpability in the creation of a bitterly segregated Black America, white society now felt comfortable enough to offer judgment from afar. Aside from the one-term interlude of Jimmy Carter's presidency, this conservative position dominated the presidency for nearly a quarter century after Lyndon B. Johnson's departure from office. When liberalism reemerged in the early nineties, it came in the form of a pro–death penalty, corporate-friendly southern governor who pledged to put a hundred thousand new police officers on America's streets, which is to say it was hardly recognizable as liberalism at all.

It was a strange and bitter irony that Bill Clinton's political ascent was in some ways facilitated by yet another riot, this one the colossal uprising that leveled swaths of Los Angeles in the aftermath of a verdict acquitting four white police officers for brutally beating a motorist named Rodney King. Unlike such incidents in the sixties, this flagrant abuse was now captured on video, yet even that proved insufficient for a jury in Simi Valley, California, to convict the officers of a single charge brought against them. On April 29, 1992, the day the verdict came down, the city of Los Angeles exploded. The destruction, estimated to be roughly three-quarters of a billion dollars, ushered in yet another commission—this one chaired by diplomat and attorney Warren Christopher—yet another report and more suggestions that would prove to be politically inert. Unlike *Kerner*, the *Christopher Report* remained narrowly tailored to the specific question of policing in Los Angeles, examining none of the broader social dynamics for which bad policing was representative. As scholar Keeanga-Yamahtta Taylor noted in the pages of *The New Yorker*,

> The period after the LA rebellion didn't usher in new initiatives to improve the quality of the lives of people who had revolted. To the contrary, the Bush White House spokesman Marlin Fitzwater blamed the uprising on social-welfare programs of previous administrations saying 'We believe that many of the root problems that have resulted in inner city difficulties were started in the sixties and seventies and they have failed.[14]

The administration presented this argument with a straight face despite Black unemployment being roughly double white unemployment in the year leading up to the uprising. Characteristically, President George H. W. Bush appeared patrician-like and out of touch in the wake of the revolt. The younger, more affable Clinton appeared empathetic and attuned, factors that helped him cement support among African American voters that fall.

The appearance of empathy was just that. Two years into his first term Clinton signed into law the 1994 Crime Bill, a punitive, lead-handed piece of legislation that was to widen racial inequities. He pushed for and signed measures meant to wean recipients off welfare, a capitulation to the canard that the system was rife with fraud and underwriting indolence. Blacks, in the white parlance of the era, were getting too much "free stuff" from the government. In his 1996 State of the Union speech Clinton informed the nation that "the era of big government is over." The renunciation was complete. Such was the state of affairs that in the election to succeed Clinton in 2000, voters complained that it was hard to tell the difference between the two patrician candidates, each the son of a US senator—Al Gore, the Democratic centrist who served as Clinton's vice president, and George W. Bush, son of the former president and a self-styled "compassionate conservative."

This state of affairs did not begin to change significantly until the stunning election of a moderate African American senator named Barack Obama in 2008 and not entirely because of forces within his control. Wary of committing unforced errors on the subject, the first Black president was generally reluctant to address race. Circumstance forced his hand. On August 9, 2014, eighteen-year-old Michael Brown was shot and killed by police officer Darren Wilson on Canfield Drive, a side street in Ferguson, a working-class suburb of St. Louis, Missouri. Months of sustained protests pushed the administration to form a task force on 21st Century Policing. The Department of Justice conducted an investigation of the police department there and filed a report that could well have been an appendix to the *Kerner Report*. The recognition that policing was just one part of a broader systemic failure began to creep its way back into public recognition. And yet, scarcely six years later, the nation once again witnessed flames of outrage in the streets, this time over the brutal asphyxiation of a handcuffed man. But unlike previous eruptions the outrage did not remain local—the flames of a single incident seemed to combust, and all at once, over the country.

This volume distills the full *Kerner Report* to its most significant and enduring parts. The case for its relevance need not be made here, current events having done so already and not for the first time. The original volume examined twenty-three disturbances and offered detailed summaries of eight of them. The riot summaries have been trimmed to include only those of Detroit and Newark, because they were the two largest-scale incidents and made the most cogent case for the commission's creation. In addition to the rapidly changing political tides, *Kerner* was also possibly a victim of its own meticulousness. The report brims with suggestions. One reason why its proposals were not realized might be that it simply made too many of them. We have judiciously trimmed the material here to retain the most vital of these suggestions and excise those that are overly specific or no longer pertinent. We have also excised the charts, indices, and sourcing references from this version, along with some sections of the original volume that were repetitive or which we judged to be less immediately pertinent to contemporary readers. Those readers who are interested in these details can consult the unexpurgated version, still widely available in libraries.

Such has been the significance of this report that the offhand mention of "Kerner" is far more likely to be a reference to the study than the late politician himself. This revised version of the report is offered in recognition of its continued value and import. But there is a conflict of interest at the heart of this endeavor. The book is published with particular hope in mind that its renewed availability might result in its observations being more thoroughly heeded. A tocsin that Americans then chose to ignore, its warnings remain strikingly relevant. Our hope is that this book may hasten the day when they no longer are.[15]

# NOTES

1. Richard Oppel Jr. and Kim Barker, "New Transcripts Reveal Last Moments of George Floyd, Jr.," *New York Times*, July 8, 2020.

2. Chao Xiong and Paul Walsh, "'World Needed to See' Says Woman Who Took Video of Man Dying Under Police Officer's Knee," *Minneapolis Star Tribune*, May 26, 2020.

3. Jacob Frey, Facebook post, May 26, 2020, 8:23 a.m., https://www.facebook.com/MayorFrey/posts/630804544173539.

4. Jacob Frey (@Jacob Frey), Twitter, "Four responding MPD officers in the death of George Floyd have been terminated. This is the right call," May 29, 2020, 3:09 p.m.; Emily Haavik, "Officers Identified in George Floyd Death, Minneapolis Mayor Calls for Charges," *KARE11*, May 27, 2020.

5. Mohammed Haddad, "Mapping US Cities Where Protests Have Erupted," aljazeera.com, June 2, 2020.

6. Seth Cohen, "Lafayette Park is America's Tiannamen Square—with One Big Difference," *Forbes*, June 4, 2020.

7. Chris McGeal, "Hopeful that Minneapolis Policing Will Change? Meet the Police Union's Chief," *Guardian*, June 5, 2020. Paul Walsh, "Derek Chauvin's Firing is Justified, Police Union Head Bob Kroll Says," *Minneapolis Star Tribune*, June 24, 2020.

8. Christopher Ingraham, "Racial Inequality in Minneapolis is Among the Worst in the Nation," *Washington Post*, May 30, 2020; "What Are Covenants?," MappingPrejudice.org. The commission's use of the phrase "moving toward" two societies was a cosmetic description of the United

xxvi *Introduction*

States—it effectively already *was* two societies, having scarcely shaken off the remnants of de jure segregation.

9. Regarding the incident with Judge Leon Kapp see Amiri Baraka, *The Autobiography of LeRoi Jones/Amiri Baraka* (Chicago: Lawrence Hill Books, 1997).

10. Peter Baker, "In Days of Discord, A President Fans the Flames," *New York Times*, May 30, 2020.

11. See Elizabeth Hinton, *From the War on Poverty to the War on Crime* (Cambridge, MA: Harvard University Press, 2017).

12. Romney's quote about Detroit was resurrected in June 2020 when his son, Utah Senator Mitt Romney, tweeted the comment in reference to the unrest that attended the murder of George Floyd. The comment was also implicitly a rebuke of President Donald Trump who had, not coincidentally, borrowed Nixon's language of "law and order" for both his 2016 and 2020 presidential campaigns.

13. Nikole Hannah Jones, "Living Apart: How the Government Betrayed a Landmark Civil Rights Law," *ProPublica*, June 25, 2015.

14. Keeanga-Yamahtta Taylor, "How Do We Change America?" NewYorker.com, June 8, 2020.

15. The report proved to be the high-water mark for Otto Kerner's career. Upon completing his service to the commission Kerner stepped down as governor of Illinois to accept an appointment to the federal bench by Lyndon B. Johnson. Five years later Kerner was convicted on multiple counts of mail fraud, perjury, and conspiracy and forced to resign from the bench. Sentenced to three years in federal prison, he began serving his term but was released early when diagnosed with terminal cancer. He died in 1976.

THE ESSENTIAL
# KERNER
# COMMISSION
# REPORT

. . . . *The only genuine, long-range solution for what has happened lies in an attack—mounted at every level—upon the conditions that breed despair and violence. All of us know what those conditions are: ignorance, discrimination, slums, poverty, disease, not enough jobs. We should attack these conditions—not because we are frightened by conflict, but because we are fired by conscience. We should attack them because there is simply no other way to achieve a decent and orderly society in America. . . .*

Lyndon Baines Johnson
Address to the Nation
July 27, 1967

# FOREWORD

This report of the National Advisory Commission on Civil Disorders responds to Executive Order 11365, issued by President Lyndon B. Johnson on July 29, 1967, and to the personal charge given to us by the President.

"Let your search," he said, "be free * * *. As best you can, find the truth and express it in your report."

We have sought to do so.

"This matter," he said, "is far, far too important for politics."

This was a bipartisan Commission and a nonpartisan effort.

"Only you," he said, "can do this job. Only if you * * * put your shoulders to the wheel can America hope for the kind of report it needs and will take to its heart."

This has been a working Commission.

To our staff, headed by David Ginsburg, Executive Director, to his deputy, Victor H. Palmieri, and to all those in government and private life who helped us, we are grateful.

OTTO KERNER
*Chairman*

JOHN V. LINDSAY
*Vice Chairman*

FRED R. HARRIS
EDWARD W. BROOKE
JAMES C. CORMAN
WILLIAM M. MCCULLOCH
I. W. ABEL
CHARLES B. THORNTON
ROY WILKINS
KATHERINE G. PEDEN
HERBERT JENKINS

# THE NATIONAL ADVISORY COMMISSION ON CIVIL DISORDERS

---

*Chairman*
OTTO KERNER
Governor of Illinois

*Vice Chairman*
JOHN V. LINDSAY
Mayor of New York City

FRED R. HARRIS
United States Senator
Oklahoma

I. W. ABEL
President
United Steelworkers of America
(AFL–CIO)

EDWARD W. BROOKE
United States Senator
Massachusetts

CHARLES B. THORNTON
Chairman of the Board and
Chief Executive Officer, Litton
Industries, Inc.

JAMES C. CORMAN
United States Representative
22d District of California

ROY WILKINS
Executive Director
National Association for the
Advancement of Colored People

WILLIAM M. McCULLOCH
United States Representative
4th District of Ohio

KATHERINE GRAHAM PEDEN
Commissioner of Commerce
State of Kentucky (1963–67)

HERBERT JENKINS
Chief of Police
Atlanta, Georgia

# SUMMARY

## INTRODUCTION

The summer of 1967 again brought racial disorders to American cities, and with them shock, fear, and bewilderment to the Nation.

The worst came during a 2-week period in July, first in Newark and then in Detroit. Each set off a chain reaction in neighboring communities.

On July 28, 1967, the President of the United States established this Commission and directed us to answer three basic questions:

What happened?

Why did it happen?

What can be done to prevent it from happening again?

To respond to these questions, we have undertaken a broad range of studies and investigations. We have visited the riot cities; we have heard many witnesses: we have sought the counsel of experts across the country.

This is our basic conclusion: Our Nation is moving toward two societies, one black, one white—separate and unequal.

Reaction to last summer's disorders has quickened the movement and deepened the division. Discrimination and segregation have long permeated much of American life: they now threaten the future of every American.

This deepening racial division is not inevitable. The movement apart can be reversed. Choice is still possible. Our principal task is to define that choice and to press for a national resolution.

To pursue our present course will involve the continuing polarization of the American community and, ultimately, the destruction of basic democratic values.

The alternative is not blind repression or capitulation to lawlessness. It is the realization of common opportunities for all within a single society.

This alternative will require a commitment to national action—compassionate, massive, and sustained, backed by the resources of the most powerful and the richest nation on this earth. From every American it will require new attitudes, new understanding, and, above all, new will.

The vital needs of the Nation must be met; hard choices must be made, and, if necessary, new taxes enacted.

Violence cannot build a better society. Disruption and disorder nourish repression, not justice. They strike at the freedom of every citizen. The community cannot—it will not—tolerate coercion and mob rule.

Violence and destruction must be ended—in the streets of the ghetto and in the lives of people.

Segregation and poverty have created in the racial ghetto a destructive environment totally unknown to most white Americans.

What white Americans have never fully understood—but what the Negro can never forget—is that white society is deeply implicated in the ghetto. White institutions created it, white institutions maintain it, and white society condones it.

It is time now to turn with all the purpose at our command to the major unfinished business of this Nation. It is time to adopt strategies for action that will produce quick and visible progress. It is time to make good the promises of American democracy to all citizens—urban and rural, white and black, Spanish-surname, American Indian, and every minority group.

Our recommendations embrace three basic principles:

- To mount programs on a scale equal to the dimension of the problems;
- To aim these programs for high impact in the immediate future in order to close the gap between promise and performance;
- To undertake new initiatives and experiments that can change the system of failure and frustration that now dominates the ghetto and weakens our society.

These programs will require unprecedented levels of funding and performance, but they neither probe deeper nor demand more than the problems which called them forth. There can be no higher priority for national action and no higher claim on the Nation's conscience.

We issue this report now, 5 months before the date called for by the President. Much remains that can be learned. Continued study is essential.

As Commissioners we have worked together with a sense of the greatest urgency and have sought to compose whatever differences exist among us. Some differences remain. But the gravity of the problem and the pressing need for action are too clear to allow further delay in the issuance of this report.

# I. WHAT HAPPENED?

## CHAPTER 1.—PROFILES OF DISORDER

The report contains profiles of a selection of the disorders that took place during the summer of 1967. These profiles are designed to indicate how the disorders happened, who participated in them, and how local officials, police forces, and the National Guard responded. Illustrative excerpts follow:

**Newark**

\* \* \* It was decided to attempt to channel the energies of the people into a nonviolent protest. While Lofton promised the crowd that a full investigation would be made of the Smith incident, the other Negro leaders began urging those on the scene to form a line of march toward the city hall.

Some persons joined the line of march. Others milled about in the narrow street. From the dark grounds of the housing project came a barrage of rocks. Some of them fell among the crowd. Others hit persons in the line of march. Many smashed the windows of the police station. The rock throwing, it was believed, was the work of youngsters: approximately 2,500 children lived in the housing project.

Almost at the same time, an old car was set afire in a

parking lot. The line of march began to disintegrate. The police, their heads protected by World War I-type helmets, sallied forth to disperse the crowd. A fire engine, arriving on the scene, was pelted with rocks. As police drove people away from the station, they scattered in all directions.

A few minutes later a nearby liquor store was broken into. Some persons, seeing a caravan of cabs appear at city hall to protest Smith's arrest, interpreted this as evidence that the disturbance had been organized, and generated rumors to that effect.

However, only a few stores were looted. Within a short period of time, the disorder appeared to have run its course.

* * * On Saturday, July 15, [Director of Police Dominick] Spina received a report of snipers in a housing project. When he arrived he saw approximately 100 National Guardsmen and police officers crouching behind vehicles, hiding in corners, and lying on the ground around the edge of the courtyard.

Since everything appeared quiet and it was broad daylight, Spina walked directly down the middle of the street. Nothing happened. As he came to the last building of the complex, he heard a shot. All around him the troopers jumped, believing themselves to be under sniper fire. A moment later a young Guardsman ran from behind a building.

The director of police went over and asked him if he had fired the shot. The soldier said "Yes," he had fired to scare a man away from a window; that his orders were to keep everyone away from windows.

Spina said he told the soldier: "Do you know what you just did? You have now created a state of hysteria. Every Guardsman up and down this street and every state policeman and every city policeman that is present thinks that somebody just fired a shot and that it is probably a sniper."

A short time later more "gunshots" were heard. Investigating, Spina came upon a Puerto Rican sitting on a wall. In reply to a question as to whether he knew "where the firing is coming from?" the man said:

"That's no firing. That's fireworks. If you look up to the fourth floor, you will see the people who are throwing down these cherry bombs."

By this time four truckloads of National Guardsmen had arrived and troopers and policemen were again crouched everywhere looking for a sniper. The director of police remained at the scene for 3 hours, and the only shot fired was the one by the Guardsman.

Nevertheless, at 6 o'clock that evening two columns of National Guardsmen and State troopers were directing mass fire at the Hayes housing project in response to what they believed were snipers. * * *

## Detroit

* * *A spirit of carefree nihilism was taking hold. To riot and destroy appeared more and more to become ends in themselves. Late Sunday afternoon it appeared to one observer that the young people were "dancing amidst the flames."

A Negro plainclothes officer was standing at an intersection when a man threw a Molotov cocktail into a business establishment at the corner. In the heat of the afternoon, fanned by the 20 to 25 miles per hour winds of both Sunday and Monday, the fire reached the home next door within minutes. As residents uselessly sprayed the flames with garden hoses, the fire jumped from roof to roof of adjacent two- and three-story buildings. Within the hour the entire block was in flames. The ninth house in the burning row belonged to the arsonist who had thrown the Molotov cocktail * * *.

* * * Employed as a private guard, 55-year-old Julius L. Dorsey, a Negro, was standing in front of a market when accosted by two Negro men and a woman. They demanded he permit them to loot the market. He ignored their

demands. They began to berate him. He asked a neighbor to call the police. As the argument grew more heated, Dorsey fired three shots from his pistol into the air.

The police radio reported: "Looters—they have rifles." A patrol car driven by a police officer and carrying three National Guardsmen arrived. As the looters fled, the law-enforcement personnel opened fire. When the firing ceased, one person lay dead.

He was Julius L. Dorsey.* * *

* * * As the riot alternately waxed and waned, one area of the ghetto remained insulated. On the northeast side the residents of some 150 square blocks inhabited by 21,000 persons had, in 1966, banded together in the Positive Neighborhood Action Committee (PNAC). With professional help from the Institute of Urban Dynamics, they had organized block clubs and made plans for the improvement of the neighborhood.* * *

When the riot broke out, the residents, through the block clubs, were able to organize quickly. Youngsters, agreeing to stay in the neighborhood, participated in detouring traffic. While many persons reportedly sympathized with the idea of a rebellion against the "system" only two small fires were set—one in an empty building.

* * * According to Lieutenant General Throckmorton and Colonel Bolling, the city, at this time, was saturated with fear. The National Guardsmen were afraid, the citizens were afraid, and the police were afraid. Numerous persons, the majority of them Negroes, were being injured by gunshots of undetermined origin. The general and his staff felt that the major task of the troops was to reduce the fear and restore an air of normalcy.

In order to accomplish this, every effort was made to establish contact and rapport between the troops and the residents. The soldiers—20 percent of whom were Negro—began helping to clean up the streets, collect garbage, and trace persons who had disappeared in the confusion. Residents in the neighborhoods responded with soup and sandwiches for the troops. In areas where the National Guard tried to establish rapport with the citizens, there was a similar response. . . .

## CHAPTER 2.—PATTERNS OF DISORDER

The "typical" riot did not take place. The disorders of 1967 were unusual, irregular, complex, and unpredictable social processes. Like most human events, they did not unfold in an orderly sequence. However, an analysis of our survey information leads to some conclusions about the riot process.

In general:

- The civil disorders of 1967 involved Negroes acting against local symbols of white American society, authority, and property in Negro neighborhoods—rather than against white persons.
- Of 164 disorders reported during the first nine months of 1967, eight (5 percent) were major in terms of violence and damage; 33 (20 percent) were serious but not major; 123 (75 percent) were minor and undoubtedly would not have received national attention as riots had the Nation not been sensitized by the more serious outbreaks.
- In the 75 disorders studied by a Senate subcommittee, 83 deaths were reported. Eighty-two percent of the deaths and more than half the injuries occurred in Newark and Detroit. About 10 percent of the dead and 36 percent of the injured were public employees, primarily law officers and firemen. The overwhelming majority of the persons killed or injured in all the disorders were Negro civilians.
- Initial damage estimates were greatly exaggerated. In Detroit, newspaper damage estimates at first ranged from $200 to $500 million; the highest recent estimate is $45 million. In Newark, early estimates ranged from $15 to $25 million. A month later damage was estimated at $10.2 million, 80 percent in inventory losses.

In the 24 disorders in 23 cities which we surveyed:

- The final incident before the outbreak of disorder, and the initial violence itself, generally took place in the evening or at night at a place in which it was normal for many people to be on the streets.
- Violence usually occurred almost immediately following the occurrence of the final precipitating incident, and then escalated rapidly. With but few exceptions, violence subsided during the day, and flared rapidly again at night. The night-day cycles continued through the early period of the major disorders.
- Disorder generally began with rock and bottle throwing and window breaking. Once store windows were broken, looting usually followed.
- Disorder did not erupt as a result of a single "triggering" or "precipitating" incident. Instead, it was generated out of an increasingly disturbed social atmosphere, in which typically a series of tension-heightening incidents over a period of weeks or months became linked in the minds of many in the Negro community with a reservoir of underlying grievances. At some point in the mounting tension, a further incident—in itself often routine or trivial—became the breaking point and the tension spilled over into violence.
- "Prior" incidents, which increased tensions and ultimately led to violence, were police actions in almost half the cases; police actions were "final" incidents before the outbreak of violence in 12 of the 24 surveyed disorders.
- No particular control tactic was successful in every situation. The varied effectiveness of control techniques emphasizes the need for advance training, planning, adequate intelligence systems, and knowledge of the ghetto community.
- Negotiations between Negroes—including young militants as well as older Negro leaders—and white officials concerning "terms of peace" occurred during virtually all the disorders surveyed. In many cases, these negotiations involved discussion of underlying grievances as well as the handling of the disorder by control authorities.

- The typical rioter was a teenager or young adult, a lifelong resident of the city in which he rioted, a high school dropout; he was, nevertheless, somewhat better educated than his nonrioting Negro neighbor, and was usually underemployed or employed in a menial job. He was proud of his race, extremely hostile to both whites and middle-class Negroes and, although informed about politics, highly distrustful of the political system.

A Detroit survey revealed that approximately 11 percent of the total residents of two riot areas admitted participation in the rioting, 20 to 25 percent identified themselves as "bystanders," over 16 percent identified themselves as "counterrioters" who urged rioters to "cool it," and the remaining 48 to 53 percent said they were at home or elsewhere and did not participate. In a survey of Negro males between the ages of 15 and 35 residing in the disturbance area in Newark, about 45 percent identified themselves as rioters, and about 55 percent as "noninvolved."

- Most rioters were young Negro males. Nearly 53 percent of arrestees were between 15 and 24 years of age; nearly 81 percent between 15 and 35.
- In Detroit and Newark about 74 percent of the rioters were brought up in the North. In contrast, of the noninvolved, 36 percent in Detroit and 52 percent in Newark were brought up in the North.
- What the rioters appeared to be seeking was fuller participation in the social order and the material benefits enjoyed by the majority of American citizens. Rather than rejecting the American system, they were anxious to obtain a place for themselves in it.
- Numerous Negro counterrioters walked the streets urging rioters to "cool it." The typical counterrioter was better educated and had higher income than either the rioter or the noninvolved.
- The proportion of Negroes in local government was substantially smaller than the Negro proportion of population. Only three of the 20 cities studied had more than one Negro legislator; none had ever had a Negro mayor or city manager. In only four cities

did Negroes hold other important policy-making positions or serve as heads of municipal departments.

- Although almost all cities had some sort of formal grievance mechanism for handling citizen complaints, this typically was regarded by Negroes as ineffective and was generally ignored.
- Although specific grievances varied from city to city, at least 12 deeply held grievances can be identified and ranked into three levels of relative intensity:

*First level of intensity:*
1. Police practices.
2. Unemployment and underemployment.
3. Inadequate housing.

*Second level of intensity:*
4. Inadequate education.
5. Poor recreation facilities and programs.
6. Ineffectiveness of the political structure and grievance mechanisms.

*Third level of intensity:*
7. Disrespectful white attitudes.
8. Discriminatory administration of justice.
9. Inadequacy of Federal programs.
10. Inadequacy of municipal services.
11. Discriminatory consumer and credit practices.
12. Inadequate welfare programs.

- The results of a three-city survey of various Federal programs—manpower, education, housing, welfare and community action—indicate that, despite substantial expenditures, the number of persons assisted constituted only a fraction of those in need.

The background of disorder is often as complex and difficult to analyze as the disorder itself. But we find that certain general conclusions can be drawn:

- Social and economic conditions in the riot cities constituted a clear pattern of severe disadvantage for Negroes compared with whites, whether the Negroes lived in the area where the riot took place or outside it. Negroes had completed fewer years of education and fewer had attended high school. Negroes were twice as likely to be unemployed and three times as likely to be in unskilled and service jobs. Negroes averaged 70 percent of the income earned by whites and were more than twice as likely to be living in poverty. Although housing cost Negroes relatively more, they had worse housing—three times as likely to be overcrowded and substandard. When compared to white suburbs, the relative disadvantage was even more pronounced.

A study of the aftermath of disorder leads to disturbing conclusions. We find that, despite the institution of some postriot programs:

- Little basic change in the conditions underlying the outbreak of disorder has taken place. Actions to ameliorate Negro grievances have been limited and sporadic; with but few exceptions, they have not significantly reduced tensions.
- In several cities, the principal official response has been to train and equip the police with more sophisticated weapons.
- In several cities, increasing polarization is evident, with continuing breakdown of interracial communication, and growth of white segregationist or black separatist groups. . . .

# II. WHY DID IT HAPPEN?

## CHAPTER 4.—THE BASIC CAUSES

In addressing the question "Why did it happen?" we shift our focus from the local to the national scene, from the particular events of the summer of 1967 to the factors within the society at large that created a mood of violence among many urban Negroes.

These factors are complex and interacting; they vary significantly in their effect from city to city and from year to year; and the consequences of one disorder, generating new grievances and new demands, become the causes of the next. Thus was created the "thicket of tension, conflicting evidence, and extreme opinions" cited by the President.

Despite these complexities, certain fundamental matters are clear.

Of these, the most fundamental is the racial attitude and behavior of white Americans toward black Americans.

Race prejudice has shaped our history decisively; it now threatens to affect our future.

White racism is essentially responsible for the explosive mixture which has been accumulating in our cities since the end of World War II. Among the ingredients of this mixture are:

- *Pervasive discrimination and segregation* in employment, education, and housing, which have resulted in the continuing exclusion of great numbers of Negroes from the benefits of economic progress.
- *Black in-migration and white exodus,* which have produced the massive and growing concentrations of impoverished Negroes in our major cities, creating a growing crisis of deteriorating facilities and services and unmet human needs.
- *The black ghettos,* where segregation and poverty converge on the young to destroy opportunity and enforce failure. Crime, drug addiction, dependency on welfare, and bitterness and resentment against society in general and white society in particular are the result.

At the same time, most whites and some Negroes outside the ghetto have prospered to a degree unparalleled in the history of civilization. Through television and other media, this affluence has been flaunted before the eyes of the Negro poor and the jobless ghetto youth.

Yet these facts alone cannot be said to have caused the disorders. Recently, other powerful ingredients have begun to catalyze the mixture:

- *Frustrated hopes* are the residue of the unfulfilled expectations aroused by the great judicial and legislative victories of the civil rights movement and the dramatic struggle for equal rights in the South.
- *A climate that tends toward approval and encouragement of violence* as a form of protest has been created by white terrorism directed against nonviolent protest; by the open defiance of

law and Federal authority by state and local officials resisting desegregation; and by some protest groups engaging in civil disobedience who turn their backs on nonviolence, go beyond the constitutionally protected rights of petition and free assembly, and resort to violence to attempt to compel alteration of laws and policies with which they disagree.

- *The frustrations of powerlessness* have led some Negroes to the conviction that there is no effective alternative to violence as a means of achieving redress of grievances, and of "moving the system." These frustrations are reflected in alienation and hostility toward the institutions of law and government and the white society which controls them, and in the reach toward racial consciousness and solidarity reflected in the slogan "Black Power."
- *A new mood* has sprung up among Negroes, particularly among the young, in which self-esteem and enhanced racial pride are replacing apathy and submission to "the system."
- *The police are not merely a "spark" factor.* To some Negroes police have come to symbolize white power, white racism, and white repression. And the fact is that many police do reflect and express these white attitudes. The atmosphere of hostility and cynicism is reinforced by a widespread belief among Negroes in the existence of police brutality and in a "double standard" of justice and protection—one for Negroes and one for whites.

To this point, we have attempted only to identify the prime components of the "explosive mixture." In the chapters that follow we seek to analyze them in the perspective of history. Their meaning, however, is clear:

In the summer of 1967, we have seen in our cities a chain reaction of racial violence. If we are heedless, none of us shall escape the consequences.

## CHAPTER 5.—PROTEST: AN HISTORICAL SKETCH

The causes of recent racial disorders are embedded in a tangle of issues and circumstances—social, economic, political, and psychological—

which arise out of the historic pattern of Negro-white relations in America.

In this chapter we trace the pattern, identify the recurrent themes of Negro protest and, most importantly, provide a perspective on the protest activities of the present era.

We describe the Negro's experience in America and the development of slavery as an institution. We show his persistent striving for equality in the face of rigidly maintained social, economic, and educational barriers, and repeated mob violence. We portray the ebb and flow of the doctrinal tides—accommodation, separatism, and self-help—and their relationship to the current theme of Black Power. . . .

## CHAPTER 6.—THE FORMATION OF
## THE RACIAL GHETTOS*

Throughout the 20th century the Negro population of the United States has been moving steadily from rural areas to urban and from South to North and West. In 1910, 91 percent of the Nation's 9.8 million Negroes lived in the South and only 27 percent of American Negroes lived in cities of 2,500 persons or more. Between 1910 and 1966 the total Negro population more than doubled, reaching 21.5 million, and the number living in metropolitan areas rose more than fivefold (from 2.6 million to 14.8 million). The number outside the South rose elevenfold (from 885,000 to 9.7 million).

Negro migration from the South has resulted from the expectation of thousands of new and highly paid jobs for unskilled workers in the North and the shift to mechanized farming in the South. However, the Negro migration is small when compared to earlier waves of European immigrants. Even between 1960 and 1966, there were 1.8 million immigrants from abroad compared to the 613,000 Negroes who arrived in the North and West from the South.

As a result of the growing number of Negroes in urban areas, natural increase has replaced migration as the primary source of

---

* The term "ghetto" as used in this Report refers to an area within a city characterized by poverty and acute social disorganization and inhabited by members of a racial or ethnic group under conditions of involuntary segregation.

Negro population increase in the cities. Nevertheless, Negro migration from the South will continue unless economic conditions there change dramatically.

Basic data concerning Negro urbanization trends indicate that:

- Almost all Negro population growth (98 percent from 1950 to 1966) is occurring within metropolitan areas, primarily within central cities.*
- The vast majority of white population growth (78 percent from 1960 to 1966) is occurring in suburban portions of metropolitan areas. Since 1960, white central-city population has declined by 1.3 million.
- As a result, central cities are becoming more heavily Negro while the suburban fringes around them remain almost entirely white.
- The 12 largest central cities now contain over two-thirds of the Negro population outside the South, and almost one-third of the Negro total in the United States.

Within the cities, Negroes have been excluded from white residential areas through discriminatory practices. Just as significant is the withdrawal of white families from, or their refusal to enter, neighborhoods where Negroes are moving or already residing. About 20 percent of the urban population of the United States changes residence every year. The refusal of whites to move into "changing" areas when vacancies occur means that most vacancies eventually are occupied by Negroes.

The result, according to a recent study, is that in 1960 the average segregation index for 207 of the largest U.S. cities was 86.2. In other words, to create an unsegregated population distribution, an average of over 86 percent of all Negroes would have to change their place of residence within the city.

---

* A "central city" is the largest city of a standard metropolitan statistical area, that is, a metropolitan area containing at least one city of 50,000 or more inhabitants.

## CHAPTER 7.—UNEMPLOYMENT, FAMILY STRUCTURE, AND SOCIAL DISORGANIZATION

Although there have been gains in Negro income nationally, and a decline in the number of Negroes below the "poverty level," the condition of Negroes in the central city remains in a state of crisis. Between 2 and 2.5 million Negroes—16 to 20 percent of the total Negro population of all central cities—live in squalor and deprivation in ghetto neighborhoods.

Employment is a key problem. It not only controls the present for the Negro American but, in a most profound way, it is creating the future as well. Yet, despite continuing economic growth and declining national unemployment rates, the unemployment rate for Negroes in 1967 was more than double that for whites.

Equally important is the undesirable nature of many jobs open to Negroes and other minorities. Negro men are more than three times as likely as white men to be in low-paying, unskilled, or service jobs. This concentration of male Negro employment at the lowest end of the occupational scale is the single most important cause of poverty among Negroes.

In one study of low-income neighborhoods, the "sub-employment rate," including both unemployment and underemployment, was about 33 percent, or 8.8 times greater than the overall unemployment rate for all U.S. workers.

Employment problems, aggravated by the constant arrival of new unemployed migrants, many of them from depressed rural areas, create persistent poverty in the ghetto. In 1966, about 11.9 percent of the Nation's whites and 40.6 percent of its nonwhites were below the poverty level defined by the Social Security Administration (in 1966, $3,335 per year for an urban family of four). Over 40 percent of the nonwhites below the poverty level live in the central cities. . . .

## CHAPTER 8.—CONDITIONS OF LIFE IN THE RACIAL GHETTO

A striking difference in environment from that of white, middle-class Americans profoundly influences the lives of residents of the ghetto.

Crime rates, consistently higher than in other areas, create a pronounced sense of insecurity. For example, in one city one low-income Negro district had 35 times as many serious crimes against persons as a high-income white district. Unless drastic steps are taken, the crime problems in poverty areas are likely to continue to multiply as the growing youth and rapid urbanization of the population outstrip police resources.

Poor health and sanitation conditions in the ghetto result in higher mortality rates, a higher incidence of major diseases, and lower availability and utilization of medical services. The infant mortality rate for non-white babies under the age of 1 month is 58 percent higher than for whites; for 1 to 12 months it is almost three times as high. The level of sanitation in the ghetto is far below that in high-income areas. Garbage collection is often inadequate. Of an estimated 14,000 cases of rat bite in the United States in 1965, most were in ghetto neighborhoods.

Ghetto residents believe they are exploited by local merchants; and evidence substantiates some of these beliefs. A study conducted in one city by the Federal Trade Commission showed that higher prices were charged for goods sold in ghetto stores than in other areas. . . .

## CHAPTER 9.—COMPARING THE IMMIGRANT AND NEGRO EXPERIENCE

In this chapter, we address ourselves to a fundamental question that many white Americans are asking: Why have so many Negroes, unlike the European immigrants, been unable to escape from the ghetto and from poverty?

We believe the following factors play a part:

- *The maturing economy.*—When the European immigrants arrived, they gained an economic foothold by providing the unskilled labor needed by industry. Unlike the immigrant, the Negro migrant found little opportunity in the city. The economy, by then matured, had little use for the unskilled labor he had to offer.
- *The disability of race.*—The structure of discrimination has stringently narrowed opportunities for the Negro and restricted

his prospects. European immigrants suffered from discrimination, but never so pervasively.

- *Entry into the political system.*—The immigrants usually settled in rapidly growing cities with powerful and expanding political machines, which traded economic advantages for political support. Ward-level grievance machinery, as well as personal representation, enabled the immigrant to make his voice heard and his power felt.

By the time the Negro arrived, these political machines were no longer so powerful or so well equipped to provide jobs or other favors, and in many cases were unwilling to share their remaining influence with Negroes. . . .

# III. WHAT CAN BE DONE?

## CHAPTER 10.—THE COMMUNITY RESPONSE

Our investigation of the 1967 riot cities establishes that virtually every major episode of violence was foreshadowed by an accumulation of unresolved grievances and by widespread dissatisfaction among Negroes with the unwillingness or inability of local government to respond.

Overcoming these conditions is essential for community support of law enforcement and civil order. City governments need new and more vital channels of communication to the residents of the ghetto; they need to improve their capacity to respond effectively to community needs before they become community grievances; and they need to provide opportunity for meaningful involvement of ghetto residents in shaping policies and programs which affect the community.

The Commission recommends that local governments:

- Develop Neighborhood Action Task Forces as joint community-government efforts through which more effective communication can be achieved, and the delivery of city services to ghetto residents improved.
- Establish comprehensive grievance-response mechanisms in order to bring all public agencies under public scrutiny.

- Bring the institutions of local government closer to the people they serve by establishing neighborhood outlets for local, state, and Federal administrative and public service agencies.
- Expand opportunities for ghetto residents to participate in the formulation of public policy and the implementation of programs affecting them through improved political representation, creation of institutional channels for community action, expansion of legal services, and legislative hearings on ghetto problems.

In this effort, city governments will require State and Federal support. The Commission recommends:

- State and Federal financial assistance for mayors and city councils to support the research, consultants, staff, and other resources needed to respond effectively to Federal program initiatives.
- State cooperation in providing municipalities with the jurisdictional tools needed to deal with their problems; a fuller measure of financial aid to urban areas; and the focusing of the interests of suburban communities on the physical, social, and cultural environment of the central city.

## CHAPTER 11.—POLICE AND THE COMMUNITY

The abrasive relationship between the police and minority communities has been a major—and explosive—source of grievance, tension, and disorder. The blame must be shared by the total society.

The police are faced with demands for increased protection and service in the ghetto. Yet the aggressive patrol practices thought necessary to meet these demands themselves create tension and hostility. The resulting grievances have been further aggravated by the lack of effective mechanisms for handling complaints against the police. Special programs for bettering police-community relations have been instituted, but these alone are not enough. Police administrators, with the guidance of public officials, and the support of the entire community, must take vigorous action to improve law enforcement and to decrease the potential for disorder.

The Commission recommends that city government and police authorities:

- Review police operations in the ghetto to ensure proper conduct by police officers, and eliminate abrasive practices
- Provide more adequate police protection to ghetto residents to eliminate their high sense of insecurity and the belief in the existence of a dual standard of law enforcement.
- Establish fair and effective mechanisms for the redress of grievances against the police and other municipal employees.
- Develop and adopt policy guidelines to assist officers in making critical decisions in areas where police conduct can create tension.
- Develop and use innovative programs to insure widespread community support for law enforcement.
- Recruit more Negroes into the regular police force, and review promotion policies to insure fair promotion for Negro officers.
- Establish a "Community Service Officer" program to attract ghetto youths between the ages of 17 and 21 to police work. These junior officers would perform duties in ghetto neighborhoods, but would not have full police authority. The Federal Government should provide support equal to 90 percent of the costs of employing CSO's on the basis of one for every 10 regular officers. . . .

## CHAPTER 15.—THE NEWS MEDIA AND THE DISORDERS

In his charge to the Commission, the President asked: "What effect do the mass media have on the riots?"

The Commission determined that the answer to the President's question did not lie solely in the performance of the press and broadcasters in reporting the riots. Our analysis had to consider also the overall treatment by the media of the Negro ghettos, community relations, racial attitudes, and poverty—day by day and month by month, year in and year out.

A wide range of interviews with Government officials, law enforcement authorities, media personnel and other citizens, including ghetto residents, as well as a quantitative analysis of riot coverage and a special conference with industry representatives, leads us to conclude that:

- Despite instances of sensationalism, inaccuracy and distortion, newspapers, radio and television tried on the whole to give a balanced, factual account of the 1967 disorders.
- Elements of the news media failed to portray accurately the scale and character of the violence that occurred last summer. The overall effect was, we believe, an exaggeration of both mood and event.
- Important segments of the media failed to report adequately on the causes and consequences of civil disorders and on the underlying problems of race relations. They have not communicated to the majority of their audience—which is white—a sense of the degradation, misery, and hopelessness of life in the ghetto.

These failings must be corrected, and the improvement must come from within the industry. Freedom of the press is not the issue. Any effort to impose governmental restrictions would be inconsistent with fundamental constitutional precepts.

We have seen evidence that the news media are becoming aware of and concerned about their performance in this field. As that concern grows, coverage will improve. But much more must be done, and it must be done soon.

The Commission recommends that the media:

- Expand coverage of the Negro community and of race problems through permanent assignment of reporters familiar with urban and racial affairs, and through establishment of more and better links with the Negro community.
- Integrate Negroes and Negro activities into all aspects of coverage and content, including newspaper articles and television programing. The news media must publish newspapers and produce programs that recognize the existence and activities of Negroes as a group within the community and as a part of the larger community.

- Recruit more Negroes into journalism and broadcasting and promote those who are qualified to positions of significant responsibility. Recruitment should begin in high schools and continue through college; where necessary, aid for training should be provided.
- Improve coordination with police in reporting riot news through advance planning, and cooperate with the police in the designation of police information officers, establishment of information centers, and development of mutually acceptable guidelines for riot reporting and the conduct of media personnel.
- Accelerate efforts to insure accurate and responsible reporting of riot and racial news, through adoption by all news-gathering organizations of stringent internal staff guidelines.
- Cooperate in the establishment of a privately organized and funded Institute of Urban Communications to train and educate journalists in urban affairs, recruit and train more Negro journalists, develop methods for improving police-press relations, review coverage of riots and racial issues, and support continuing research in the urban field. . . .

# PREFACE

## I

The summer of 1967 brought racial disorder again to American cities, deepening the bitter residue of fear and threatening the future of all Americans.

We are charged by the President with the responsibility to examine this condition and to speak the truth as we see it. Two fundamental questions confront us:

> How can we as a people end the resort to violence while we
>   build a better society?
> How can the Nation realize the promise of a single
>   society—one nation indivisible—which yet remains
>   unfulfilled?

Violence surely cannot build that society. Disruption and disorder will nourish not justice but repression. Those few who would destroy civil order and the rule of law strike at the freedom of every citizen. They must know that the community cannot and will not tolerate coercion and mob action.

We have worked together these past months with a sense of the greatest urgency. Although much remains that can be learned, we have determined to say now what we already have learned. We do this in the hope that the American public will understand the nature and gravity of the problem and that those who have power to act—at all levels of government and in all sections of the community—will listen and respond.

This sense of urgency has led us to consolidate in this single report the interim and final reports called for by the President. To accomplish this, it has been necessary to do without the benefit of some studies still under way which will not be completed for months to come. Certain of these studies—a 15-city survey of Negro and white attitudes, a special survey of attitudes of community leaders, elected officials, administrators and teachers, a report on the application of mediation techniques, and a further analysis of riot arrestees—will be issued later, with other materials, as supplemental reports.

We believe that to wait until midsummer to present our findings and recommendations may be to forfeit whatever opportunity exists for this report to affect, this year, the dangerous climate of tension and apprehension that pervades our cities.

# II

Last summer over 150 cities reported disorders in Negro—and in some instances, Puerto Rican—neighborhoods. These ranged from minor disturbances to major outbursts involving sustained and widespread looting and destruction of property. The worst came during a 2-week period in July when large-scale disorders erupted first in Newark and then in Detroit, each setting off a chain reaction in neighboring communities.

It was in this troubled and turbulent setting that the President of the United States established this Commission. He called upon it "to guide the country through a thicket of tension, conflicting evidence and extreme opinions."

In his charge, the President framed the Commission's mandate in these words:

> "We need to know the answers to three basic questions about these riots:
> —What happened?
> —Why did it happen?
> —What can be done to prevent it from happening again and again?"

The three parts of this report offer answers to these questions.

Part I tells "What happened?" Chapter 1 is a profile of the 1967 disorders told through a narrative of the summer's events in 10 of the 23 cities surveyed by the Commission. Chapter 2 calls on data from all 23 cities to construct an analytical profile. Chapter 3 is the report of the Commission on the issue of conspiracy.

Part II responds to the question, "Why did it happen?" Early in our investigation it became clear that the disorders were not the result of contemporary conditions alone; Chapter 5 identifies some of the historical factors that are an essential part of the background of last summer's outbreaks. Chapters 6 through 9 deal with present conditions, examining the impact of ghetto formation, unemployment, and family structures, and conditions of life in the ghettos, and the differences between the Negro experience and that of other urban immigrant groups.

Part III contains our answer to the question, "What can be done?" Our recommendations begin with organizing the community to respond more effectively to ghetto needs and then proceed with police-community relations, control of disorders, the administration of justice under emergency conditions, compensation for property damage, the role of the news media, and national action in the critical areas of employment, education, welfare and housing.

In formulating this report, we have attempted to draw on all relevant sources. During closed hearings held from August through December, we heard over 130 witnesses, including Federal, state and local officials, experts from the military establishment and law enforcement agencies, universities and foundations, Negro leaders, and representatives of the business community. We personally visited eight cities in which major disturbances had occurred. We met together for 24 days to review and revise the several drafts of our report. Through our staff, we also undertook field surveys in 23 cities in which disorders occurred during the summer of 1967, and took sworn testimony in nine of the cities investigated and from Negro leaders and militants across the country. Expert consultants and advisers supplemented the work of our staff in all the areas covered in our report.

# III

Much of our report is directed to the condition of those Americans who are also Negroes and to the social and economic environment in which they live—many in the black ghettos of our cities. But this Nation is confronted with the issue of justice for all its people—white as well as black, rural as well as urban. In particular, we are concerned for those who have continued to keep faith with society in the preservation of public order—the people of Spanish surname, the American Indian and other minority groups to whom this country owes so much.

We wish it to be clear that in focusing on the Negro, we do not mean to imply any priority of need. It will not do to fight misery in the black ghetto and leave untouched the reality of injustice and deprivation elsewhere in our society. The first priority is order and justice for all Americans.

In speaking of the Negro, we do not speak of "them." We speak of us—for the freedoms and opportunities of all Americans are diminished and imperiled when they are denied to some Americans. The tragic waste of human spirit and resources, the unrecoverable loss to the Nation which this denial has already caused—and continues to produce—no longer can be ignored or afforded.

Two premises underlie the work of the Commission:

- That this Nation cannot abide violence and disorder if it is to ensure the safety of its people and their progress in a free society.
- That this Nation will deserve neither safety nor progress unless it can demonstrate the wisdom and the will to undertake decisive action against the root causes of racial disorder.

This report is addressed to the institutions of government and to the conscience of the Nation, but even more urgently, to the mind and heart of each citizen. The responsibility for decisive action, never more clearly demanded in the history of our country, rests on all of us.

We do not know whether the tide of racial disorder has begun to recede. We recognize as we must that the conditions underlying the disorders will not be obliterated before the end of this year or the end of the next and that so long as these conditions exist a potential for disorder remains. But we believe that the likelihood of disorder can be markedly lessened by an American commitment to confront those conditions and eliminate them—a commitment so clear that Negro citizens will know its truth and accept its goal. The most important step toward domestic peace is an act of will; this country can do for its people what it chooses to do.

The pages that follow set forth our conclusions and the facts upon which they are based. Our plea for civil order and our recommendations for social and economic change are a call to national action. We are aware of the breadth and scope of those recommendations, but they neither probe deeper nor demand more than the problems which call them forth.

PART I

# WHAT HAPPENED?

# CHAPTER 1

# PROFILES OF
# DISORDER

—

## INTRODUCTION

The President directed the Commission to produce "a profile of the riots—of the rioters, of their environment, of their victims, of their causes and effects."

In response to this mandate the Commission constructed profiles of the riots in 10 of the 23 cities under investigation. Brief summaries of what were often conflicting views and perceptions of confusing episodes, they are, we believe, a fair and accurate picture of what happened.

From the profiles, we have sought to build a composite view of the riots as well as of the environment out of which they erupted.

The summer of 1967 was not the beginning of the current wave of disorders. Omens of violence had appeared much earlier.

### 1963–64
In 1963, serious disorders, involving both whites and Negroes, broke out in Birmingham, Savannah, Cambridge, Md., Chicago, and Philadelphia. Sometimes the mobs battled each other; more often they fought the police.

The most violent encounters took place in Birmingham. Police used dogs, firehoses, and cattle prods against marchers, many of whom were children. White racists shot at Negroes and bombed Negro residences. Negroes retaliated by burning white-owned businesses in Negro areas. On a quiet Sunday morning, a bomb exploded beneath a Negro church. Four young girls in a Sunday school class were killed.

In the spring of 1964, the arrest and conviction of civil rights demonstrators provoked violence in Jacksonville. A shot fired from a passing car killed a Negro woman. When a bomb threat forced evacuation of an all-Negro high school, the students stoned policemen and firemen and burned the cars of newsmen. For the first time, Negroes used Molotov cocktails in setting fires.

Two weeks later, at a demonstration protesting school segregation in Cleveland, a bulldozer accidentally killed a young white minister. When police moved in to disperse a crowd composed primarily of Negroes, violence erupted.

In late June, white segregationists broke through police lines and attacked civil rights demonstrators in St. Augustine, Florida. In Philadelphia, Mississippi, law enforcement officers were implicated in the lynch murders of three civil rights workers. On July 10, Ku Klux Klansmen shot and killed a Negro U.S. Army lieutenant colonel, Lemuel Penn, as he was driving through Georgia.

On July 16, in New York City, several young Negroes walking to summer school classes became involved in a dispute with a white building superintendent. When an off-duty police lieutenant intervened, a 15-year-old boy attacked him with a knife. The officer shot and killed the boy.

A crowd of teenagers gathered and smashed store windows. Police arrived in force and dispersed the group.

On the following day, the Progressive Labor Movement, a Marxist-Leninist organization, printed and passed out inflammatory leaflets charging the police with brutality.

On the second day after the shooting, a rally called by the Congress of Racial Equality to protest the Mississippi lynch murders developed into a march on a precinct police station. The crowd clashed with the police; one person was killed, and 12 police officers and 19 citizens were injured.

For several days thereafter, the pattern was repeated: despite exhortations of Negro community leaders against violence, protest rallies became uncontrollable. Police battled mobs in Harlem and in the Bedford-Stuyvesant section of Brooklyn. Firemen fought fires started with Molotov cocktails. When bricks and bottles were thrown, police responded with gunfire. Widespread looting followed and many persons were injured.

A week later, a riot broke out in Rochester when police tried to arrest an intoxicated Negro youth at a street dance. After 2 days of violence, the National Guard restored order.

During the first 2 weeks of August, disorders took place in three New Jersey communities: Jersey City, Elizabeth, and Paterson.

On August 15, when a white liquor store owner in the Chicago suburb of Dixmoor had a Negro woman arrested for stealing a bottle of whiskey, he was accused of having manhandled her. A crowd gathered in front of the store, broke the store window, and threw rocks at passing cars. The police restored order. The next day, when the disturbance was renewed, a Molotov cocktail set the liquor store afire. Several persons were injured.

The final violence of the summer occurred in Philadelphia. A Negro couple's car stalled at an intersection in an area known as "The Jungle"—where, with almost 2,000 persons living in each block, there is the greatest incidence of crime, disease, unemployment, and poverty in the city. When two police officers, one white and one black, attempted to move the car, the wife of the owner became abusive, and the officers arrested her. Police officers and Negro spectators gathered at the scene. Two nights of rioting, resulting in extensive damage, followed.

## 1965

In the spring of 1965, the Nation's attention shifted back to the South. When civil rights workers staged a nonviolent demonstration in Selma, Alabama, police and state troopers forcibly interrupted their march. Within the next few weeks racists murdered a white clergyman and a white housewife active in civil rights.

In the small Louisiana town of Bogalusa, when Negro demonstrators attacked by whites received inadequate police protection, the

Negroes formed a self-defense group called the "Deacons for Defense and Justice."

As late as the second week of August, there had been few disturbances outside the South. But, on the evening of August 11, as Los Angeles sweltered in a heat wave, a highway patrolman halted a young Negro driver for speeding. The young man appeared intoxicated, and the patrolman arrested him. As a crowd gathered, law enforcement officers were called to the scene. A highway patrolman mistakenly struck a bystander with his billy club. A young Negro woman, who was accused of spitting on the police, was dragged into the middle of the street.

When the police departed, members of the crowd began hurling rocks at passing cars, beating white motorists, and overturning cars and setting them on fire. The police reacted hesitantly. Actions they did take further inflamed the people on the streets.

The following day, the area was calm. Community leaders attempting to mediate between Negro residents and the police received little cooperation from municipal authorities. That evening the previous night's pattern of violence was repeated.

Not until almost 30 hours after the initial flareup did window smashing, looting, and arson begin. Yet the police utilized only a small part of their forces.

Few police were on hand the next morning when huge crowds gathered in the business district of Watts, 2 miles from the location of the original disturbance, and began looting. In the absence of police response, the looting became bolder and spread into other areas. Hundreds of women and children from five housing projects clustered in or near Watts took part. Around noon, extensive firebombing began. Few white persons were attacked; the principal intent of the rioters now seemed to be to destroy property owned by whites in order to drive white "exploiters" out of the ghetto.

The chief of police asked for National Guard help, but the arrival of the military units was delayed for several hours. When the Guardsmen arrived, they, together with police, made heavy use of firearms. Reports of "sniper fire" increased. Several persons were killed by mistake. Many more were injured.

Thirty-six hours after the first Guard units arrived, the main force of the riot had been blunted. Almost 4,000 persons were arrested. Thirty-four were killed and hundreds injured. Approximately $35 million in damage had been inflicted.

The Los Angeles riot, the worst in the United States since the Detroit riot of 1943, shocked all who had been confident that race relations were improving in the North, and evoked a new mood in Negro ghettos across the country.

## 1966

The events of 1966 made it appear that domestic turmoil had become part of the American scene.

In March, a fight between several Negroes and Mexican-Americans resulted in a new flareup in Watts. In May, after a police officer accidentally shot and killed a Negro, demonstrations by Negro militants again increased tension in Los Angeles.

Evidence was accumulating that a major proportion of riot participants were youths. Increasing race pride, skepticism about their job prospects, and dissatisfaction with the inadequacy of their education, caused unrest among students in Negro colleges and high schools throughout the country. Students and youths were the principal participants in at least six of the 13 spring and early summer disorders of 1966.

July 12, 1966, was a hot day in Chicago. Negro youngsters were playing in water gushing from an illegally opened fire hydrant. Two police officers, arriving on the scene, closed the hydrant. A Negro youth turned it on again, and the police officers arrested him. A crowd gathered. Police reinforcements arrived. As the crowd became unruly, seven Negro youth were arrested.

Rumors spread that the arrested youths had been beaten and that police were turning off fire hydrants in Negro neighborhoods but leaving them on in white areas. Sporadic window breaking, rock throwing, and firebombing lasted for several hours. Most of the participants were teenagers.

In Chicago, as in other cities, the long-standing grievances of the Negro community needed only minor incidents to trigger violence.

In 1961 when Negroes, after being evacuated from a burning tenement, had been sheltered in a church in an all-white area, a crowd of residents had gathered and threatened to attack the church unless the Negroes were removed.

Segregated schools and housing had led to repeated picketing and marches by civil rights organizations. When marchers had gone into white neighborhoods, they had been met on several occasions by KKK signs and crowds throwing eggs and tomatoes. In 1965, when a Chicago firetruck had killed a Negro woman in an accident, Negroes had congregated to protest against the fire station's all-white complement. Rock throwing and looting had broken out. More than 170 persons were arrested in 2 days.

On the evening of July 13, 1966, the day after the fire hydrant incident, rock throwing, looting and fire-bombing began again. For several days thereafter, the pattern of violence was repeated. Police responding to calls were subjected to random gunfire. Rumors spread. The press talked in highly exaggerated terms of "guerrilla warfare" and "sniper fire."

Before the police and 4,200 National Guardsmen managed to restore order, scores of civilians and police had been injured. There were 533 arrests, including 155 juveniles. Three Negroes were killed by stray bullets, among them a 13-year-old boy and a 14-year-old pregnant girl.

Less than a week later, Ohio National Guardsmen were mobilized to deal with an outbreak of rioting that continued for 4 nights in the Hough section of Cleveland. It is probable that Negro extremists, although they neither instigated nor organized the disorder, exploited and enlarged it. Amidst widespread reports of "sniper fire," four Negroes, including one young woman, were killed; many others, several children among them, were injured. Law enforcement officers were responsible for two of the deaths, a white man firing from a car for a third, and a group of young white vigilantes for the fourth.

Some news media keeping "tally sheets" of the disturbances began to apply the term "riot" to acts of vandalism and relatively minor disorders.

At the end of July, the National States Rights Party, a white extremist organization that advocates deporting Negroes and other minorities, preached racial hatred at a series of rallies in Baltimore. Bands of white youths were incited into chasing and beating Negroes. A court order halted the rallies.

Forty-three disorders and riots were reported during 1966. Although there were considerable variations in circumstances, intensity, and length, they were usually ignited by a minor incident fueled by antagonism between the Negro population and the police.

## Spring, 1967

In the spring of 1967, disorders broke out at three Southern Negro universities at which SNCC (Student Nonviolent Coordinating Committee), a militant antiwhite organization, had been attempting to organize the students.

On Friday, April 7, learning that Stokely Carmichael was speaking at two primarily Negro universities, Fisk and Tennessee A&I, in Nashville, and receiving information that some persons were preparing to riot, the police adopted an emergency riot plan. On the following day, Carmichael and others, including South Carolina Senator Strom Thurmond, spoke at a symposium at Vanderbilt University.

That evening, the Negro operator of a restaurant located near Fisk University summoned police to arrest an allegedly intoxicated Negro soldier.

Within a few minutes, students, many of them members of SNCC, began to picket the restaurant. A squad of riot police arrived and soon became the focus of attention. Spectators gathered. When a city bus was halted and attacked by members of the crowd, a Negro police lieutenant fired five shots into the air.

Rocks and bottles were thrown and additional police were called into the area. Officers fired a number of shots over the heads of the crowd. The students and spectators gradually dispersed.

On the following evening, after negotiations between students and police broke down, crowds again began forming. Police fired over their heads, and shots were fired back at the police. On the fringes of the campus, several white youths aimed shots at a police patrol wagon.

A few days later, when police raided the home of several young Negro militants, they confiscated a half-dozen bottles prepared as Molotov cocktails.

About a month later, students at Jackson State College, in Jackson, Mississippi, were standing around after a political rally when two Negro police officers pursued a speeding car, driven by a Negro student, onto the campus. When the officers tried to arrest the driver, the students interfered. The police called for reinforcements. A crowd of several hundred persons quickly gathered, and a few rocks were thrown.

On the following evening, an even larger crowd assembled. When police attempted to disperse it by gunfire, three persons were hit. One of them, a young Negro, died the next day. The National Guard restored order.

Six days later, on May 16, two separate Negro protests were taking place in Houston. One group was picketing a garbage dump in a Negro residential neighborhood, where a Negro child had drowned. Another was demonstrating at a junior high school on the grounds that Negro students were disciplined more harshly than white.

That evening college students who had participated in the protests returned to the campus of Texas Southern University. About 50 of them were grouped around a 21-year-old student, D.W., a Vietnam veteran, who was seeking to stimulate further protest action. A dispute broke out, and D.W. reportedly slapped another student. When the student threatened D.W., he left, armed himself with a pistol, and returned.

In response to the report of a disturbance, two unmarked police cars with four officers arrived. Two of the officers questioned D.W., discovered he was armed with a pistol, and arrested him.

A short time later, when one of the police cars returned to the campus, it was met by rocks and bottles thrown by students. As police called for reinforcements, sporadic gunshots reportedly came from the men's dormitory. The police returned the fire.

For several hours, gunfire punctuated unsuccessful attempts by community leaders to negotiate a truce between the students and the police.

When several tar barrels were set afire in the street and shooting broke out again, police decided to enter the dormitory. A patrolman, struck by a ricocheting bullet, was killed. After clearing all 480 occupants from the building, police searched it and found one shotgun and two .22 caliber pistols. The origin of the shot that killed the officer was not determined.

As the summer of 1967 approached, Americans, conditioned by 3 years of reports of riots, expected violence. But they had no answers to hard questions: What was causing the turmoil? Was it organized and, if so, by whom? Was there a pattern to the disorders? . . .

# IV. NEWARK

The last outburst in Atlanta occurred on Tuesday night, June 20. That same night, in Newark, N.J., a tumultuous meeting of the planning board took place. Until 4 a.m., speaker after speaker from the Negro ghetto arose to denounce the city's intent to turn over 150 acres in the heart of the central ward as a site for the State's new medical and dental college.

The growing opposition to the city administration by vocal black residents had paralyzed both the planning board and the board of education. Tension had been rising so steadily throughout the northern New Jersey area that, in the first week of June, Col. David Kelly, head of the state police, had met with municipal police chiefs to draw up plans for state police support of city police wherever a riot developed. Nowhere was the tension greater than in Newark.

Founded in 1666, the city, part of the Greater New York City port complex, rises from the salt marshes of the Passaic River. Although in 1967 Newark's population of 400,000 still ranked it 30th among American municipalities, for the past 20 years the white middle class had been deserting the city for the suburbs.

In the late 1950's, the desertions had become a rout. Between 1960 and 1967, the city lost a net total of more than 70,000 white residents. Replacing them in vast areas of dilapidated housing where living conditions, according to a prominent member of the County Bar Association, were so bad that "people would be kinder to their pets," were Negro migrants, Cubans, and Puerto Ricans. In 6 years, the city switched from 65 percent white to 52 percent Negro and 10 percent Puerto Rican and Cuban.

The white population, nevertheless, retained political control of the city. On both the city council and the board of education, seven of nine members were white. In other key boards, the disparity was equal or greater. In the central ward, where the medical college controversy raged, the Negro constituents and their white councilman found themselves on opposite sides of almost every crucial issue.

The municipal administration lacked the ability to respond quickly enough to navigate the swiftly changing currents. Even had it had great astuteness, it would have lacked the financial resources to affect significantly the course of events.

In 1962, seven-term Congressman Hugh Addonizio had forged an Italian-Negro coalition to overthrow longtime Irish control of the city hall. A liberal in Congress, Addonizio, when he became mayor, had opened his door to all people. Negroes, who had been excluded from the previous administration, were brought into the government. The police department was integrated.

Nevertheless, progress was slow. As the Negro population increased, more and more of the politically oriented found the progress inadequate.

The Negro-Italian coalition began to develop strains over the issue of the police. The police were largely Italian, the persons they arrested were largely Negro. Community leaders agreed that, as in many police forces, there was a small minority of officers who abused their responsibility. This gave credibility to the cries of "brutality!" voiced periodically by ghetto Negroes.

In 1965, Mayor Addonizio, acknowledging that there was "a small group of misguided individuals" in the department, declared that "it is vital to establish once and for all, in the minds of the public, that charges of alleged police brutality will be thoroughly investigated and the appropriate legal or punitive action be taken if the charges are found to be substantiated."

Pulled one way by the Negro citizens who wanted a police review board, and the other by the police, who adamantly opposed it, the mayor decided to transfer "the control and investigation of complaints of police brutality out of the hands of both the police and the public and into the hands of an agency that all can support—the Federal Bureau of Investigation," and to send "a copy of any charge of police brutality * * * directly to the Prosecutor's office." However, the FBI could act only if there had been a violation of a person's federal civil rights. No complaint was ever heard of again.

Nor was there much redress for other complaints. The city had no money with which to redress them.

The city had already reached its legal bonding limit, yet expenditures continued to outstrip income. Health and welfare costs, per capita, were 20 times as great as for some of the surrounding communities. Cramped by its small land area of 23.6 square miles—one-third of which was taken up by Newark Airport and unusable marshland—and surrounded by independent jurisdictions, the city had nowhere to expand.

Taxable property was contracting as land, cleared for urban renewal, lay fallow year after year. Property taxes had been increased, perhaps, to the point of diminishing return. By the fall of 1967, they were to reach $661.70 on a $10,000 house—double that of suburban communities.* As a result, people were refusing either to own or to renovate property in the city. Seventy-four percent of white and 87 percent of Negro families lived in rental housing. Whoever was able to move to the suburbs, moved. Many of these persons, as downtown areas were cleared and new office buildings were constructed, continued to work in the city. Among them were a large proportion of the people from whom a city normally draws its civic leaders, but who, after moving out, tended to cease involving themselves in the community's problems.

During the daytime Newark more than doubled its population—and was, therefore, forced to provide services for a large number of people who contributed nothing in property taxes. The city's per capita outlay for police, fire protection, and other municipal services continued to increase. By 1967 it was twice that of the surrounding area.

Consequently, there was less money to spend on education. Newark's per capita outlay on schools was considerably less than that of surrounding communities. Yet within the city's school system were 78,000 children, 14,000 more than 10 years earlier.

Twenty thousand pupils were on double sessions. The dropout rate was estimated to be as high as 33 percent. Of 13,600 Negroes between the ages of 16 and 19, more than 6,000 were not in school. In

---

* The legal tax rate is $7.76 per $100 of market value. However, because of inflation, a guideline of 85.27 percent of market value is used in assessing, reducing the true tax rate to $6.617 per $100.

1960 over half of the adult Negro population had less than an eighth grade education.

The typical ghetto cycle of high unemployment, family breakup, and crime was present in all its elements. Approximately 12 percent of Negroes were without jobs. An estimated 40 percent of Negro children lived in broken homes. Although Newark maintained proportionately the largest police force of any major city, its crime rate was among the highest in the Nation. In narcotics violations it ranked fifth nationally. Almost 80 percent of the crimes were committed within 2 miles of the core of the city, where the central ward is located. A majority of the criminals were Negro. Most of the victims, likewise, were Negro. The Mafia was reputed to control much of the organized crime.

Under such conditions a major segment of the Negro population became increasingly militant. Largely excluded from positions of traditional political power, Negroes, tutored by a handful of militant social activists who had moved into the city in the early 1960's, made use of the antipoverty program, in which poor people were guaranteed representation, as a political springboard. This led to friction between the United Community Corporation, the agency that administered the antipoverty program, and the city administration.

When it became known that the secretary of the board of education intended to retire, the militants proposed for the position the city's budget director, a Negro with a master's degree in accounting. The mayor, however, had already nominated a white man. Since the white man had only a high school education, and at least 70 percent of the children in the school system were Negro, the issue of who was to obtain the secretaryship, an important and powerful position, quickly became a focal issue.

Joined with the issue of the 150-acre medical school site, the area of which had been expanded to triple the original request—an expansion regarded by the militants as an effort to dilute black political power by moving out Negro residents—the board of education battle resulted in a confrontation between the mayor and the militants. Both sides refused to alter their positions.

Into this impasse stepped a Washington Negro named Albert Roy Osborne. A flamboyant, 42-year-old former wig salesman who called himself Colonel Hassan Jeru-Ahmed and wore a black beret, he presided over a mythical "Blackman's Volunteer Army of Liberation." Articulate and magnetic, the self-commissioned "colonel" proved to be a one-man show. He brought Negro residents flocking to board of education and planning board meetings. The Colonel spoke in violent terms, and backed his words with violent action. At one meeting he tore the tape from the official stenographic recorder.

It became more and more evident to the militants that, though they might not be able to prevail, they could prevent the normal transaction of business. Filibustering began. A Negro former State assemblyman held the floor for more than 4 hours. One meeting of the board of education began at 5 p.m., and did not adjourn until 3:23 a.m. Throughout the months of May and June, speaker after speaker warned that if the mayor persisted in naming a white man as secretary to the board of education and in moving ahead with plans for the medical school site, violence would ensue. The city administration played down the threats.

On June 27, when a new secretary to the board of education was to be named, the state police set up a command post in the Newark armory.

The militants, led by the local CORE (Congress of Racial Equality) chapter, disrupted and took over the board of education meeting. The outcome was a stalemate. The incumbent secretary decided to stay on another year. No one was satisfied.

At the beginning of July there were 24,000 unemployed Negroes within the city limits. Their ranks were swelled by an estimated 20,000 teenagers, many of whom, with school out and the summer recreation program curtailed due to a lack of funds, had no place to go.

On July 8, Newark and East Orange police attempted to disperse a group of Black Muslims. In the melee that followed, several police officers and Muslims suffered injuries necessitating medical treatment. The resulting charges and countercharges heightened the tension between police and Negroes.

Early on the evening of July 12, a cabdriver named John Smith began, according to police reports, tailgating a Newark police car. Smith was an unlikely candidate to set a riot in motion. Forty years old, a Georgian by birth, he had attended college for a year before entering the Army in 1950. In 1953 he had been honorably discharged with the rank of corporal. A chess-playing trumpet player, he had worked as a musician and a factory hand before, in 1963, becoming a cabdriver.

As a cabdriver, he appeared to be a hazard. Within a relatively short period of time he had eight or nine accidents. His license was revoked. When, with a woman passenger in his cab, he was stopped by the police, he was in violation of that revocation.

From the high-rise towers of the Reverend William P. Hayes housing project, the residents can look down on the orange-red brick facade of the Fourth Precinct Police Station and observe every movement. Shortly after 9:30 p.m., people saw Smith, who either refused or was unable to walk, being dragged out of a police car and into the front door of the station.

Within a few minutes, at least two civil rights leaders received calls from a hysterical woman declaring a cabdriver was being beaten by the police. When one of the persons at the station notified the cab company of Smith's arrest, cabdrivers all over the city began learning of it over their cab radios.

A crowd formed on the grounds of the housing project across the narrow street from the station. As more and more people arrived, the description of the beating purportedly administered to Smith became more and more exaggerated. The descriptions were supported by other complaints of police malpractice that, over the years, had been submitted for investigation—but had never been heard of again.

Several Negro community leaders, telephoned by a civil rights worker and informed of the deteriorating situation, rushed to the scene. By 10:15 p.m., the atmosphere had become so potentially explosive that Kenneth Melchior, the senior police inspector on the night watch, was called. He arrived at approximately 10:30 p.m.

Met by a delegation of civil rights leaders and militants who requested the right to see and interview Smith, Inspector Melchior acceded to their request.

When the delegation was taken to Smith, Melchior agreed with their observations that, as a result of injuries Smith had suffered, he needed to be examined by a doctor. Arrangements were made to have a police car transport him to the hospital.

Both within and outside of the police station, the atmosphere was electric with hostility. Carloads of police officers arriving for the 10:45

p.m. change of shifts were subjected to a gauntlet of catcalls, taunts, and curses.

Joined by Oliver Lofton, administrative director of the Newark Legal Services Project, the Negro community leaders inside the station requested an interview with Inspector Melchior. As they were talking to the inspector about initiating an investigation to determine how Smith had been injured, the crowd outside became more and more unruly. Two of the Negro spokesmen went outside to attempt to pacify the people.

There was little reaction to the spokesmen's appeal that the people go home. The second of the two had just finished speaking from atop a car when several Molotov cocktails smashed against the wall of the police station.

With the call of "Fire!" most of those inside the station, police officers and civilians alike, rushed out of the front door. The Molotov cocktails had splattered to the ground; the fire was quickly extinguished.

Inspector Melchior had a squad of men form a line across the front of the station. The police officers and the Negroes on the other side of the street exchanged volleys of profanity.

Three of the Negro leaders, Timothy Still of the United Community Corporation, Robert Curvin of CORE, and Lofton, requested they be given another opportunity to disperse the crowd. Inspector Melchior agreed to let them try and provided a bullhorn. It was apparent that the several hundred persons who had gathered in the street and on the grounds of the housing project were not going to disperse. Therefore, it was decided to attempt to channel the energies of the people into a nonviolent protest. While Lofton promised the crowd that a full investigation would be made of the Smith incident, the other Negro leaders urged those on the scene to form a line of march toward the city hall.

Some persons joined the line of march. Others milled about in the narrow street. From the dark grounds of the housing project came a barrage of rocks. Some of them fell among the crowd. Others hit persons in the line of march. Many smashed the windows of the police station. The rock throwing, it was believed, was the work of youngsters; approximately 2,500 children lived in the housing project.

Almost at the same time, an old car was set afire in a parking lot. The line of march began to disintegrate. The police, their heads protected by World War I-type helmets, sallied forth to disperse the crowd. A fire engine, arriving on the scene, was pelted with rocks. As police drove people away from the station, they scattered in all directions.

A few minutes later, a nearby liquor store was broken into. Some persons, seeing a caravan of cabs appear at City Hall to protest Smith's arrest, interpreted this as evidence that the disturbance had been organized, and generated rumors to that effect.

However, only a few stores were looted. Within a short period of time the disorder ran its course.

The next afternoon, Thursday, July 13, the mayor described it as an isolated incident. At a meeting with Negro leaders to discuss measures to defuse the situation, he agreed to appoint the first Negro police captain, and announced that he would set up a panel of citizens to investigate the Smith arrest. To one civil rights leader, this sounded like "the playback of a record," and he walked out. Other observers reported that the mayor seemed unaware of the seriousness of the tensions.

The police were not. Unknown to the mayor, Dominick Spina, the Director of Police, had extended shifts from 8 hours to 12, and was in the process of mobilizing half the strength of the department for that evening. The night before, Spina had arrived at the Fourth Precinct Police Station at approximately midnight, and had witnessed the latter half of the disturbance. Earlier in the evening he had held the regularly weekly "open house" in his office. This was intended to give any person who wanted to talk to him an opportunity to do so. Not a single person had shown up.

As director of police, Spina had initiated many new programs: police-precinct councils, composed of the police precinct captain and business and civic leaders, who would meet once a month to discuss mutual problems; Junior Crimefighters; a Boy Scout Explorer program for each precinct; mandatory human relations training for every officer; a Citizens' Observer Program, which permitted citizens to ride in police cars and observe activities in the stations; a Police Cadet program; and others.

Many of the programs initially had been received enthusiastically, but—as was the case with the "open house"—interest had fallen off.

In general, the programs failed to reach the hard-core unemployed, the disaffected, the school dropouts—of whom Spina estimates there are 10,000 in Essex County—that constitute a major portion of the police problem.

Reports and rumors, including one that Smith had died, circulated through the Negro community. Tension continued to rise. Nowhere was the tension greater than at the Spirit House, the gathering place for Black Nationalists, Black Power advocates, and militants of every hue. Black Muslims, Orthodox Moslems, and members of the United Afro-American Association, a new and growing organization that follows, in general, the teachings of the late Malcolm X, came regularly to mingle and exchange views. Antiwhite playwright LeRoi Jones held workshops. The two police-Negro clashes, coming one on top of the other, coupled with the unresolved political issues, had created a state of crisis.

On Thursday, inflammatory leaflets were circulated in the neighborhoods of the Fourth Precinct. A "Police Brutality Protest Rally" was announced for early evening in front of the Fourth Precinct Station. Several television stations and newspapers sent news teams to interview people. Cameras were set up. A crowd gathered.

A picket line was formed to march in front of the police station. Between 7 and 7:30 p.m., James Threatt, executive director of the Newark Human Rights Commission, arrived to announce to the people the decision of the mayor to form a citizens group to investigate the Smith incident, and to elevate a Negro to the rank of captain.

The response from the loosely milling mass of people was derisive. One youngster shouted "Black Power!" Rocks were thrown at Threatt, a Negro. The barrage of missiles that followed placed the police station under siege.

After the barrage had continued for some minutes, police came out to disperse the crowd. According to witnesses, there was little restraint of language or action by either side. A number of police officers and Negroes were injured.

As on the night before, once the people had been dispersed, reports of looting began to come in. Soon the glow of the first fire was seen.

Without enough men to establish control, the police set up a perimeter around a 2-mile stretch of Springfield Avenue, one of the principal business districts, where bands of youths roamed up and down smashing windows. Grocery and liquor stores, clothing and furniture stores, drugstores and cleaners, appliance stores and pawnshops were the principal targets. Periodically, police officers would appear and fire their weapons over the heads of looters and rioters. Laden with stolen goods, people began returning to the housing projects.

Near midnight, activity appeared to taper off. The mayor told reporters the city had turned the corner.

As news of the disturbances had spread, however, people had flocked into the streets. As they saw stores being broken into with impunity, many bowed to temptation and joined the looting.

Without the necessary personnel to make mass arrests, police were shooting into the air to clear stores. A Negro boy was wounded by a .22 caliber bullet said to have been fired by a white man riding in a car. Guns were reported stolen from a Sears, Roebuck store. Looting, fires, and gunshots were reported from a widening area. Between 2 and 2:30 a.m. on Friday, July 14, the mayor decided to request Gov. Richard J. Hughes to dispatch the state police and National Guard troops. The first elements of the state police arrived with a sizeable contingent before dawn.

During the morning the Governor and the mayor, together with the police and National Guard officers, made a reconnaissance of the area. The police escort guarding the officials arrested looters as they went. By early afternoon the National Guard had set up 137 road-blocks, and state police and riot teams were beginning to achieve control. Command of antiriot operations was taken over by the Governor, who decreed a "hard line" in putting down the riot.

As a result of technical difficulties, such as the fact that the city and state police did not operate on the same radio wave-lengths, the three-way command structure—city police, state police and National Guard—worked poorly.

At 3:30 p.m. that afternoon, the family of Mrs. D. J. was standing near the upstairs windows of their apartment, watching looters run in and out of a furniture store on Springfield Avenue. Three carloads of police rounded the corner. As the police yelled at the looters, they began running.

The police officers opened fire. A bullet smashed the kitchen window in Mrs. D. J.'s apartment. A moment later she heard a cry from the bedroom. Her 3-year-old daughter, Debbie, came running into the room. Blood was streaming down the left side of her face: the bullet had entered her eye. The child spent the next 2 months in the hospital. She lost the sight of her left eye and the hearing in her left ear.

Simultaneously, on the street below, Horace W. Morris, an associate director of the Washington Urban League who had been visiting relatives in Newark, was about to enter a car for the drive to Newark Airport. With him were his two brothers and his 73-year-old stepfather, Isaac Harrison. About 60 persons had been on the street watching the looting. As the police arrived, three of the looters cut directly in front of the group of spectators. The police fired at the looters. Bullets plowed into the spectators. Everyone began running. As Harrison, followed by the family, headed toward the apartment building in which he lived, a bullet kicked his legs out from under him. Horace Morris lifted him to his feet. Again he fell. Mr. Morris' brother, Virgil, attempted to pick the old man up. As he was doing so, he was hit in the left leg and right forearm. Mr. Morris and his other brother managed to drag the two wounded men into the vestibule of the building, jammed with 60 to 70 frightened, angry Negroes.

Bullets continued to spatter against the walls of the buildings. Finally, as the firing died down, Morris—whose stepfather died that evening—yelled to a sergeant that innocent people were being shot.

"Tell the black bastards to stop shooting at us," the sergeant, according to Morris, replied.

"They don't have guns; no one is shooting at you," Morris said.

"You shut up, there's a sniper on the roof," the sergeant yelled.

A short time later, at approximately 5 p.m., in the same vicinity, a police detective was killed by a small caliber bullet. The origin of the shot could not be determined. Later during the riot, a fireman was killed by a .30 caliber bullet. Snipers were blamed for the deaths of both.

At 5:30 p.m., on Beacon Street, W. F. told J. S., whose 1959 Pontiac he had taken to the station for inspection, that his front brake needed fixing. J. S., who had just returned from work, went to the car which was parked in the street, jacked up the front end, took the wheel off, and got under the car.

The street was quiet. More than a dozen persons were sitting on porches, walking about, or shopping. None heard any shots. Suddenly several state troopers appeared at the corner of Springfield and Beacon. J. S. was startled by a shot clanging into the side of the garbage can next to his car. As he looked up he saw a state trooper with his rifle pointed at him. The next shot struck him in the right side.

At almost the same instant, K. G., standing on a porch, was struck in the right eye by a bullet. Both he and J. S. were critically injured.

At 8 p.m., Mrs. L. M. bundled her husband, her husband's brother, and her four sons into the family car to drive to a restaurant for dinner. On the return trip her husband, who was driving, panicked as he approached a National Guard roadblock. He slowed the car, then quickly swerved around. A shot rang out. When the family reached home, everyone began piling out of the car. Ten-year-old Eddie failed to move. Shot through the head, he was dead.

Although, by nightfall, most of the looting and burning had ended, reports of sniper fire increased. The fire was, according to New Jersey National Guard reports, "deliberately or otherwise inaccurate." Maj. Gen. James F. Cantwell, Chief of Staff of the New Jersey National Guard, testified before an Armed Services Subcommittee of the House of Representatives that "there was too much firing initially against snipers" because of "confusion when we were finally called on for help and our thinking of it as a military action."

"As a matter of fact," Director of Police Spina told the Commission, "down in the Springfield Avenue area it was so bad that, in my opinion, Guardsmen were firing upon police and police were firing back at them * * *. I really don't believe there was as much sniping as we thought * * *. We have since compiled statistics indicating that there were 79 specified instances of sniping."

Several problems contributed to the misconceptions regarding snipers: the lack of communications; the fact that one shot might be reported half a dozen times by half a dozen different persons as it caromed and reverberated a mile or more through the city; the fact that the National Guard troops lacked riot training. They were, said a police official, "young and very scared," and had had little contact with Negroes.

Within the Guard itself contact with Negroes had certainly been limited. Although, in 1949, out of a force of 12,529 men there had been 1,183 Negroes, following the integration of the Guard in the 1950's the number had declined until, by July of 1967, there were 303 Negroes in a force of 17,529 men.

On Saturday, July 15, Spina received a report of snipers in a housing project. When he arrived he saw approximately 100 National Guardsmen and police officers crouching behind vehicles, hiding in corners and lying on the ground around the edge of the courtyard.

Since everything appeared quiet and it was broad daylight, Spina walked directly down the middle of the street. Nothing happened. As he came to the last building of the complex, he heard a shot. All around him the troopers jumped, believing themselves to be under sniper fire. A moment later a young Guardsman ran from behind a building.

The director of police went over and asked him if he had fired the shot. The soldier said yes, he had fired to scare a man away from a window; that his orders were to keep everyone away from windows.

Spina said he told the soldier: "Do you know what you just did? You have now created a state of hysteria. Every Guardsman up and down this street and every state policeman and every city policeman that is present thinks that somebody just fired a shot and that it is probably a sniper."

A short time later more "gunshots" were heard. Investigating, Spina came upon a Puerto Rican sitting on a wall. In reply to a question as to whether he knew "where the firing is coming from?" the man said: "That's no firing. That's fireworks. If you look up to the fourth floor, you will see the people who are throwing down these cherry bombs."

By this time, four truckloads of National Guardsmen had arrived and troopers and policemen were again crouched everywhere, looking for a sniper. The director of police remained at the scene for three hours, and the only shot fired was the one by the guardsman.

Nevertheless, at six o'clock that evening two columns of National Guardsmen and state troopers were directing mass fire at the Hayes Housing project in response to what they believed were snipers.

On the 10th floor, Eloise Spellman, the mother of several children, fell, a bullet through her neck.

Across the street, a number of persons, standing in an apartment window, were watching the firing directed at the housing project.

Suddenly, several troopers whirled and began firing in the general direction of the spectators. Mrs. Hattie Gainer, a grandmother, sank to the floor.

A block away Rebecca Brown's 2-year-old daughter was standing at the window. Mrs. Brown rushed to drag her to safety. As Mrs. Brown was, momentarily, framed in the window, a bullet spun into her back.

All three women died.

A number of eye witnesses, at varying times and places, reported seeing bottles thrown from upper story windows. As these would land at the feet of an officer he would turn and fire. Thereupon, other officers and Guardsmen up and down the street would join in.

In order to protect his property, B. W. W., the owner of a Chinese laundry, had placed a sign saying "Soul Brother" in his window. Between 1 and 1:30 a.m., on Sunday, July 16, he, his mother, wife, and brother, were watching television in the back room. The neighborhood had been quiet. Suddenly, B. W. W. heard the sound of jeeps, then shots.

Going to an upstairs window he was able to look out into the street. There he observed several jeeps, from which soldiers and state troopers were firing into stores that had "Soul Brother" signs in the windows. During the course of three nights, according to dozens of eye witness reports, law enforcement officers shot into and smashed windows of businesses that contained signs indicating they were Negro-owned.

At 11 p.m., on Sunday, July 16, Mrs. Lucille Pugh looked out of the window to see if the streets were clear. She then asked her 11-year-old son, Michael, to take the garbage out. As he reached the street and was illuminated by a street light, a shot rang out. He died.

By Monday afternoon, July 17, state police and National Guard forces were withdrawn. That evening, a Catholic priest saw two Negro men walking down the street. They were carrying a case of soda and two bags of groceries. An unmarked car with five police officers pulled up beside them. Two white officers got out of the car. Accusing the Negro men of looting, the officers made them put the groceries on the sidewalk, then kicked the bags open, scattering their contents all over the street.

Telling the men, "Get out of here," the officers drove off. The Catholic priest went across the street to help gather up the groceries. One of the men turned to him: "I've just been back from Vietnam 2 days," he said, "and this is what I get. I feel like going home and getting a rifle and shooting the cops."

Of the 250 fire alarms, many had been false, and 13 were considered by the city to have been "serious." Of the $10,251,000 damage total, four-fifths was due to stock loss. Damage to buildings and fixtures was less than $2 million.

Twenty-three persons were killed—a white detective, a white fireman, and 21 Negroes. One was 73-year-old Isaac Harrison. Six were women. Two were children. . . .

# VIII. DETROIT

On Saturday evening, July 22, the Detroit Police Department raided five "blind pigs." The blind pigs had had their origin in prohibition days, and survived as private social clubs. Often, they were after-hours drinking and gambling spots.

The fifth blind pig on the raid list, the United Community and Civic League at the corner of 12th Street and Clairmount, had been raided twice before. Once 10 persons had been picked up; another time, 28. A Detroit vice squad officer had tried but failed to get in shortly after 10 o'clock Saturday night. He succeeded, on his second attempt, at 3:45 Sunday morning.

The Tactical Mobile Unit, the Police Department's crowd control squad, had been dismissed at 3 a.m. Since Sunday morning traditionally is the least troublesome time for police in Detroit—and all over the country—only 193 officers were patroling the streets. Of these, 44 were in the 10th precinct where the blind pig was located.

Police expected to find two dozen patrons in the blind pig. That night, however, it was the scene of a party for several servicemen, two of whom were back from Vietnam. Instead of two dozen patrons, police found 82. Some voiced resentment at the police intrusion.

An hour went by before all 82 could be transported from the scene. The weather was humid and warm—the temperature that day was to rise to 86—and despite the late hour, many people were still on the street. In short order, a crowd of about 200 gathered.

In November of 1965, George Edwards, Judge of the United States Court of Appeals for the Sixth Circuit, and Commissioner of the Detroit Police Department from 1961 to 1963, had written in the *Michigan Law Review:*

> It is clear that in 1965 no one will make excuses for any city's inability to foresee the possibility of racial trouble. * * * Although local police forces generally regard themselves as public servants with the responsibility of maintaining law and order, they tend to minimize this attitude when they are patrolling areas that are heavily populated with Negro citizens. There, they tend to view each person on the streets as a potential criminal or enemy, and all too often that attitude is reciprocated. Indeed, hostility between the Negro communities in our large cities and the police departments, is the major problem in law enforcement in this decade. It has been a major cause of all recent race riots.

At the time of Detroit's 1943 race riot, Judge Edwards told Commission investigators, there was "open warfare between the Detroit Negroes and the Detroit Police Department." As late as 1961, he had thought that "Detroit was the leading candidate in the United States for a race riot."

There was a long history of conflict between the police department and citizens. During the labor battles of the 1930's, union members had come to view the Detroit Police Department as a strike-breaking force. The 1943 riot, in which 34 persons died, was the bloodiest in the United States in a span of two decades.

Judge Edwards and his successor, Commissioner Ray Girardin, attempted to restructure the image of the department. A Citizens Complaint Bureau was set up to facilitate the filing of complaints by citizens against officers. In practice, however, this Bureau appeared to work little better than less enlightened and more cumbersome procedures in other cities.

On 12th Street, with its high incidence of vice and crime, the issue of police brutality was a recurrent theme. A month earlier, the killing of a prostitute had been determined by police investigators to be the work of a pimp. According to rumors in the community, the crime had been committed by a vice squad officer.

At about the same time, the killing of Danny Thomas, a 27-year-old Negro Army veteran, by a gang of white youths had inflamed the community. The city's major newspapers played down the story in hope that the murder would not become a cause for increased tensions. The intent backfired. A banner story in the *Michigan Chronicle*, the city's Negro newspaper, began: "As James Meredith marched again Sunday to prove a Negro could walk in Mississippi without fear, a young woman who saw her husband killed by a white gang, shouting: 'Niggers keep out of Rouge Park,' lost her baby.

"Relatives were upset that the full story of the murder was not being told, apparently in an effort to prevent the incident from sparking a riot."

Some Negroes believed that the daily newspapers' treatment of the story was further evidence of the double standard: playing up crimes by Negroes, playing down crimes committed against Negroes.

Although police arrested one suspect for murder, Negroes questioned why the entire gang was not held. What, they asked, would have been the result if a white man had been killed by a gang of Negroes? What if Negroes had made the kind of advances toward a white woman that the white men were rumored to have made toward Mrs. Thomas?

The Thomas family lived only four or five blocks from the raided blind pig.

A few minutes after 5 a.m., just after the last of those arrested had been hauled away, an empty bottle smashed into the rear window of a police car. A litter basket was thrown through the window of a store. Rumors circulated of excess force used by the police during the raid. A youth, whom police nicknamed "Mr. Greensleeves" because of the color of his shirt, was shouting: "We're going to have a riot!" and exhorting the crowd to vandalism.

At 5:20 a.m., Commissioner Girardin was notified. He immediately called Mayor Jerome Cavanagh. Seventeen officers from other areas were ordered into the 10th Precinct. By 6 a.m., police strength had grown to 369 men. Of these, however, only 43 were committed to the immediate riot area. By that time, the number of persons on

12th Street was growing into the thousands and widespread window-smashing and looting had begun.

On either side of 12th Street were neat, middle-class districts. Along 12th Street itself, however, crowded apartment houses created a density of more than 21,000 persons per square mile, almost double the city average.

The movement of people when the slums of "Black Bottom" had been cleared for urban renewal had changed 12th Street from an integrated community into an almost totally black one, in which only a number of merchants remained white. Only 18 percent of the residents were homeowners. Twenty-five percent of the housing was considered so substandard as to require clearance. Another 19 percent had major deficiencies.

The crime rate was almost double that of the city as a whole. A Detroit police officer told Commission investigators that prostitution was so widespread that officers made arrests only when soliciting became blatant. The proportion of broken families was more than twice that in the rest of the city.

By 7:50 a.m., when a 17-man police commando unit attempted to make the first sweep, an estimated 3,000 persons were on 12th Street. They offered no resistance. As the sweep moved down the street, they gave way to one side, and then flowed back behind it.

A shoe store manager said he waited vainly for police for 2 hours as the store was being looted. At 8:25 a.m., someone in the crowd yelled, "The cops are coming!" The first flames of the riot billowed from the store. Firemen who responded were not harassed. The flames were extinguished.

By midmorning, 1,122 men—approximately a fourth of the police department—had reported for duty. Of these, 540 were in or near the six-block riot area. One hundred eight officers were attempting to establish a cordon. There was, however, no interference with looters, and police were refraining from the use of force.

Commissioner Girardin said: "If we had started shooting in there * * * not one of our policemen would have come out alive. I am convinced it would have turned into a race riot in the conventional sense."

According to witnesses, police at some roadblocks made little effort to stop people from going in and out of the area. Bantering took place between police officers and the populace, some still in pajamas. To some observers, there seemed at this point to be an atmosphere of apathy. On the one hand, the police failed to interfere with the looting. On the other, a number of older, more stable residents, who had seen the street deteriorate from a prosperous commercial thoroughfare to one ridden by vice, remained aloof.

Because officials feared that the 12th Street disturbance might be a diversion, many officers were sent to guard key installations in other sections of the city. Belle Isle, the recreation area in the Detroit River that had been the scene of the 1943 riot, was sealed off.

In an effort to avoid attracting people to the scene, some broadcasters cooperated by not reporting the riot, and an effort was made to downplay the extent of the disorder. The facade of "business as usual" necessitated the detailing of numerous police officers to protect the 50,000 spectators that were expected at that afternoon's New York Yankees–Detroit Tigers baseball game.

Early in the morning, a task force of community workers went into the area to dispel rumors and act as counterrioters. Such a task force had been singularly successful at the time of the incident in the Kercheval district in the summer of 1966, when scores of people had gathered at the site of an arrest. Kercheval, however, has a more stable population, fewer stores, less population density, and the city's most effective police-community relations program.

The 12th Street area, on the other hand, had been determined, in a 1966 survey conducted by Dr. Ernest Harburg of the Psychology Department of the University of Michigan, to be a community of high stress and tension. An overwhelming majority of the residents indicated dissatisfaction with their environment.

Of the interviewed, 93 percent said they wanted to move out of the neighborhood; 73 percent felt that the streets were not safe; 91 percent believed that a person was likely to be robbed or beaten at night; 58 percent knew of a fight within the last 12 months in which a weapon had been employed; 32 percent stated that they themselves owned a weapon; 57 percent were worried about fires.

A significant proportion believed municipal services to be inferior: 36 percent were dissatisfied with the schools; 43 percent with the city's contribution to the neighborhood; 77 percent with the recreational facilities; 78 percent believed police did not respond promptly when they were summoned for help.

U.S. Representative John Conyers, Jr., a Negro, was notified about the disturbance at his home a few blocks from 12th Street, at 8:30 a.m. Together with other community leaders, including Hubert G. Locke, a Negro and assistant to the commissioner of police, he began to drive around the area. In the side streets, he asked people to stay in their homes. On 12th Street, he asked them to disperse. It was, by his own account, a futile task.

Numerous eyewitnesses interviewed by Commission investigators tell of the carefree mood with which people ran in and out of stores, looting and laughing, and joking with the police officers. Stores with "Soul Brother" signs appeared no more immune than others. Looters paid no attention to residents who shouted at them and called their actions senseless. An epidemic of excitment [sic] had swept over the persons on the street.

Congressman Conyers noticed a woman with a baby in her arms; she was raging, cursing "whitey" for no apparent reason.

Shortly before noon, Congressman Conyers climbed atop a car in the middle of 12th Street to address the people. As he began to speak, he was confronted by a man in his fifties whom he had once, as a lawyer, represented in court. The man had been active in civil rights. He believed himself to have been persecuted as a result, and it was Conyers' opinion that he may have been wrongfully jailed. Extremely bitter, the man was inciting the crowd and challenging Conyers: "Why are you defending the cops and the establishment? You're just as bad as they are!"

A police officer in the riot area told Commission investigators that neither he nor his fellow officers were instructed as to what they were supposed to be doing. Witnesses tell of officers standing behind sawhorses as an area was being looted—and still standing there much later, when the mob had moved elsewhere. A squad from the commando unit, wearing helmets with face-covering visors and carrying bayonet-tipped carbines, blockaded a street several blocks from the scene of the riot. Their appearance drew residents into the street. Some began to harangue them and to question why they were in an area where there was no trouble. Representative Conyers convinced the police department to remove the commandos.

By that time, a rumor was threading through the crowd that a man had been bayoneted by the police. Influenced by such stories, the crowd became belligerent. At approximately 1 p.m., stonings accelerated. Numerous officers reported injuries from rocks, bottles, and other objects thrown at them. Smoke billowed upward from four fires, the first since the one at the shoe store early in the morning. When firemen answered the alarms, they became the target for rocks and bottles.

At 2 p.m., Mayor Cavanagh met with community and political leaders at police headquarters. Until then there had been hope that, as the people blew off steam, the riot would dissipate. Now the opinion was nearly unanimous that additional forces would be needed.

A request was made for state police aid. By 3 p.m., 360 officers were assembling at the armory. At that moment looting was spreading from the 12th Street area to other main thoroughfares.

There was no lack of the disaffected to help spread it. Although not yet as hard-pressed as Newark, Detroit was, like Newark, losing population. Its prosperous middle-class whites were moving to the suburbs and being replaced by unskilled Negro migrants. Between 1960 and 1967, the Negro population rose from just under 30 percent to an estimated 40 percent of the total.

In a decade, the school system had gained 50,000 to 60,000 children. Fifty-one percent of the elementary school classes were overcrowded. Simply to achieve the statewide average, the system needed 1,650 more teachers and 1,000 additional classrooms. The combined cost would be $63 million.

Of 300,000 school children, 171,000, or 57 percent, were Negro. According to the Detroit superintendent of schools, 25 different school districts surrounding the city spent up to $500 more per pupil per year than Detroit. In the inner city schools, more than half the pupils who entered high school became dropouts.

The strong union structure had created excellent conditions for most working men, but had left others, such as civil service and Government workers, comparatively disadvantaged and dissatisfied. In June, the "Blue Flu" had struck the city as police officers, forbidden to strike, had staged a sick-out. In September, the teachers were to go on strike. The starting wages for a plumber's helper were almost equal to the salary of a police officer or teacher.

Some unions, traditionally closed to Negroes, zealously guarded training opportunities. In January of 1967, the school system notified six apprenticeship trades it would not open any new apprenticeship classes unless a large number of Negroes were included. By fall, some of the programs were still closed.

High school diplomas from inner-city schools were regarded by personnel directors as less than valid. In July, unemployment was at a 5-year peak. In the 12th Street area, it was estimated to be between 12 and 15 percent for Negro men and 30 percent or higher for those under 25.

The more education a Negro had, the greater the disparity between his income and that of a white with the same level of education. The income of whites and Negroes with a seventh-grade education was about equal. The median income of whites with a high school diploma was $1,600 more per year than that of Negroes. White college graduates made $2,600 more. In fact, so far as income was concerned, it made very little difference to a Negro man whether he had attended school for 8 years or for 12. In the fall of 1967, a study conducted at one inner-city high school, Northwestern, showed that, although 50 percent of the dropouts had found work, 90 percent of the 1967 graduating class was unemployed.

Mayor Cavanagh had appointed many Negroes to key positions in his administration, but in elective offices the Negro population was still underrepresented. Of nine councilmen, one was a Negro. Of seven school board members, two were Negroes.

Although Federal programs had brought nearly $360 million to the city between 1962 and 1967, the money appeared to have had little impact at the grassroots. Urban renewal, for which $38 million had been allocated, was opposed by many residents of the poverty area.

Because of its financial straits, the city was unable to produce on promises to correct such conditions as poor garbage collection and bad street lighting, which brought constant complaints from Negro residents.

On 12th Street, Carl Perry, the Negro proprietor of a drugstore and photography studio, was dispensing ice cream, sodas, and candy to the youngsters streaming in and out of his store. For safekeeping, he had brought the photography equipment from his studio, in the next block, to the drugstore. The youths milling about repeatedly assured him that, although the market next door had been ransacked, his place of business was in no danger.

In midafternoon, the market was set afire. Soon after, the drug store went up in flames.

State Representative James Del Rio, a Negro, was camping out in front of a building he owned when two small boys, neither more than 10 years old, approached. One prepared to throw a brick through a window. Del Rio stopped him: "That building belongs to me," he said.

"I'm glad you told me, baby, because I was just about to bust you in!" the youngster replied.

Some evidence that criminal elements were organizing spontaneously to take advantage of the riot began to manifest itself. A number of cars were noted to be returning again and again, their occupants methodically looting stores. Months later, goods stolen during the riot were still being peddled.

A spirit of carefree nihilism was taking hold. To riot and to destroy appeared more and more to become ends in themselves. Late Sunday afternoon, it appeared to one observer that the young people were "dancing amidst the flames."

A Negro plainclothes officer was standing at an intersection when a man threw a Molotov cocktail into a business establishment at the corner. In the heat of the afternoon, fanned by the 20 to 25 m.p.h. winds of both Sunday and Monday, the fire reached the home next door within minutes. As residents uselessly sprayed the flames with garden hoses, the fire jumped from roof to roof of adjacent two- and three-story buildings. Within the hour, the entire block was in flames. The ninth house in the burning row belonged to the arsonist who had thrown the Molotov cocktail.

In some areas, residents organized rifle squads to protect firefighters. Elsewhere, especially as the wind-whipped flames began to overwhelm the Detroit Fire Department and more and more residences burned, the firemen were subjected to curses and rock-throwing.

Because of a lack of funds, on a per capita basis the department is one of the smallest in the Nation. In comparison to Newark, where approximately 1,000 firemen patrol an area of 16 square miles with a population of 400,000, Detroit's 1,700 firemen must cover a city of

140 square miles with a population of 1.6 million. Because the department had no mutual aid agreement with surrounding communities, it could not quickly call in reinforcements from outlying areas, and it was almost 9 p.m. before the first arrived. At one point, out of a total of 92 pieces of Detroit firefighting equipment and 56 brought in from surrounding communities, only four engine companies were available to guard areas of the city outside of the riot perimeter.

As the afternoon progressed, the fire department's radio carried repeated messages of apprehension and orders of caution:

> There is no police protection here at all; there isn't a policeman in the area. * * * If you have trouble at all, pull out! * * * We're being stoned at the scene. It's going good. We need help! * * * Protect yourselves! Proceed away from the scene. * * * Engine 42 over at Linwood and Gladstone. They are throwing bottles at us so we are getting out of the area. * * * All companies without police protection—all companies without police protection—orders are to withdraw, do not try to put out the fires. I repeat—all companies without police protection orders are to withdraw, do not try to put out the fires!

It was 4:30 p.m. when the firemen, some of them exhausted by the heat, abandoned an area of approximately 100 square blocks on either side of 12th Street to await protection from police and National Guardsmen.

During the course of the riot, firemen were to withdraw 283 times.

Fire Chief Charles J. Quinlan estimated that at least two-thirds of the buildings were destroyed by spreading fires rather than fires set at the scene. Of the 683 structures involved, approximately one-third were residential, and in few, if any, of these was the fire set originally.

Governor George Romney flew over the area between 8:30 and 9 p.m. "It looked like the city had been bombed on the west side and there was an area two-and-a-half miles by three-and-a-half miles with major fires, with entire blocks in flames," he told the Commission.

In the midst of chaos, there were some unexpected individual responses.

Twenty-four-year-old E.G., a Negro born in Savannah, Ga., had come to Detroit in 1965 to attend Wayne State University. Rebellion had been building in him for a long time because,

> You just had to bow down to the white man. * * * When the insurance man would come by he would always call out to my mother by her first name and we were expected to smile and greet him happily. * * * Man, I know he would never have thought of me or my father going to his home and calling his wife by her first name. Then I once saw a white man slapping a young pregnant Negro woman on the street with such force that she just spun around and fell. I'll never forget that.

When a friend called to tell him about the riot on 12th Street, E. G. went there expecting "a true revolt," but was disappointed as soon as he saw the looting begin: "I wanted to see the people really rise up in revolt. When I saw the first person coming out of the store with things in his arms, I really got sick to my stomach and wanted to go home. Rebellion against the white suppressors is one thing, but one measly pair of shoes or some food completely ruins the whole concept."

E. G. was standing in a crowd, watching firemen work, when Fire Chief Alvin Wall called out for help from the spectators. E. G. responded. His reasoning was: "No matter what color someone is, whether they are green or pink or blue, I'd help them if they were in trouble. That's all there is to it."

He worked with the firemen for 4 days, the only Negro in an all-white crew. Elsewhere, at scattered locations, a half dozen other Negro youths pitched in to help the firemen.

At 4:20 p.m., Mayor Cavanagh requested that the National Guard be brought into Detroit. Although a major portion of the Guard was in its summer encampment 200 miles away, several hundred troops were conducting their regular week-end drill in the city. That circumstance obviated many problems. The first troops were on the streets by 7 p.m.

At 7:45 p.m., the mayor issued a proclamation instituting a 9 p.m. to 5 a.m. curfew. At 9:07 p.m., the first sniper fire was reported.

Following his aerial survey of the city, Governor Romney, at or shortly before midnight, proclaimed that "a state of public emergency exists" in the cities of Detroit, Highland Park and Hamtramck.

At 4:45 p.m., a 68-year-old white shoe repairman, George Messerlian, had seen looters carrying clothes from a cleaning establishment next to his shop. Armed with a saber, he had rushed into the street, flailing away at the looters. One Negro youth was nicked on the shoulder. Another, who had not been on the scene, inquired as to what had happened. After he had been told, he allegedly replied: "I'll get the old man for you!"

Going up to Messerlian, who had fallen or been knocked to the ground, the youth began to beat him with a club. Two other Negro youths dragged the attacker away from the old man. It was too late. Messerlian died 4 days later in the hospital.

At 9:15 p.m., a 16-year-old Negro boy, superficially wounded while looting, became the first reported gunshot victim.

At midnight, Sharon George, a 23-year-old white woman, together with her two brothers, was a passenger in a car being driven by her husband. After having dropped off two Negro friends, they were returning home on one of Detroit's main avenues when they were slowed by a milling throng in the street. A shot fired from close range struck the car. The bullet splintered in Mrs. George's body. She died less than 2 hours later.

An hour before midnight, a 45-year-old white man, Walter Grzanka, together with three white companions, went into the street. Shortly thereafter, a market was broken into. Inside the show window, a Negro man began filling bags with groceries and handing them to confederates outside the store. Grzanka twice went over to the store, accepted bags, and placed them down beside his companions across the street. On the third occasion he entered the market. When he emerged, the market owner, driving by in his car, shot and killed him.

In Grzanka's pockets, police found seven cigars, four packages of pipe tobacco, and nine pairs of shoelaces.

Before dawn, four other looters were shot, one of them accidentally while struggling with a police officer. A Negro youth and a National Guardsman were injured by gunshots of undetermined origin. A private guard shot himself while pulling his revolver from his pocket. In the basement of the 13th Precinct Police Station, a cue ball, thrown by an unknown assailant, cracked against the head of a sergeant.

At about midnight, three white youths, armed with a shotgun, had gone to the roof of their apartment building, located in an all-white block, in order, they said, to protect the building from fire. At 2:45 a.m., a patrol car, carrying police officers and National Guardsmen, received a report of "snipers on the roof." As the patrol car arrived, the manager of the building went to the roof to tell the youths they had better come down.

The law enforcement personnel surrounded the building, some going to the front, others to the rear. As the manager, together with the three youths, descended the fire escape in the rear, a National Guardsman, believing he heard shots from the front, fired. His shot killed 23-year-old Clifton Pryor.

Early in the morning, a young white fireman and a 49-year-old Negro homeowner were killed by fallen power lines.

By 2 a.m. Monday, Detroit police had been augmented by 800 State Police officers and 1,200 National Guardsmen. An additional 8,000 Guardsmen were on the way. Nevertheless, Governor Romney and Mayor Cavanagh decided to ask for Federal assistance. At 2:15 a.m., the mayor called Vice President Hubert Humphrey, and was referred to Attorney General Ramsey Clark. A short time thereafter, telephone contact was established between Governor Romney and the attorney general.*

There is some difference of opinion about what occurred next. According to the attorney general's office, the governor was advised of the seriousness of the request and told that the applicable Federal statute required that, before Federal troops could be brought into the city, he would have to state that the situation had deteriorated to the point that local and state forces could no longer maintain law and order. According to the governor, he was under the impression that he was being asked to declare that a "state of insurrection" existed in the city.

---

* A little over two hours earlier, at 11:55 p.m., Mayor Cavanagh had informed the U.S. Attorney General that a "dangerous situation existed in the city." Details are set forth in the final report of Cyrus R. Vance, covering the Detroit riot, released on September 12, 1967.

The governor was unwilling to make such a declaration, contending that, if he did, insurance policies would not cover the loss incurred as a result of the riot. He and the mayor decided to re-evaluate the need for Federal troops.

Contact between Detroit and Washington was maintained throughout the early morning hours. At 9 a.m., as the disorder still showed no sign of abating, the governor and the mayor decided to make a renewed request for Federal troops.

Shortly before noon, the President of the United States authorized the sending of a task force of paratroops to Selfridge Air Force Base, near the city. A few minutes past 3 p.m., Lt. Gen. John L. Throckmorton, commander of Task Force Detroit, met Cyrus Vance, former Deputy Secretary of Defense, at the air base. Approximately an hour later, the first Federal troops arrived at the air base.

After meeting with state and municipal officials, Mr. Vance, General Throckmorton, Governor Romney, and Mayor Cavanagh, made a tour of the city, which lasted until 7:15 p.m. During this tour Mr. Vance and General Throckmorton independently came to the conclusion that—since they had seen no looting or sniping, since the fires appeared to be coming under control, and since a substantial number of National Guardsmen had not yet been committed—injection of Federal troops would be premature.

As the riot alternately waxed and waned, one area of the ghetto remained insulated. On the northeast side, the residents of some 150 square blocks inhabited by 21,000 persons had, in 1966, banded together in the Positive Neighborhood Action Committee (PNAC). With professional help from the Institute of Urban Dynamics, they had organized block clubs and made plans for the improvement of the neighborhood. In order to meet the need for recreational facilities, which the city was not providing, they had raised $3,000 to purchase empty lots for playgrounds. Although opposed to urban renewal, they had agreed to cosponsor with the Archdiocese of Detroit a housing project to be controlled jointly by the archdiocese and PNAC.

When the riot broke out, the residents, through the block clubs, were able to organize quickly. Youngsters, agreeing to stay in the neighborhood, participated in detouring traffic. While many persons reportedly sympathized with the idea of a rebellion against the "system," only two small fires were set—one in an empty building.

During the daylight hours Monday, nine more persons were killed by gunshots elsewhere in the city, and many others were seriously or critically injured. Twenty-three-year-old Nathaniel Edmonds, a Negro, was sitting in his backyard when a young white man stopped his car, got out, and began an argument with him. A few minutes later, declaring he was "going to paint his picture on him with a shotgun," the white man allegedly shotgunned Edmonds to death.

Mrs. Nannie Pack and Mrs. Mattie Thomas were sitting on the porch of Mrs. Pack's house when police began chasing looters from a nearby market. During the chase officers fired three shots from their shotguns. The discharge from one of these accidentally struck the two women. Both were still in the hospital weeks later.

Included among those critically injured when they were accidentally trapped in the line of fire were an 8-year-old Negro girl and a 14-year-old white boy.

As darkness settled Monday, the number of incidents reported to police began to rise again. Although many turned out to be false, several involved injuries to police officers, National Guardsmen, and civilians by gunshots of undetermined origin.

Watching the upward trend of reported incidents, Mr. Vance and General Throckmorton became convinced Federal troops should be used, and President Johnson was so advised. At 11:20 p.m., the President signed a proclamation federalizing the Michigan National Guard and authorizing the use of the paratroopers.

At this time, there were nearly 5,000 Guardsmen in the city, but fatigue, lack of training, and the haste with which they had had to be deployed reduced their effectiveness. Some of the Guardsmen traveled 200 miles and then were on duty for 30 hours straight. Some had never received riot training and were given on-the-spot instructions on mob control—only to discover that there were no mobs, and that the situation they faced on the darkened streets was one for which they were unprepared.

Commanders committed men as they became available, often in small groups. In the resulting confusion, some units were lost in the city. Two Guardsmen assigned to an intersection on Monday were discovered still there on Friday.

Lessons learned by the California National Guard two years earlier in Watts regarding the danger of overreaction and the necessity of great restraint in using weapons had not, apparently, been passed on to the Michigan National Guard. The young troopers could not be expected to know what a danger they were creating by the lack of fire discipline, not only to the civilian population but to themselves.

A Detroit newspaper reporter who spent a night riding in a command jeep told a Commission investigator of machine guns being fired accidentally, street lights being shot out by rifle fire, and buildings being placed under siege on the sketchiest reports of sniping. Troopers would fire, and immediately from the distance there would be answering fire, sometimes consisting of tracer bullets.

In one instance, the newsman related, a report was received on the jeep radio that an Army bus was pinned down by sniper fire at an intersection. National Guardsmen and police, arriving from various directions, jumped out and began asking each other: "Where's the sniper fire coming from?" As one Guardsman pointed to a building, everyone rushed about, taking cover. A soldier, alighting from a jeep, accidentally pulled the trigger on his rifle. As the shot reverberated through the darkness, an officer yelled: "What's going on?" "I don't know," came the answer. "Sniper, I guess."

Without any clear authorization or direction, someone opened fire upon the suspected building. A tank rolled up and sprayed the building with .50-caliber tracer bullets. Law enforcement officers rushed into the surrounded building and discovered it empty. "They must be firing one shot and running," was the verdict.

The reporter interviewed the men who had gotten off the bus and were crouched around it. When he asked them about the sniping incident, he was told that someone had heard a shot. He asked "Did the bullet hit the bus?" The answer was: "Well, we don't know."

Bracketing the hour of midnight Monday, heavy firing, injuring many persons and killing several, occurred in the southeastern sector, which was to be taken over by the paratroopers at 4 a.m., Tuesday, and which was, at this time, considered to be the most active riot area in the city.

Employed as a private guard, 55-year-old Julius L. Dorsey, a Negro, was standing in front of a market when accosted by two Negro men and a woman. They demanded he permit them to loot the market. He ignored their demands. They began to berate him. He asked a neighbor to call the police. As the argument grew more heated, Dorsey fired three shots from his pistol into the air.

The police radio reported: "Looters, they have rifles." A patrol car driven by a police officer and carrying three National Guardsmen arrived. As the looters fled, the law enforcement personnel opened fire. When the firing ceased, one person lay dead.

He was Julius L. Dorsey.

In two areas—one consisting of a triangle formed by Mack, Gratiot, and E. Grand Boulevard, the other surrounding Southeastern High School—firing began shortly after 10 p.m. and continued for several hours.

In the first of the areas, a 22-year-old Negro complained that he had been shot at by snipers. Later, a half dozen civilians and one National Guardsman were wounded by shots of undetermined origin.

Henry Denson, a passenger in a car, was shot and killed when the vehicle's driver, either by accident or intent, failed to heed a warning to halt at a National Guard roadblock.

Similar incidents occurred in the vicinity of Southeastern High School, one of the National Guard staging areas. As early as 10:20 p.m., the area was reported to be under sniper fire. Around midnight there were two incidents, the sequence of which remains in doubt.

Shortly before midnight, Ronald Powell, who lived three blocks east of the high school and whose wife was, momentarily, expecting a baby, asked the four friends with whom he had been spending the evening to take him home. He, together with Edward Blackshear, Charles Glover, and John Leroy climbed into Charles Dunson's station wagon for the short drive. Some of the five may have been drinking, but none was intoxicated.

To the north of the high school, they were halted at a National Guard roadblock, and told they would have to detour around the school and a fire station at Mack and St. Jean Streets because of the firing that had been occurring. Following orders, they took a circuitous route and approached Powell's home from the south.

On Lycaste Street, between Charlevoix and Goethe, they saw a jeep sitting at the curb. Believing it to be another roadblock, they slowed down. Simultaneously a shot rang out. A National Guardsmen fell, hit in the ankle.

Other National Guardsmen at the scene thought the shot had come from the station wagon. Shot after shot was directed against the vehicle, at least 17 of them finding their mark. All five occupants were injured, John Leroy fatally.

At approximately the same time, firemen, police, and National Guardsmen at the corner of Mack and St. Jean Streets, 2½ blocks away, again came under fire from what they believed were rooftop snipers to the southeast, the direction of Charlevoix and Lycaste. The police and guardsmen responded with a hail of fire.

When the shooting ceased, Carl Smith, a young firefighter, lay dead. An autopsy determined that the shot had been fired at street level, and, according to police, probably had come from the southeast.

At 4 a.m., when paratroopers, under the command of Col. A. R. Bolling, arrived at the high school, the area was so dark and still that the colonel thought, at first, that he had come to the wrong place. Investigating, he discovered National Guard troops, claiming they were pinned down by sniper fire, crouched behind the walls of the darkened building.

The colonel immediately ordered all of the lights in the building turned on and his troops to show themselves as conspicuously as possible. In the apartment house across the street, nearly every window had been shot out, and the walls were pockmarked with bullet holes. The colonel went into the building and began talking to the residents, many of whom had spent the night huddled on the floor. He reassured them no more shots would be fired.

According to Lieutenant General Throckmorton and Colonel Bolling, the city, at this time, was saturated with fear. The National Guardsmen were afraid, the residents were afraid, and the police were afraid. Numerous persons, the majority of them Negroes, were being injured by gunshots of undetermined origin. The general and his staff felt that the major task of the troops was to reduce the fear and restore an air of normalcy.

In order to accomplish this, every effort was made to establish contact and rapport between the troops and the residents. Troopers—20 percent of whom were Negro—began helping to clean up the streets, collect garbage, and trace persons who had disappeared in the confusion. Residents in the neighborhoods responded with soup and sandwiches for the troops. In areas where the National Guard tried to establish rapport with the citizens, there was a similar response.

Within hours after the arrival of the paratroops, the area occupied by them was the quietest in the city, bearing out General Throckmorton's view that the key to quelling a disorder is to saturate an area with "calm, determined, and hardened professional soldiers." Loaded weapons, he believes, are unnecessary. Troopers had strict orders not to fire unless they could see the specific person at whom they were aiming. Mass fire was forbidden.

During five days in the city, 2,700 Army troops expended only 201 rounds of ammunition, almost all during the first few hours, after which even stricter fire discipline was enforced. (In contrast, New Jersey National Guardsmen and state police expended 13,326 rounds of ammunition in three days in Newark.) Hundreds of reports of sniper fire—most of them false—continued to pour into police headquarters; the Army logged only 10. No paratrooper was injured by a gunshot. Only one person was hit by a shot fired by a trooper. He was a young Negro who was killed when he ran into the line of fire as a trooper, aiding police in a raid on an apartment, aimed at a person believed to be a sniper.

General Throckmorton ordered the weapons of all military personnel unloaded, but either the order failed to reach many National Guardsmen, or else it was disobeyed.

Even as the general was requesting the city to relight the streets, Guardsmen continued shooting out the lights, and there were reports of dozens of shots being fired to dispatch one light. At one such location, as Guardsmen were shooting out the street lights, a radio newscaster reported himself to be pinned down by "sniper fire."

On the same day that the general was attempting to restore normalcy by ordering street barricades taken down, Guardsmen on one street were not only, in broad daylight, ordering people off the street, but off their porches and away from the windows. Two persons who failed to respond to the order quickly enough were shot, one of them fatally.

The general himself reported an incident of a Guardsman "firing across the bow" of an automobile that was approaching a roadblock.

As in Los Angeles 2 years earlier, roadblocks that were ill-lighted and ill-defined—often consisting of no more than a trash barrel or similar object with Guardsmen standing nearby—proved a continuous hazard to motorists. At one such roadblock, National Guard Sgt. Larry Post, standing in the street, was caught in a sudden crossfire as his fellow Guardsmen opened up on a vehicle. He was the only soldier killed in the riot.

With persons of every description arming themselves, and guns being fired accidentally or on the vaguest pretext all over the city, it became more and more impossible to tell who was shooting at whom. Some firemen began carrying guns. One accidentally shot and wounded a fellow fireman. Another injured himself.

The chaos of a riot, and the difficulties faced by police officers, are demonstrated by an incident that occurred at 2 a.m., Tuesday.

A unit of 12 officers received a call to guard firemen from snipers. When they arrived at the corner of Vicksburg and Linwood in the 12th Street area, the intersection was well-lighted by the flames completely enveloping one building. Sniper fire was directed at the officers from an alley to the north, and gun flashes were observed in two buildings.

As the officers advanced on the two buildings, Patrolman Johnie Hamilton fired several rounds from his machinegun. Thereupon, the officers were suddenly subjected to fire from a new direction, the east. Hamilton, struck by four bullets, fell, critically injured, in the intersection. As two officers ran to his aid, they too were hit.

By this time other units of the Detroit Police Department, state police, and National Guard had arrived on the scene, and the area was covered with a hail of gunfire.

In the confusion the snipers who had initiated the shooting escaped.

At 9:15 p.m., Tuesday, July 25, 38–year-old Jack Sydnor, a Negro, came home drunk. Taking out his pistol, he fired one shot into an alley. A few minutes later, the police arrived. As his common-law wife took refuge in a closet, Sydnor waited, gun in hand, while the police forced open the door. Patrolman Roger Poike, the first to enter, was shot by Sydnor. Although critically injured, the officer managed to get off six shots in return. Police within the building and on the street then poured a hail of fire into the apartment. When the shooting ceased,

Sydnor's body, riddled by the gunfire, was found lying on the ground outside a window.

Nearby, a state police officer and a Negro youth were struck and seriously injured by stray bullets. As in other cases where the origin of the shots was not immediately determinable, police reported them as "shot by sniper."

Reports of "heavy sniper fire" poured into police headquarters from the two blocks surrounding the apartment house where the battle with Jack Sydnor had taken place. National Guard troops with two tanks were dispatched to help flush out the snipers.

Shots continued to be heard throughout the neighborhood. At approximately midnight—there are discrepancies as to the precise time—a machinegunner on a tank, startled by several shots, asked the assistant gunner where the shots were coming from. The assistant gunner pointed toward a flash in the window of an apartment house from which there had been earlier reports of sniping.

The machinegunner opened fire. As the slugs ripped through the window and walls of the apartment, they nearly severed the arm of 21-year-old Valerie Hood. Her 4-year-old niece, Tonya Blanding, toppled dead, a .50-caliber bullet hole in her chest.

A few seconds earlier, 19-year-old Bill Hood, standing in the window, had lighted a cigarette.

Down the street, a bystander was critically injured by a stray bullet. Simultaneously, the John C. Lodge Freeway, two blocks away, was reported to be under sniper fire. Tanks and National Guard troops were sent to investigate. At the Harlan House Motel, 10 blocks from where Tonya Blanding had died a short time earlier, Mrs. Helen Hall, a 51-year-old white businesswoman, opened the drapes of the fourth floor hall window. Calling out to other guests, she exclaimed: "Look at the tanks!"

She died seconds later as bullets began to slam into the building. As the firing ceased, a 19-year-old Marine, carrying a Springfield rifle, burst into the building. When, accidentally, he pushed the rifle barrel through a window, firing commenced anew. A police investigation showed that the Marine, who had just decided to "help out" the law enforcement personnel, was not involved in the death of Mrs. Hall.

R. R., a white 27-year-old coin dealer, was the owner of an

expensive, three-story house on L Street, an integrated middle-class neighborhood. In May of 1966, he and his wife and child had moved to New York and had rented the house to two young men. After several months, he had begun to have problems with his tenants. On one occasion, he reported to his attorney that he had been threatened by them.

In March of 1967, R. R. instituted eviction proceedings. These were still pending when the riot broke out. Concerned about the house, R. R. decided to fly to Detroit. When he arrived at the house on Wednesday, July 26, he discovered the tenants were not at home.

He then called his attorney, who advised him to take physical possession of the house and, for legal purposes, to take witnesses along.

Together with his 17-year-old brother and another white youth, R. R. went to the house, entered, and began changing the locks on the doors. For protection they brought a .22 caliber rifle, which R. R.'s brother took into the cellar and fired into a pillow in order to test it.

Shortly after 8 p.m., R. R. called his attorney to advise him that the tenants had returned, and he had refused to admit them. Thereupon, R. R. alleged, the tenants had threatened to obtain the help of the National Guard. The attorney relates that he was not particularly concerned. He told R. R. that if the National Guard did appear he should have the officer in charge call him (the attorney).

At approximately the same time, the National Guard claims it received information to the effect that several men had evicted the legal occupants of the house, and intended to start sniping after dark.

A National Guard column was dispatched to the scene. Shortly after 9 p.m., in the half-light of dusk, the column of approximately 30 men surrounded the house. A tank took position on a lawn across the street. The captain commanding the column placed in front of the house an explosive device similar to a firecracker. After setting this off in order to draw the attention of the occupants to the presence of the column, he called for them to come out of the house. No attempt was made to verify the truth or falsehood of the allegations regarding snipers.

When the captain received no reply from the house, he began counting to 10. As he was counting, he said, he heard a shot, the origin of which he could not determine. A few seconds, later he heard another shot and saw a "fire streak" coming from an upstairs window. He thereupon gave the order to fire.

According to the three young men, they were on the second floor of the house and completely bewildered by the barrage of fire that was unleashed against it. As hundreds of bullets crashed through the first- and second-story windows and richocheted [sic] off the walls, they dashed to the third floor. Protected by a large chimney, they huddled in a closet until, during a lull in the firing, they were able to wave an item of clothing out of the window as a sign of surrender. They were arrested as snipers.

The firing from rifles and machine guns had been so intense that in a period of a few minutes it inflicted an estimated $10,000 worth of damage. One of a pair of stone columns was shot nearly in half.

Jailed at the 10th precinct station sometime Wednesday night, R. R. and his two companions were taken from their cell to an "alley court," police slang for an unlawful attempt to make prisoners confess. A police officer, who has resigned from the force, allegedly administered such a severe beating to R. R. that the bruises still were visible 2 weeks later.

R. R.'s 17-year-old brother had his skull cracked open, and was thrown back into the cell. He was taken to a hospital only when other arrestees complained that he was bleeding to death.

At the preliminary hearing 12 days later, the prosecution presented only one witness, the National Guard captain who had given the order to fire. The police officer who had signed the original complaint was not asked to take the stand. The charges against all three of the young men were dismissed.

Nevertheless, the morning after the original incident, a major metropolitan newspaper in another section of the country composed the following banner story from wire service reports:

DETROIT, *July 27* (*Thursday*).—Two National Guard tanks ripped a sniper's haven with machine guns Wednesday night and flushed out three shaggy-haired white youths. Snipers attacked a guard command post and Detroit's racial riot set a modern record for bloodshed. The death toll soared to 36, topping the Watts bloodbath of 1966 in which 35 died and making Detroit's insurrection the most deadly racial riot in modern U.S. history. * * *

In the attack on the sniper's nest, the Guardsmen poured hundreds of rounds of .50 caliber machine gun fire into the home, which authorities said housed arms and ammunition used by West Side sniper squads.

Guardsmen recovered guns and ammunition. A reporter with the troopers said the house, a neat brick home in a neighborhood of $20,000 to $50,000 homes, was torn apart by the machine gun and rifle fire.

Sniper fire crackled from the home as the Guard unit approached. It was one of the first verified reports of sniping by whites. * * *

A pile of loot taken from riot-ruined stores was recovered from the sniper's haven, located ten blocks from the heart of the 200-square block riot zone.

Guardsmen said the house had been identified as a store-house of arms and ammunition for snipers. Its arsenal was regarded as an indication that the sniping—or at least some of it—was organized.

As hundreds of arrestees were brought into the 10th precinct station, officers took it upon themselves to carry on investigations and to attempt to extract confessions. Dozens of charges of police brutality emanated from the station as prisoners were brought in uninjured, but later had to be taken to the hospital.

In the absence of the precinct commander, who had transferred his headquarters to the riot command post at a nearby hospital, discipline vanished. Prisoners who requested that they be permitted to notify someone of their arrest were almost invariably told that: "The telephones are out of order." Congressman Conyers and State Representative Del Rio, who went to the station hoping to coordinate with the police the establishing of a community patrol, were so upset by what they saw that they changed their minds and gave up on the project.

A young woman, brought into the station, was told to strip. After she had done so, and while an officer took pictures with a Polaroid camera, another officer came up to her and began fondling her. The negative of one of the pictures, fished out of a wastebasket, subsequently was turned over to the mayor's office.

Citing the sniper danger, officers throughout the department had taken off their bright metal badges. They also had taped over the license plates and the numbers of the police cars. Identification of individual officers became virtually impossible.

On a number of occasions officers fired at fleeing looters, then made little attempt to determine whether their shots had hit anyone. Later some of the persons were discovered dead or injured in the street.

In one such case police and National Guardsmen were interrogating a youth suspected of arson when, according to officers, he attempted to escape. As he vaulted over the hood of an automobile, an officer fired his shotgun. The youth disappeared on the other side of the car. Without making an investigation, the officers and Guardsmen returned to their car and drove off.

When nearby residents called police, another squad car arrived to pick up the body. Despite the fact that an autopsy disclosed the youth had been killed by five shotgun pellets, only a cursory investigation was made, and the death was attributed to "sniper fire." No police officer at the scene during the shooting filed a report.

Not until a Detroit newspaper editor presented to the police the statements of several witnesses claiming that the youth had been shot by police after he had been told to run did the department launch an investigation. Not until 3 weeks after the shooting did an officer come forward to identify himself as the one who had fired the fatal shot.

Citing conflicts in the testimony of the score of witnesses, the Detroit Prosecutor's office declined to press charges.

Prosecution is proceeding in the case of three youths in whose shotgun deaths law enforcement personnel were implicated following a report that snipers were firing from the Algiers Motel. In fact, there is little evidence that anyone fired from inside the building. Two witnesses say that they had seen a man, standing outside of the motel, fire two shots from a rifle. The interrogation of other persons revealed that law enforcement personnel then shot out one or more street lights. Police patrols responded to the shots. An attack was launched on the motel.

The picture is further complicated by the fact that this incident occurred at roughly the same time that the National Guard was directing fire at the apartment house in which Tonya Blanding was killed. The apartment house was only six blocks distant from and in a direct line with the motel.

The killings occurred when officers began on-the-spot questioning of the occupants of the motel in an effort to discover weapons used in the "sniping." Several of those questioned reportedly were beaten. One was a Negro ex-paratrooper who had only recently been honorably discharged, and had gone to Detroit to look for a job.

Although by late Tuesday looting and fire-bombing had virtually ceased, between 7 and 11 p.m. that night there were 444 reports of incidents. Most were reports of sniper fire.

During the daylight hours of July 26, there were 534 such reports. Between 8:30 and 11 p.m., there were 255. As they proliferated, the pressure on law enforcement officers to uncover the snipers became intense. Homes were broken into. Searches were made on the flimsiest of tips. A Detroit newspaper headline aptly proclaimed: "Everyone's Suspect in No Man's Land."

Before the arrest of a young woman IBM operator in the city assessor's office brought attention to the situation on Friday, July 28, any person with a gun in his home was liable to be picked up as a suspect.

Of the 27 persons charged with sniping, 22 had charges against them dismissed at preliminary hearings, and the charges against two others were dismissed later. One pleaded guilty to possession of an unregistered gun and was given a suspended sentence. Trials of two are pending.

In all, more than 7,200 persons were arrested. Almost 3,000 of these were picked up on the second day of the riot, and by midnight Monday 4,000 were incarcerated in makeshift jails. Some were kept as long as 30 hours on buses. Others spent days in an underground garage without toilet facilities. An uncounted number were people who had merely been unfortunate enough to be on the wrong street at the wrong time. Included were members of the press whose attempts to show their credentials had been ignored. Released later, they were chided for not having exhibited their identification at the time of their arrests.

The booking system proved incapable of adequately handling the large number of arrestees. People became lost for days in the maze of different detention facilities. Until the later stages, bail was set deliberately high, often at $10,000 or more. When it became apparent that this policy was unrealistic and unworkable, the prosecutor's office began releasing on low bail or on their own recognizance hundreds of those who had been picked up. Nevertheless, this fact was not publicized for fear of antagonizing those who had demanded a high-bail policy.

Of the 43 persons who were killed during the riot, 33 were Negro and 10 were white. Seventeen were looters, of whom two were white. Fifteen citizens (of whom four were white), one white National Guardsman, one white fireman, and one Negro private guard died as the result of gunshot wounds. Most of these deaths appear to have been accidental, but criminal homicide is suspected in some.

Two persons, including one fireman, died as a result of fallen power-lines. Two were burned to death. One was a drunken gunman; one an arson suspect. One white man was killed by a rioter. One police officer was felled by a shotgun blast when a gun, in the hands of another officer, accidentally discharged during a scuffle with a looter.

Action by police officers accounted for 20 and, very likely, 21 of the deaths; action by the National Guard for seven, and, very likely, nine; action by the Army for one. Two deaths were the result of action by store-owners. Four persons died accidentally. Rioters were responsible for two, and perhaps three of the deaths; a private guard for one. A white man is suspected of murdering a Negro youth. The perpetrator of one of the killings in the Algiers Motel remains unknown.

Damage estimates, originally set as high as $500 million, were quickly scaled down. The city assessor's office placed the loss—excluding business stock, private furnishings, and the buildings of churches and charitable institutions—at approximately $22 million. Insurance payments, according to the State Insurance Bureau, will come to about $32 million, representing an estimated 65 to 75 percent of the total loss.

By Thursday, July 27, most riot activity had ended. The paratroopers were removed from the city on Saturday. On Tuesday, August 1, the curfew was lifted and the National Guard moved out.

## METHODOLOGY—PROFILES OF DISORDER

Construction of the Profiles of Disorder began with surveys by field teams in 23 cities. From an analysis of the documents compiled and field interviews, 10 of the 23, a fair cross section of the cities, were chosen for intensive further investigation.

A special investigating group was dispatched to each city under study to conduct in-depth interviews of persons previously questioned and others that had come to our attention as a result of the analysis. Additional documents were obtained. In the process of acquisition, analysis, and distillation of information, the special investigating group made several trips to each city. In the meantime, the regular field teams continued to conduct their surveys and report additional information.

The approximately 1,200 persons interviewed represent a cross section of officials, observers, and participants involved in the riot process—from mayors, police chiefs, and army officers to Black Power advocates and rioters. Experts in diverse fields, such as taxation, fire fighting, and psychology, were consulted. Testimony presented to the Commission in closed hearings was incorporated.

Many official documents were used in compiling chronologies and corroborating statements made by witnesses. These included but were not limited to police department and other law enforcement agencies' after-action reports, logs, incident reports, injury reports, and reports of homicide investigations; after-action reports of U.S. Army and National Guard units; FBI reports; fire department logs and reports; and reports from Prosecutors' offices and other investigating agencies.

About 1,500 pages of depositions were taken from 90 witnesses to substantiate each of the principal items in the Profiles.

Since some information was supplied to the Commission on a confidential basis, a fully annotated, footnoted copy of the Profiles cannot be made public at this time, but will be deposited in the Archives of the United States.

# CHAPTER 2

# PATTERNS OF DISORDER

———

## INTRODUCTION

The President asked the Commission to answer several specific questions about the nature of riots:

- The kinds of communities in which they occurred;
- The characteristics—including age, education, and job history—of those who rioted and those who did not;
- The ways in which groups of lawful citizens can be encouraged to help cool the situation;
- The relative impact of various depressed conditions in the ghetto which stimulated people to riot;
- The impact of Federal and other programs on those conditions;
- The effect on rioting of police-community relationships;
- The parts of the community which suffered the most as a result of the disorders.

The Profiles in the foregoing chapter portray the nature and extent of 10 of the disorders which took place during the summer of 1967. This chapter seeks in these events, and in the others which we surveyed, a set of common elements to aid in understanding what happened and in answering the President's questions.

This chapter also considers certain popular conceptions about riots. Disorders are often discussed as if there were a single type. The "typical" riot of recent years is sometimes seen as a massive uprising against white people, involving widespread burning, looting, and sniping, either by all ghetto Negroes or by an uneducated, Southern-born Negro underclass of habitual criminals or "riffraff". An agitator at a protest demonstration, the coverage of events by the news media, or an isolated "triggering" or "precipitating" incident, is often identified as the primary spark of violence. A uniform set of stages is sometimes posited, with a succession of confrontations and withdrawals by two cohesive groups, the police on one side and a riotous mob on the other. Often it is assumed that there was no effort within the Negro community to reduce the violence. Sometimes the only remedy prescribed is application of the largest possible police or control force, as early as possible.

What we have found does not validate these conceptions. We have been unable to identify constant patterns in all aspects of civil disorders. We have found that they are unusual, irregular, complex, and, in the present state of knowledge, unpredictable social processes. Like many human events, they do not unfold in orderly sequences.

Moreover, we have examined the 1967 disorders within a few months after their occurrence and under pressing time limitations. While we have collected information of considerable immediacy, analysis will undoubtedly improve with the passage and perspective of time and with the further accumulation and refinement of data. To facilitate further analysis we have appended much of our data to this report.

We have categorized the information now available about the 1967 disorders as follows:

- The pattern of violence over the nation: severity, location, timing, and numbers of people involved;
- The riot process in a sample of 24 disorders we have surveyed:* prior events, the development of violence, the various control

* [All footnotes in this chapter are omitted intentionally.]

efforts on the part of officials and the community, and the relationship between violence and control efforts;

- The riot participants: a comparison of rioters with those who sought to limit the disorder and with those who remained uninvolved;
- The setting in which the disorders occurred: social and economic conditions, local governmental structure, the scale of Federal programs, and the grievance reservoir in the Negro community;
- The aftermath of disorder: the ways in which communities responded after order was restored in the streets.

Based upon information derived from our surveys, we offer the following generalizations:

1. No civil disorder was "typical" in all respects. Viewed in a national framework, the disorders of 1967 varied greatly in terms of violence and damage: while a relatively small number were major under our criteria and a somewhat larger number were serious, most of the disorders would have received little or no national attention as "riots" had the Nation not been sensitized by the more serious outbreaks.

2. While the civil disorders of 1967 were racial in character, they were not *inter*racial. The 1967 disorders, as well as earlier disorders of the recent period, involved action within Negro neighborhoods against symbols of white American society—authority and property—rather than against white persons.

3. Despite extremist rhetoric, there was no attempt to subvert the social order of the United States. Instead, most of those who attacked white authority and property seemed to be demanding fuller participation in the social order and the material benefits enjoyed by the vast majority of American citizens.

4. Disorder did not typically erupt without preexisting causes as a result of a single "triggering" or "precipitating" incident. Instead, it developed out of an increasingly disturbed social atmosphere, in which typically a series of tension-heightening incidents over a period of weeks or months became linked in the minds of many in the Negro community with a shared reservoir of underlying grievances.

5. There was, typically, a complex relationship between the series of incidents and the underlying grievances. For example, grievances about allegedly abusive police practices, unemployment and underemployment, housing, and other conditions in the ghetto, were often aggravated in the minds of many Negroes by incidents involving the police, or the inaction of municipal authorities on Negro complaints about police action, unemployment, inadequate housing or other conditions. When grievance-related incidents recurred and rising tensions were not satisfactorily resolved, a cumulative process took place in which prior incidents were readily recalled and grievances reinforced. At some point in the mounting tension, a further incident—in itself often routine or even trivial—became the breaking point, and the tension spilled over into violence.

6. Many grievances in the Negro community result from the discrimination, prejudice and powerlessness which Negroes often experience. They also result from the severely disadvantaged social and economic conditions of many Negroes as compared with those of whites in the same city and, more particularly, in the predominantly white suburbs.

7. Characteristically, the typical rioter was not a hoodlum, habitual criminal or riffraff; nor was he a recent migrant, a member of an uneducated underclass or a person lacking broad social and political concerns. Instead, he was a teenager or young adult, a lifelong resident of the city in which he rioted, a high school dropout—but somewhat better educated than his Negro neighbor—and almost invariably underemployed or employed in a menial job. He was proud of his race, extremely hostile to both whites and middle-class Negroes and, though informed about politics, highly distrustful of the political system and of political leaders.

8. Numerous Negro counterrioters walked the streets urging rioters to "cool it." The typical counterrioter resembled in many respects the majority of Negroes, who neither rioted nor took action against the rioters, that is, the noninvolved. But certain differences are crucial: the counterrioter was better educated and had higher income than either the rioter or the noninvolved.

9. Negotiations between Negroes and white officials occurred during virtually all the disorders surveyed. The negotiations often involved young, militant Negroes as well as older, established leaders. Despite a setting of chaos and disorder, negotiations in many cases involved discussion of underlying grievances as well as the handling of the disorder by control authorities.

10. The chain we have identified—discrimination, prejudice, disadvantaged conditions, intense and pervasive grievances, a series of tension-heightening incidents, all culminating in the eruption of disorder at the hands of youthful, politically-aware activists—must be understood as describing the central trend in the disorders, not as an explanation of all aspects of the riots or of all rioters. Some rioters, for example, may have shared neither the conditions nor the grievances of their Negro neighbors; some may have coolly and deliberately exploited the chaos created by others; some may have been drawn into the melee merely because they identified with, or wished to emulate, others. Nor do we intend to suggest that the majority of the rioters, who shared the adverse conditions and grievances, necessarily articulated in their own minds the connection between that background and their actions.

11. The background of disorder in the riot cities was typically characterized by severely disadvantaged conditions for Negroes, especially as compared with those for whites; a local government often unresponsive to these conditions; Federal programs which had not yet reached a significantly large proportion of those in need; and the resulting reservoir of pervasive and deep grievance and frustration in the ghetto.

12. In the immediate aftermath of disorder, the status quo of daily life before the disorder generally was quickly restored. Yet, despite some notable public and private efforts, little basic change took place in the conditions underlying the disorder. In some cases, the result was increased distrust between blacks and whites, diminished interracial communication, and growth of Negro and white extremist groups.

# I. THE PATTERN OF VIOLENCE AND DAMAGE

## LEVELS OF VIOLENCE AND DAMAGE

Because definitions of civil disorder vary widely, between 51 and 217 disorders were recorded by various agencies as having occured [sic] during the first 9 months of 1967. From these sources we have developed a list of 164 disorders which occurred during that period. We have ranked them in three categories of violence and damage, utilizing such criteria as the degree and duration of violence, the number of active participants, and the level of law enforcement response:

### Major Disorders

Eight disorders, 5 percent of the total, were major. These were characterized generally by a combination of the following factors: (1) many fires, intensive looting, and reports of sniping; (2) violence lasting more than 2 days; (3) sizeable crowds; and (4) use of National Guard or Federal forces as well as other control forces.

### Serious Disorders

Thirty-three disorders, 20 percent of the total, were serious but not major. These were characterized generally by: (1) isolated looting, some fires, and some rock throwing; (2) violence lasting between 1 and 2 days; (3) only one sizeable crowd or many small groups and (4) use of state police though generally not National Guard or Federal forces.

### Minor Disorders

One hundred and twenty-three disorders, 75 percent of the total, were minor. These would not have been classified as "riots" or received wide press attention without national conditioning to a "riot" climate. They were characterized generally by: (1) a few fires or broken windows; (2) violence lasting generally less than 1 day; (3) participation by only small numbers of people; and (4) use, in most cases, only of local police or police from a neighboring community.

The 164 disorders which we have categorized occurred in 128 cities. Twenty-five (20 percent) of the cities had two or more disturbances.

New York had five separate disorders, Chicago had four, six cities had three and 17 cities had two. Two cities which experienced a major disorder—Cincinnati and Tampa—had subsequent disorders; Cincinnati had two more. However, in these two cities the later disorders were less serious than the earlier ones. In only two cities were later disorders more severe.

Three conclusions emerge from the data:

- The significance of the 1967 disorders cannot be minimized. The level of disorder was major or serious, in terms of our criteria, on 41 occasions in 39 cities.
- The level of disorder, however, has been exaggerated. Three-fourths of the disorders were relatively minor and would not have been regarded as nationally-newsworthy "riots" in prior years.
- The fact that a city had experienced disorder earlier in 1967 did not immunize it from further violence.

## DISTRIBUTION IN TERMS OF TIME, AREA AND SIZE OF COMMUNITY

### Time

In 1967, disorders occurred with increasing frequency as summer approached and tapered off as it waned. More than 60 percent of the 164 disorders occurred in July alone.

### Disorders by Month and Level

| Month (1967) | Number of major disorders | Number of serious disorders | Number of minor disorders | Totals |
|---|---|---|---|---|
| January | | | 1 | 1 |
| February | | | | |
| March | | 1 | | 1 |
| April | | 1 | 3 | 4 |
| May | | 3 | 8 | 11 |
| June | 3 | 3 | 10 | 16 |
| July | 5 | 22 | 76 | 103 |

Disorders by Month and Level *Continued*

| Month (1967) | Number of major disorders | Number of serious disorders | Number of minor disorders | Totals |
|---|---|---|---|---|
| August | | 3 | 14 | 17 |
| September | | | 11 | 11 |
| Total | 8 | 33 | 123 | 164 |

## Area
The violence was not limited to any one section of the country.

Disorders by Region and Level

| Region | Number of major disorders | Number of serious disorders | Number of minor disorders | Total (percent) |
|---|---|---|---|---|
| East | 3 | 10 | 44 | 35 |
| Midwest | 4 | 11 | 44 | 36 |
| South and border | 1 | 7 | 19 | 16 |
| West | | 5 | 16 | 13 |
| Total | 8 | 33 | 123 | 100 |

When timing and location are considered together, other relationships appear. Ninety-eight disorders can be grouped into 23 clusters, which consist of two or more disturbances occurring within 2 weeks and within a few hundred miles of each other.

"Clustering" was particularly striking for two sets of cities. The first, centered on Newark, consisted of disorders in 14 New Jersey cities. The second, centered on Detroit, consisted of disturbances in seven cities in Michigan and one in Ohio.

## Size of Community
The violence was not limited to large cities. Seven of the eight major disorders occurred in communities with populations of 250,000 or more. But 37 (23 percent) of the disorders reviewed occurred in communities with populations of 50,000 or less; and 67 disorders (41 percent) occurred in communities with populations of 100,000 or less, including nine (about 22 percent) of the 41 serious or major disturbances.

Disorders by Level and City Population

| City population (in thousands) | Number of major disorders | Number of serious disorders | Number of minor disorders | Totals |
|---|---|---|---|---|
| 0–50 | 1 | 5 | 31 | 37 |
| 50–100 | 0 | 3 | 27 | 30 |
| 100–250 | 0 | 8 | 23 | 31 |
| 250–500 | 5 | 10 | 15 | 30 |
| 500–1,000 | 1 | 4 | 10 | 15 |
| Over 1,000 | 1 | 3 | 13 | 17 |
| Totals | 8 | 33 | 119 | 160 |

## DEATH, INJURY AND DAMAGE

In its study of 75 disturbances in 67 cities, the Permanent Subcommittee on Investigations of the Senate Committee on Government Operations reported 83 deaths and 1,897 injuries. Deaths occurred in 12 of these disturbances. More than 80 percent of the deaths and more than half the injuries occurred in Newark and Detroit. In more than 60 percent of the disturbances, no deaths and no more than 10 injuries were reported.

Substantial damage to property also tended to be concentrated in a relatively small number of cities. Of the disorders which the Commission surveyed, significant damage resulted in Detroit ($40–$45 million), Newark ($10.2 million), and Cincinnati (more than $1 million). In each of nine cities, damage was estimated at less than $100,000.

Fire caused extensive damage in Detroit and Cincinnati, two of the three cities which suffered the greatest destruction of property. Newark had relatively little loss from fire but extensive inventory loss from looting and damage to stock.

Damage estimates made at the time of the Newark and Detroit disorders were later greatly reduced. Early estimates in Newark ranged from $15 to $25 million; a month later the estimate was revised to $10.2 million. In Detroit, newspaper damage estimates at first ranged from $200 million to $500 million; the highest recent estimate is $45 million.

What we have said should not obscure three important factors.

First, the dollar cost of the disorders should be increased by the extraordinary administrative expenses of municipal, state and Federal Governments. Second, deaths and injuries are not the sole measures of the cost of civil disorders in human terms. For example, the cost of dislocation of people—though clearly not quantifiable in dollars and cents—was a significant factor in Detroit, the one case in which many residences were destroyed. Other human costs—fear, distrust, and alienation—were incurred in every disorder. Third, even a relatively low level of violence and damage in absolute terms may seriously disrupt a small or medium-sized community.

## VICTIMS OF VIOLENCE

Of the 83 persons who died in the 75 disorders studied by the Permanent Subcommittee on Investigations, about 10 percent were public officials, primarily law officers and firemen. Among the injured, public officials made up 38 percent. The overwhelming majority of the civilians killed and injured were Negroes.

Retail businesses suffered a much larger proportion of the damage during the disorders than public institutions, industrial properties, or private residences. In Newark, 1,029 establishments, affecting some 4,492 employers and employees, suffered damage to buildings or loss of inventory or both. Those which suffered the greatest loss through looting, in descending order of loss, were liquor, clothing, and furniture stores.

White-owned businesses are widely believed to have been damaged much more frequently than those owned by Negroes. In at least nine of the cities studied, the damage seems to have been, at least in part, the result of deliberate attacks on white-owned businesses characterized in the Negro community as unfair or disrespectful toward Negroes.

Not all the listed damage was purposeful or was caused by rioters. Some was a byproduct of violence. In certain instances police and fire department control efforts caused damage. The New Jersey Commission on Civil Disorders has found that in Newark, retributive action was taken against Negro-owned property by control forces. Some damage was accidental. In Detroit some fire damage, especially to residences, may have been caused primarily by a heavy wind.

Public institutions generally were not targets of serious attacks, but police and fire equipment was damaged in at least 15 of the 23 cities.

Of the cities surveyed, significant damage to residences occurred only in Detroit. In at least nine of the 22 other cities there was minor damage to residences, often resulting from fires in adjacent businesses.

## II. THE RIOT PROCESS

The Commission has found no "typical" disorder in 1967 in terms of intensity of violence and extensiveness of damage. To determine whether, as is sometimes suggested, there was a typical "riot process," we examined 24 disorders which occurred during 1967 in 20 cities and three university settings. We have concentrated on four aspects of that process:

- The accumulating reservoir of grievances in the Negro community;
- "Precipitating" incidents and their relationship to the reservoir of grievances;
- The development of violence after its initial outbreak;
- The control effort, including official force, negotiation, and persuasion.

We found a common social process operating in all 24 disorders in certain critical respects. These events developed similarly, over a period of time and out of an accumulation of grievances and increasing tension in the Negro community. Almost invariably, they exploded in ways related to the local community and its particular problems and conflicts. But once violence erupted, there began a complex interaction of many elements—rioters, official control forces, counterrioters—in which the differences between various disorders were more pronounced than the similarities.

## THE RESERVOIR OF GRIEVANCES IN
## THE NEGRO COMMUNITY

Our examination of the background of the surveyed disorders revealed a typical pattern of deeply held grievances which were widely shared by many members of the Negro community. The specific content of the expressed grievances varied somewhat from city to city. But in general, grievances among Negroes in all the cities related to prejudice, discrimination, severely disadvantaged living conditions, and a general sense of frustration about their inability to change those conditions.

Specific events or incidents exemplified and reinforced the shared sense of grievance. News of such incidents spread quickly throughout the community and added to the reservoir. Grievances about police practices, unemployment and underemployment, housing, and other objective conditions in the ghetto were aggravated in the minds of many Negroes by the inaction of municipal authorities.

Out of this reservoir of grievance and frustration, the riot process began in the cities which we surveyed.

## PRECIPITATING INCIDENTS

In virtually every case a single "triggering" or "precipitating" incident can be identified as having immediately preceded—within a few hours and in generally the same location—the outbreak of disorder. But this incident was usually a relatively minor, even trivial one, by itself substantially disproportionate to the scale of violence that followed. Often it was an incident of a type which had occurred frequently in the same community in the past without provoking violence.

We found that violence was generated by an increasingly disturbed social atmosphere, in which typically not one, but a series of incidents occurred over a period of weeks or months prior to the outbreak of disorder. Most cities had three or more such incidents; Houston had 10 over a 5-month period. These earlier or prior incidents were linked in the minds of many Negroes to the preexisting reservoir of underlying grievances. With each such incident, frustration and tension grew until at some point a final incident, often similar to the incidents preceding it, occurred and was followed almost immediately by violence.

As we see it, the prior incidents and the reservoir of underlying grievances contributed to a cumulative process of mounting tension that spilled over into violence when the final incident occurred. In this sense the entire chain—the grievances, the series of prior tension-heightening incidents, and the final incident—was the "precipitant" of disorder.

This chain describes the central trend in the disorders we surveyed and not necessarily all aspects of the riots or of all rioters. For example, incidents have not always increased tension; and tension has not always resulted in violence. We conclude only that both processes did occur in the disorders we examined.

Similarly, we do not suggest that all rioters shared the conditions or the grievances of their Negro neighbors: some may deliberately have exploited the chaos created out of the frustration of others; some may have been drawn into the melee merely because they identified with, or wished to emulate, others. Some who shared the adverse conditions and grievances did not riot.

We found that the majority of the rioters did share the adverse conditions and grievances, although they did not necessarily articulate in their own minds the connection between that background and their actions.

Newark and Detroit presented typical sequences of prior incidents, a buildup of tensions, a final incident, and the outbreak of violence:

## NEWARK

**Prior Incidents**

*1965:* A Newark policeman shot and killed an 18-year-old Negro boy. After the policeman had stated that he had fallen and his gun had discharged accidentally, he later claimed that the youth had assaulted another officer and was shot as he fled. At a hearing it was decided that the patrolman had not used excessive force. The patrolman remained on duty, and his occasional assignment to Negro areas was a continuing source of irritation in the Negro community.

*April 1967:* Approximately 15 Negroes were arrested while picketing a grocery store which they claimed sold bad meat and used unfair credit practices.

*Late May, early June:* Negro leaders had for several months voiced strong opposition to a proposed medical-dental center to be built on 150 acres of land in the predominantly Negro central ward. The dispute centered mainly around the lack of relocation provisions for those who would be displaced by the medical center. The issue became extremely volatile in late May when public "blight hearings" were held regarding the land to be condemned. The hearings became a public forum in which many residents spoke against the proposed center. The city did not change its plan.

*Late May, June:* The mayor recommended appointment of a white city councilman who had no more than a high school education to the position of secretary to the board of education. Reportedly, there was widespread support from both whites and Negroes for a Negro candidate who held a master's degree and was considered more qualified. The mayor did not change his recommendation. Ultimately, the original secretary retained his position and neither candidate was appointed.

*July 8:* Several Newark policemen, allegedly including the patrolman involved in the 1965 killing, entered East Orange to assist the East Orange police during an altercation with a group of Negro men.

**Final Incident**

*July 12, approximately 9:30 p.m.:* A Negro cab driver was injured during or after a traffic arrest in the heart of the central ward. Word spread quickly, and a crowd gathered in front of the Fourth Precinct stationhouse across the street from a large public housing project.

**Initial Violence**

*Same day, approximately 11:30 p.m.:* The crowd continued to grow until it reached 300 to 500 people. One or two Molotov cocktails were thrown at the stationhouse. Shortly after midnight the police dispersed the crowd, and window-breaking and looting began a few minutes later. By about 1 a.m., the peak level of violence for the first night was reached.

## DETROIT

**Prior Incidents**

*August 1966:* A crowd formed during a routine arrest of several Negro youths in the Kercheval section of the city. Tensions were high for several hours, but no serious violence occurred.

*June 1967:* A Negro prostitute was shot to death on her front steps. Rumors in the Negro community attributed the killing to a vice-squad officer. A police investigation later reportedly unearthed leads to a disgruntled pimp. No arrests were made.

*June 26:* A young Negro man on a picnic was shot to death while reportedly trying to protect his pregnant wife from assault by seven white youths. The wife witnessed the slaying and miscarried shortly thereafter. Of the white youths, only one was charged. The others were released.

**Final Incident**

*July 23, approximately 3:45 a.m.:* Police raided a "blind pig," a type of night club in the Negro area which served drinks after hours. Eighty persons were in the club—more than the police had anticipated—attending a party for several servicemen, two of whom had recently returned from Vietnam. A crowd of about 200 persons gathered as the police escorted the patrons into the police wagons.

**Initial Violence**

*Approximately 5:00 a.m.:* As the last police cars drove away from the "blind pig," the crowd began to throw rocks. By 8:00 a.m., looting had become widespread. Violence continued to increase throughout the day, and by evening reached a peak level for the first day.

In the 24 disorders surveyed, the events identified as tension-heightening incidents, whether prior or final, involved issues which generally paralleled the grievances we found in these cities. The incidents identified were of the following types:

## Police Actions

Some 40 percent of the prior incidents involved allegedly abusive or discriminatory police actions. Most of the police incidents began routinely and involved a response to, at most, a few persons rather than a large group.

A typical incident occurred in Bridgeton, N.J., 5 days before the disturbance when two police officers went to the home of a young Negro man to investigate a nonsupport complaint. A fight ensued when the officers attempted to take the man to the police station, and the Negro was critically injured and partially paralyzed. A Negro minister representing the injured man's family asked for suspension of the two officers involved pending investigation. This procedure had been followed previously when three policemen were accused of collusion in the robbery of a white-owned store. The Negro's request was not granted.

Police actions were also identified as the final incident preceding 12 of the 24 disturbances. Again, in all but two cases, the police action which became the final incident began routinely.

The final incident in Grand Rapids occurred when police attempted to apprehend a Negro driving an allegedly stolen car. A crowd of 30 to 40 Negro spectators gathered. The suspect had one arm in a cast, and some of the younger Negroes in the crowd intervened because they thought the police were handling him too roughly.

## Protest Activities

Approximately 22 percent of the prior incidents involved Negro demonstrations, rallies, and protest meetings. Only five involved appearances by nationally known Negro militants.

Protest rallies and meetings were also identified as the final incident preceding five disturbances. Nationally known Negro militants spoke at two of these meetings; in the other three only local leaders were involved. A prior incident involving alleged police brutality was the principal subject of each of three rallies. Inaction of municipal authorities was the topic for two other meetings.

## White Racist Activities

About 17 percent of the prior incidents involved activities by whites intended to discredit or intimidate Negroes or violence by whites against

Negroes. These included some 15 cross-burnings in Bridgeton, the harrassment [*sic*] of Negro college students by white teenagers in Jackson, Mississippi, and, in Detroit, the slaying of a Negro by a group of white youths. No final incidents were classifiable as racist activity.

## Previous Disorders in the Same City

In this category were approximately 16 percent of the prior incidents, including seven previous disorders, the handling of which had produced a continuing sense of grievance. There were other incidents, usually of minor violence, which occurred prior to seven disorders and were seen by the Negro community as precursors of the subsequent disturbance. Typically, in Plainfield the night before the July disorder, a Negro youth was injured in an altercation between white and Negro teenagers. Tensions rose as a result. No final incidents were identified in this category.

## Disorders in Other Cities

Local media coverage and rumors generated by the Newark and Detroit riots were specifically identified as prior incidents in four cases. However, these major disorders appeared to be important factors in all the disorders which followed them.

Media coverage and rumors generated by the major riots in nearby Newark and Plainfield were the only identifiable final incidents preceding five nearby disorders. In these cases there was a substantial mobilization of police and extensive patrolling of the ghetto area in anticipation of violence.

## Official City Actions

Approximately 14 percent of the prior incidents were identified as action, or in some cases, inaction of city officials other than police or the judiciary. Typically, in Cincinnati 2 months prior to the disturbance, approximately 200 representatives (mostly Negroes) of the innercity community councils sought to appear before the city council to request summer recreation funds. The council permitted only one person from the group to speak, and then only briefly, on the ground that the group had not followed the proper procedure for placing the issue on the agenda.

No final incidents were identified in this category.

**Administration of Justice**

Eight of the prior incidents involved cases of allegedly discriminatory administration of justice. Typical was a case in Houston a month-and-a-half before the disorder. Three civil rights advocates were arrested for leading a protest and for their participation in organizing a boycott of classes at the predominantly Negro Texas Southern University. Bond was set at $25,000 each. The court refused for several days to reduce bond, even though TSU officials dropped the charges they had originally pressed.

There were no final incidents identified involving the administration of justice.

In a unique case in New Haven, the shooting of a Puerto Rican by a white man was identified as the final incident before violence.

Finally, we have noted a marked relationship between prior and final incidents within each city. In most of the cities surveyed, the final incident was of the same type as one or more of the prior incidents. For example, police actions were identified as both the final incident and one or more prior incidents preceding seven disturbances. Rallies or meetings to protest police actions involved in a prior incident were identified as the final incident preceding three additional disturbances. The cumulative reinforcement of grievances and heightening of tensions found in all instances were particularly evident in these cases.

## THE DEVELOPMENT OF VIOLENCE

Once the series of precipitating incidents culminated in violence, the riot process did not follow a uniform pattern in the 24 disorders surveyed. However, some similarities emerge.

The final incident before the outbreak of disorder, and the initial violence itself, generally occurred at a time and place in which it was normal for many people to be on the streets. In most of the 24 disorders, groups generally estimated at 50 or more persons were on the street at the time and place of the first outbreak.

In all 24 disturbances, including the three university-related disorders, the initial disturbance area consisted of streets with relatively high concentrations of pedestrian and automobile traffic at the time. In all but two cases—Detroit and Milwaukee—violence started between 7 p.m. and 12:30 a.m., when the largest numbers of pedestrians could be expected. Ten of the 24 disorders erupted on Friday night, Saturday, or Sunday.

In most instances, the temperature during the day on which violence first erupted was quite high. This contributed to the size of the crowds on the street, particularly in areas of congested housing.

Major violence occurred in all 24 disorders during the evening and night hours, between 6 p.m. and 6 a.m., and in most cases between 9 p.m. and 3 a.m. In only a few disorders, including Detroit and Newark, did substantial violence occur or continue during the daytime. Generally, the night-day cycles continued in daily succession through the early period of the disorder.

At the beginning of disorder, violence generally flared almost immediately after the final precipitating incident. It then escalated quickly to its peak level, in the case of 1-night disorders, and to the first night peak in the case of continuing disorders. In Detroit and Newark, the first outbreaks began within two hours and reached severe, although not the highest, levels within 3 hours.

In almost all of the subsequent night-day cycles, the change from relative order to a state of disorder by a number of people typically occurred extremely rapidly—within 1 or 2 hours at the most.

Nineteen of the surveyed disorders lasted more than 1 night. In 10 of these, violence peaked on the first night, and the level of activity on subsequent nights was the same or less. In the other nine disorders, however, the peak was reached on a subsequent night.

Disorder generally began with less serious violence against property, such as rock and bottle-throwing and window-breaking. These were usually the materials and the targets closest to hand at the place of the initial outbreak.

Once store windows were broken, looting usually followed. Whether fires were set only after looting occurred is unclear. Reported instances of fire-bombing and Molotov cocktails in the 24 disorders appeared to occur as frequently during one cycle of violence as during another in disorders which continued through more than one cycle. However, fires seemed to break out more frequently during the middle cycles of riots lasting several days. Gunfire and sniping were also reported more frequently during the middle cycles.

## THE CONTROL EFFORT

What type of community response is most effective once disorder erupts is clearly a critically important question. Chapter 12, "Control of Disorder," . . . consider[s] this question at length. We consider in this section the variety of control responses, official and unofficial, utilized in the 24 surveyed disorders, including:

- Use or threatened use of local official force;
- Use or threatened use of supplemental official force from other jurisdictions;
- Negotiations between officials and representatives from the Negro community;
- On-the-street persuasion by "counterrioters."

Disorders are sometimes discussed as if they consisted of a succession of confrontations and withdrawals by two cohesive groups, the police or other control force on one side and a riotous mob on the other. Often it is assumed that there was no effort within the Negro community to reduce the violence. Sometimes the only remedy prescribed is mobilization of the largest possible police or control force as early as possible.

None of these views is accurate. We found that:

- A variety of different control forces employed a variety of tactics, often at the same time, and often in a confused situation;
- Substantial non-force control efforts, such as negotiations and on-the-street persuasion by "counterrioters," were usually underway, often simultaneously with forcible control efforts; counterrioter activity often was carried on by Negro residents of the disturbance area, sometimes with and frequently without official recognition;
- No single tactic appeared to be effective in containing or reducing violence in all situations.

**Local Official Force**

In 20 of the 24 disorders, the primary effort to restore order at the beginning of violence was made entirely by local police. In 10 cases no additional outside force was called for after the initial response. In only a few cases was the initial control force faced with crowds too large to control.

The police approach to the initial outbreak of disorder in the surveyed cities was generally cautious. Three types of response were employed. One was dispersal (clearing the area, either by arrests or by scattering crowds), used in 10 cases. Another was reconnaissance (observing and evaluating developments), used in eight cases. In half of these instances, they soon withdrew from the disturbance area, generally because they believed they were unable to cope with the disorder. The third was containment (preventing movement in or out of a cordoned or barricaded area), used in six cases.

No uniform result from utilizing any of the three control approaches is apparent. In at least half of the 24 cases, it can reasonably be said that the approach taken by the police failed to prevent the continuation of violence. To the extent that their effectiveness is measurable, the conclusion appears to hold for subsequent police control responses as well. There is also evidence in some instances of over-response in subsequent cycles of violence.

The various tactical responses we have described are not mutually exclusive, and in many instances combinations were employed. The most common were attempts at dispersal in the disturbance area and a simultaneous cordon or barricade at the routes leading from the disturbance area to the central commercial area of the city, either to contain the disturbance or to prevent persons outside the area from entering it, or both.

In 11 disorders a curfew was imposed at some time, either as the major dispersal technique or in combination with other techniques.

In only four disorders was tear gas used at any point as a dispersal technique.

Only Newark and New Haven used a combination of all three means of control—cordon, curfew, and tear gas.

## Supplemental Official Force

In nine disturbances—involving a wide variation in the intensity of violence—additional control forces were brought in after there had been serious violence which local police had been unable to handle alone. In every case, further violence occurred, often more than once and often of equal or greater intensity than before.

The result was the same when extra forces were mobilized before serious violence. In four cities where this was done, violence nonetheless occurred, in most cases more than once, and often of equal or greater intensity than in the original outbreak.

In the remaining group of seven cities, no outside control forces were called, because the level and duration of violence were lower. Outbreaks in these cities nevertheless followed the same random pattern as in the cities which used outside forces.

## Negotiation

In 21 of the 24 disturbances surveyed, discussion or negotiation occurred during the disturbance. These took the form of relatively formal meetings between government officials and Negroes during which grievances and issues were discussed and means were sought to restore order.

Such meetings were usually held either immediately before or soon after the outbreak of violence. Meetings often continued beyond the first or second day of the disorder and, in a few instances, through the entire period of the disorder.

The Negro participants in these meetings usually were established leaders in the Negro community, such as city councilmen or members of human relations commissions, ministers, or officers of civil rights or other community organizations. However, Negro youths participated in over one-third of these meetings. In a few disorders both youths and adult Negro leaders participated, sometimes without the participation of local officials.

Employees of community action agencies occasionally participated, either as intermediaries or as participants. In some cases they provided the meeting place.

Discussions usually included issues generated by the disorder itself, such as the treatment by the police of those arrested. In 12 cases, prior ghetto grievances, such as unemployment and inadequate recreational facilities, were included as subjects. Often both disorder-related and prior grievances were discussed, with the focus generally shifting from the former to the latter as the disorder continued.

How effective these meetings were is, as in the case of forcible response, impossible to gauge. Again, much depends on who participated, timing, and other responses being made at the same time.

## Counterrioters

In all but six of the 24 disorders, Negro private citizens were active on the streets attempting to restore order primarily by means of persuasion. In a Detroit survey of riot area residents over the age of 15, some 14 percent stated that they had been active as counterrioters.

Counterrioters sometimes had some form of official recognition from either the mayor or a human relations council. Police reaction in these cases varied from total opposition to close cooperation. In most cases, some degree of official authorization was given before the activity of the counterrioters began, and in a smaller number of cases, their activity was not explicitly authorized but merely condoned by the authorities.

Distinctive insignia were worn by the officially recognized counterrioters in at least a few cities. In Dayton and Tampa, the white helmets issued to the counter-rioters have made the name "White Hats" synonymous with counter-rioters.

Public attention has centered on the officially recognized counterrioters. However, counter-rioters are known to have acted independently, without official recognition, in a number of cities.

Counterrioters generally included young men, ministers, community action agency and other antipoverty workers, and well-known ghetto residents. Their usual technique was to walk through the disturbance area urging people to "cool it," although they often took other positive action as well, such as distributing food.

How effective the counterrioters were is difficult to estimate. Authorities in several cities indicated that they believed they were helpful.

## III. THE RIOT PARTICIPANT

It is sometimes assumed that the rioters were criminal types, over-active social deviants, or riffraff—recent migrants, members of an uneducated underclass, alienated from responsible Negroes, and without broad social or political concerns. It is often implied that there was no effort within the Negro community to attempt to reduce the violence.

We have obtained data on participation from four different sources:

- Eyewitness accounts from more than 1,200 interviews in our staff reconnaissance survey of 20 cities;
- Interview surveys based on probability samples of riot area residents in the two major riot cities—Detroit and Newark—designed to elicit anonymous self-identification of participants as rioters, counterrioters or noninvolved;
- Arrest records from 22 cities; and
- A special study of arrestees in Detroit

Only partial information is available on the total numbers of participants. In the Detroit survey, approximately 11 percent of the sampled residents over the age of 15 in the two disturbance areas admittedly participated in rioting; another 20 to 25 percent admitted to having been bystanders but claimed that they had not participated; approximately 16 percent claimed they had engaged in counterriot activity; and the largest proportion (48 to 53 percent) claimed they were at home or elsewhere and did not participate. However, a large proportion of the Negro community apparently believed that more was gained than lost through rioting, according to the Newark and Detroit surveys.

Greater precision is possible in describing the characteristics of those who participated. We have combined the data from the four sources to construct a profile of the typical rioter and to compare him with the counterrioter and the noninvolved.

## THE PROFILE OF A RIOTER

The typical rioter in the summer of 1967 was a Negro, unmarried male between the ages of 15 and 24. He was in many ways very different from the stereotype. He was not a migrant. He was born in the state and was a lifelong resident of the city in which the riot took place. Economically his position was about the same as his Negro neighbors who did not actively participate in the riot.

Although he had not, usually, graduated from high school, he was somewhat better educated than the average inner-city Negro, having at least attended high school for a time.

Nevertheless, he was more likely to be working in a menial or low status job as an unskilled laborer. If he was employed, he was not working full time and his employment was frequently interrupted by periods of unemployment.

He feels strongly that he deserves a better job and that he is barred from achieving it, not because of lack of training, ability, or ambition, but because of discrimination by employers.

He rejects the white bigot's stereotype of the Negro as ignorant and shiftless. He takes great pride in his race and believes that in some respects Negroes are superior to whites. He is extremely hostile to whites, but his hostility is more apt to be a product of social and economic class than of race; he is almost equally hostile toward middle class Negroes.

He is substantially better informed about politics than Negroes who were not involved in the riots. He is more likely to be actively engaged in civil rights efforts, but is extremely distrustful of the political system and of political leaders.

## THE PROFILE OF THE COUNTERRIOTER

The typical counterrioter, who risked injury and arrest to walk the streets urging rioters to "cool it," was an active supporter of existing social institutions. He was, for example, far more likely than either the rioter or the noninvolved to feel that this country is worth defending in a major war. His actions and his attitudes reflected his substantially greater stake in the social system; he was considerably better educated and more affluent than either the rioter or the noninvolved. He was somewhat more likely than the rioter, but less likely than the noninvolved, to have been a migrant. In all other respects he was identical to the noninvolved.

## CHARACTERISTICS OF PARTICIPANTS

### Race
Of the arrestees 83 percent were Negroes; 15 percent were whites. Our interviews in 20 cities indicate that almost all rioters were Negroes.

### Age
The survey data from Detroit, the arrest records, and our interviews in 20 cities, all indicate that the rioters were late teenagers or young adults. In the Detroit survey, 61.3 percent of the self-reported rioters were between the ages of 15 and 24, and 86.3 percent were between 15 and 35. The arrest data indicate that 52.5 percent of the arrestees were between 15 and 24, and 80.8 percent were between 15 and 35.

Of the noninvolved, by contrast, only 22.6 percent in the Detroit survey were between 15 and 24, and 38.3 percent were between 15 and 35.

### Sex
In the Detroit survey, 61.4 percent of the self-reported rioters were male. Arrestees, however, were almost all male—89.3 percent. Our interviews in 20 cities indicate that the majority of rioters were male. The large difference in proportion between the Detroit survey data and the arrestee figures probably reflects either selectivity in the arrest process or less dramatic, less provocative riot behavior by women.

### Family Structure
Three sources of available information—the Newark survey, the Detroit arrest study, and arrest records from four cities—indicate a tendency for rioters to be single. The Newark survey indicates that rioters were single—56.2 percent—more often than the noninvolved—49.6 percent.

The Newark survey also indicates that rioters were more likely to have been divorced or separated—14.2 percent—than the noninvolved—6.4 percent. However, the arrest records from four cities indicate that only a very small percentage of those arrested fall into this category.

In regard to the structure of the family in which he was raised, the self-reported rioter, according to the Newark survey, was not significantly different from many of his Negro neighbors who did not actively participate in the riot. Twenty-five and five-tenths percent of the self-reported rioters and 23 percent of the noninvolved were brought up in homes where no adult male lived.

## Region of Upbringing

Both survey data and arrest records demonstrate unequivocally that those brought up in the region in which the riot occurred are much more likely to have participated in the riots. The percentage of self-reported rioters brought up in the North is almost identical for the Detroit survey—74.4 percent—and the Newark survey—74 percent. By contrast, of the noninvolved, 36 percent in Detroit and 52.4 percent in Newark were brought up in the region in which the disorder occurred.

Data available from five cities on the birthplace of arrestees indicate that 63 percent of the arrestees were born in the North. Although birthplace is not necessarily identical with place of upbringing, the data are sufficiently similar to provide strong support for the conclusion.

Of the self-reported counterrioters, however, 47.5 percent were born in the North, according to the Detroit survey, a figure which places them between self-reported rioters and the noninvolved. Apparently, a significant consequence of growing up in the South is the tendency toward noninvolvement in a riot situation, while involvement in a riot, either in support of or against existing social institutions, was more common among those born in the North.

## Residence

Rioters are not only more likely than the noninvolved to have been born in the region in which the riot occurred, but they are also more likely to have been long-term residents of the city in which the disturbance took place. The Detroit survey data indicate that 59.4 percent of the self-reported rioters, but only 34.6 percent of the noninvolved, were born in Detroit. The comparable figures in the Newark survey are 53.5 percent and 22.5 percent.

Outsiders who temporarily entered the city during the riot might have left before the surveys were conducted and therefore may be underestimated in the survey data. However, the arrest data, which is contemporaneous with the riot, suggest that few outsiders were involved: 90 percent of those arrested resided in the riot city, 7 percent lived in the same state, and only 1 percent were from outside the state. Our interviews in 20 cities corroborate these conclusions.

### Income

In the Detroit and Newark survey data, income level alone does not seem to correlate with self-reported riot participation. The figures from the two cities are not directly comparable since respondents were asked for individual income in Detroit and family income in Newark. More Detroit self-reported rioters (38.6 percent) had annual incomes under $5,000 per year than the noninvolved (30.3 percent), but even this small difference disappears when the factor of age is taken into account.

In the Newark data, in which the age distributions of self-reported rioters and the noninvolved are more similar, there is almost no difference between the rioters, 32.6 percent of whom had annual incomes under $5,000, and the noninvolved, 29.4 percent of whom had annual incomes under $5,000.

The similarity in income distribution should not, however, lead to the conclusion that more affluent Negroes are as likely to riot as poor Negroes. Both surveys were conducted in disturbance areas where incomes are considerably lower than in the city as a whole and the surrounding metropolitan area. Nevertheless, the data show that rioters are not necessarily the poorest of the poor.

While income fails to distinguish self-reported rioters from those who were not involved, it does distinguish counterrioters from rioters and the noninvolved. Less than 9 percent of both those who rioted and those not involved earned more than $10,000 annually. Yet almost 20 percent of the counterrioters earned this amount or more. In fact, there were no male self-reported counterrioters in the Detroit survey who earned less than $5,000 annually. In the Newark sample there were seven respondents who owned their own homes; none of them participated in the riot. While extreme poverty does not necessarily move a man to riot, relative affluence seems at least to inhibit him from attacking the existing social order and may motivate him to take considerable risks to protect it.

## Education

Level of schooling is strongly related to participation. Those with some high school education were more likely to riot than those who had only finished grade school. In the Detroit survey, 93 percent of the self-reported rioters had gone beyond grade school, compared with 72.1 percent of the noninvolved. In the Newark survey the comparable figures are 98.1 and 85.7 percent. The majority of self-reported rioters were not, however, high school graduates.

The counterrioters were clearly the best educated of the three groups. Approximately twice as many counterrioters had attended college as had the noninvolved, and half again as many counterrioters had attended college as rioters. Considered with the information on income, the data suggest that counterrioters were probably well on their way into the middle class.

Education and income are the only factors which distinguish the counterrioter from the noninvolved. Apparently, a high level of education and income not only prevents rioting but is more likely to lead to active, responsible opposition to rioting.

## Employment

The Detroit and Newark surveys, the arrest records from four cities, and the Detroit arrest study all indicate that there are no substantial differences in unemployment between the rioters and the noninvolved.

Unemployment levels among both groups were extremely high. In the Detroit survey, 29.6 percent of the self-reported rioters were unemployed; in the Newark survey, 29.7 percent; in the four-city arrest data, 33.2 percent; and in the Detroit arrest study, 21.8 percent. The unemployment rates for the noninvolved in the Detroit and Newark surveys were 31.5 and 19.0 percent.

Self-reported rioters were more likely to be only intermittently employed, however, than the noninvolved. Respondents in Newark were asked whether they had been unemployed for as long as a month or more during the last year. Sixty-one percent of the self-reported rioters, but only 43.4 percent of the noninvolved, answered, "yes."

Despite generally higher levels of education, rioters were more likely than the noninvolved to be employed in unskilled jobs. In the Newark survey, 50 percent of the self-reported rioters, but only 39.6 percent of the noninvolved, had unskilled jobs.

## Attitudes about Employment

The Newark survey data indicate that self-reported rioters were more likely to feel dissatisfied with their present jobs than were the noninvolved.

Only 29.3 percent of the rioters, compared with 44.4 percent of the noninvolved, thought their present jobs appropriate for them in responsibility and pay. Of the self-reported rioters, 67.6 percent, compared with 56.1 percent of the noninvolved, felt that it was impossible to obtain the kind of job they wanted. Of the self-reported rioters, 69 percent, as compared with 50 percent of the noninvolved, felt that racial discrimination was the major obstacle to finding better employment. Despite this feeling, surprising numbers of rioters (76.9 percent) responded that "getting what you want out of life is a matter of ability, not being in the right place at the right time."

## Racial Attitudes

The Detroit and Newark surveys indicate that rioters have strong feelings of racial pride, if not racial superiority. In the Detroit survey, 48.6 percent of the self-reported rioters said that they felt Negroes were more dependable than whites. Only 22.4 percent of the noninvolved stated this. In Newark, the comparable figures were 45 and 27.8 percent. The Newark survey data indicate that rioters wanted to be called "black" rather than "Negro" or "colored" and were somewhat more likely than the noninvolved to feel that all Negroes should study African history and languages.

To what extent this racial pride antedated the riot or was produced by the riot is impossible to determine from the survey data. Certainly the riot experience seems to have been associated with increased pride in the minds of many participants. This was vividly illustrated by the statement of a Detroit rioter:

> INTERVIEWER: You said you were feeling good when you
> followed the crowds?
> RESPONDENT: I was feeling proud, man, at the fact that I was
> a Negro. I felt like I was a first-class citizen. I didn't feel
> ashamed of my race because of what they did.

Similar feelings were expressed by an 18-year-old Detroit girl who reported that she had been a looter:

> INTERVIEWER: What is the Negro then if he's not American?
> RESPONDENT: A Negro, he's considered a slave to the white
> folks. But half of them know that they're slaves and feel
> that they can't do nothing about it because they're just
> going along with it. But most of them they seem to get it
> in their heads now how the white folks treat them and how
> they've been treating them and how they've been slaves for
> the white folks. * * *

Along with increased racial pride there appears to be intense hostility toward whites. Self-reported rioters in both the Detroit and Newark surveys were more likely to feel that civil rights groups with white and Negro leaders would do better without the whites. In Detroit, 36.1 percent of the self-reported rioters thought that this statement was true, while only 21.1 percent of the noninvolved thought so. In the Newark survey, 51.4 percent of the self-reported rioters agreed; 33.1 percent of the noninvolved shared this opinion.

Self-reported rioters in Newark were also more likely to agree with the statement, "Sometimes I hate white people." Of the self-reported rioters, 72.4 percent agreed; of the noninvolved, 50 percent agreed.

The intensity of the self-reported rioters' racial feelings may suggest that the recent riots represented traditional interracial hostilities. Two sources of data suggest that this interpretation is probably incorrect. First, the Newark survey data indicate that rioters were almost as hostile to middle-class Negroes as they were to whites. Seventy-one and four-tenths percent of the self-reported rioters, but only 59.5 percent of the noninvolved, agreed with the statement, "Negroes who make a lot of money like to think they are better than other Negroes." Perhaps even more significant, particularly in light of the rioters' strong feelings of racial pride, is that 50.5 percent of the self-reported rioters agreed that "Negroes who make a lot of money are just as bad as white people." Only 35.2 percent of the noninvolved shared this opinion.

Second, the arrest data show that the great majority of those arrested during the disorders were generally charged with a crime relating to looting or curfew violations. Only 2.4 percent of the arrests were for assault and 0.1 percent were for homicide, but 31.3 percent of the arrests were for breaking and entering—crimes directed against white property rather than against individual whites.

## Political Attitudes and Involvement

Respondents in the Newark survey were asked about relatively simple items of political information, such as the race of prominent local and national political figures. In general, the self-reported rioters were much better informed than the noninvolved. For example, self-reported rioters were more likely to know that one of the 1966 Newark mayoral candidates was a Negro. Of the rioters, 77.1 percent—but only 61.6 percent of the noninvolved—identified him correctly. The overall scores on a series of similar questions also reflect the self-reported rioters' higher levels of information.

Self-reported rioters were also more likely to be involved in activities associated with Negro rights. At the most basic level of political participation, they were more likely than the noninvolved to talk frequently about Negro rights. In the Newark survey, 53.8 percent of the self-reported rioters, but only 34.9 percent of the noninvolved, said that they talked about Negro rights nearly every day.

The self-reported rioters also were more likely to have attended a meeting or participated in civil rights activity. Of the rioters, 39.3 percent—but only 25.7 percent of the noninvolved—reported that they had engaged in such activity.

In the Newark survey, respondents were asked how much they thought they could trust the local government. Only 4.8 percent of the self-reported rioters, compared with 13.7 percent of the noninvolved, said that they felt they could trust it most of the time; 44.2 percent of the self-reported rioters and 33.9 percent of the noninvolved reported that they could almost never trust the government.

In the Detroit survey, self-reported rioters were much more likely to attribute the riot to anger about politicians and police than were the noninvolved. Of the self-reported rioters, 43.2 percent—but only 19.6 percent of the noninvolved—said anger against politicians had a great deal to do with causing the riot. Of the self-reported rioters, 70.5 percent, compared with 48.8 percent of the noninvolved, believed that anger against the police had a great deal to do with causing the riot.

Perhaps the most revealing and disturbing measure of the rioters' anger at the social and political system was their response to a question asking whether they thought "the country was worth fighting for in the event of a major world war." Of the self-reported rioters, 39.4 percent in Detroit and 52.8 percent in Newark shared a negative view. In contrast, 15.5 percent of the noninvolved in Detroit and 27.8 percent of the noninvolved in Newark shared this sentiment. Almost none of the self-reported counterrioters in Detroit—3.3 percent—agreed with the self-reported rioters.

Some comments of interviewees are worthy of note:

> Not worth fighting for—if Negroes had an equal chance it would be worth fighting for.
>
> Not worth fighting for—I am not a true citizen so why should I?
>
> Not worth fighting for—because my husband came back from Vietnam and nothing had changed.

## IV. THE BACKGROUND OF DISORDER

In response to the President's questions to the Commission about the riot environment, we have gathered information on the pre-riot conditions in 20 of the cities surveyed. We have sought to analyze the backgrounds of the disorders in terms of four basic groupings of information:

- The social and economic conditions as described in the 1960 census, with particular reference to the area of each city in which the disturbance took place;
- Local governmental structure and its organizational capacity to respond to the needs of the people, particularly those living in the most depressed conditions;
- The extent to which Federal programs assisted in meeting these needs; and
- The nature of the grievances in the ghetto community.

It is sometimes said that conditions for Negroes in the riot cities have improved over the years and are not materially different from conditions for whites; that local government now seeks to accommodate the demands of Negroes and has created many mechanisms for redressing legitimate complaints; that Federal programs now enable most Negroes who so desire, to live comfortably through welfare, housing, employment or antipoverty assistance; and that grievances are harbored only by a few malcontents and agitators.

Our findings show the contrary. In the riot cities we surveyed, we found that Negroes were severely disadvantaged, especially as compared with whites; that local government is often unresponsive to this fact; that Federal programs have not yet reached a significantly large proportion of those in need; and that these facts create a reservoir of unredressed grievances and frustration in the ghetto.

## THE PATTERN OF DISADVANTAGE

Social and economic conditions in the riot cities constituted a clear pattern of severe disadvantage for Negroes as compared with whites, whether the Negroes lived in the disturbance area or outside of it. When ghetto conditions are compared with those for whites in the suburbs, the relative disadvantage for Negroes is even greater.

In all the cities surveyed, the Negro population increased between 1950 and 1960 at a median rate of 75 percent.

Meanwhile, the white population decreased in more than half the cities—including six which experienced the most severe disturbances in 1967. The increase in nonwhite population in four of these cities was so great that their total population increased despite the decrease in white population. These changes were attributable in large part to heavy in-migration of Negroes from rural poverty areas and movement of whites from the central cities to the suburbs.

In all the cities surveyed:

- The percentage of Negro population in the disturbance area exceeded the percentage of Negro population in the entire city. In some cases it was twice, and in nine instances triple, the city-wide percentage.
- The Negro population was invariably younger than the white population.
- Negroes had completed fewer years of education and proportionately fewer had attended high school than whites.
- A larger percentage of Negroes than whites were in the labor force.
- Yet they were twice as likely to be unemployed as whites.
- In cities where they had greater opportunities to work at skilled or semi-skilled jobs, proportionately more Negro men tended to be working, or looking for work, than white men. Conversely, the proportion of men working, or looking for work, tended to be lower among Negroes than whites in cities that offered the least opportunities for skilled or semi-skilled labor.
- Among the employed, Negroes were more than three times as likely to be in unskilled and service jobs as whites.
- Negroes earned less than whites in all the surveyed cities, averaging barely 70 percent of white income, and were more than twice as likely to be living in poverty.
- A smaller proportion of Negro children than white children under 18 were living with both parents.
- However, family "responsibility" was strongly related to opportunity. In cities where the proportion of Negro men in better-than-menial jobs was higher, median Negro family income was higher, and the proportion of children under 18 living with both parents was also higher. Both family income and family structure showed greater weakness in cities where job opportunities were more restricted to unskilled jobs.

- Fewer Negroes than whites owned their own homes. Among nonhomeowners, Negroes paid the same rents, yet they paid a higher share of their incomes for rent than did whites. Although housing cost Negroes relatively more, their housing was three times as likely to be overcrowded and substandard as dwellings occupied by whites.

## LOCAL GOVERNMENTAL STRUCTURE

In the riot cities surveyed, we found that:

- All major forms of local government were represented.
- In a substantial minority of instances, a combination of at-large election of legislators and a "weak-mayor" system resulted in fragmentation of political responsibility and accountability.
- The proportion of Negroes in government was substantially smaller than the Negro proportion of population.
- Almost all the cities had some formal grievance machinery, but typically it was regarded by most Negroes interviewed as ineffective and was generally ignored.

All major forms of municipal government were represented in the 20 cities examined. Fourteen had a mayor-city council form of government, five had a council-city manager, and one had a commission.

The division of power between the legislative and executive branches varied widely from city to city. Of the mayor-council cities, eight could be characterized as "strong mayor/weak city council" systems in the sense that the mayor had broad appointive and veto powers. Five could be characterized as "weak mayor/strong council" forms, where the city council had broad appointive and veto powers. In one city, Milwaukee, such powers appeared to be evenly balanced.

In 17 of the 20 cities, mayors were elected directly. Mayors were parttime in eight cities. Almost all the cities had a principal executive, either a mayor or a city manager, who earned a substantial annual salary. Terms of office for mayors ranged from 2 to 4 years.

In eight cities, all legislators were elected at large and therefore represented no particular legislative ward or district. Six of these cities also had either a city manager or a "weak-mayor" form of government. In these cases, there was heavy reliance upon the city council as the principal elected policymaking authority. This combination of factors appeared to produce even less identification by citizens with any particular elected official than in the 12 cities which elected all legislators from wards or districts or used a combination of election by districts and at large.

The proportion of Negroes in the governments of the 20 cities was substantially smaller than the median proportion of Negro population—16 percent. Ten percent of the legislators in the surveyed cities were Negroes. Only in New Brunswick and Phoenix was the proportion of legislators who were Negroes as great as the percentage of the total population that was nonwhite. Six cities had no Negro legislators. Only three cities had more than one Negro legislator: Newark and Plainfield had two, and New Haven had five. None of the 20 cities had or had ever had a Negro mayor or city manager. In only four cities did Negroes hold other important policymaking positions or serve as heads of other municipal departments. In seven cities Negro representatives had been elected to the State legislature.

In 17 of the cities, however, Negroes were serving on boards of education. In all 17 cities which had human relations councils or similar organizations, Negroes were represented on the boards of such organizations.

One of the most surprising findings is that in 17 of the 20 surveyed riot cities, some formal grievance machinery existed before the 1967 disorders—a municipal human relations council or similar organization authorized to receive citizen complaints about racial or other discrimination by public and private agencies. Existence of these formal channels, however, did not necessarily achieve their tension-relieving purpose. They were seldom regarded as effective by Negroes who were interviewed. The councils generally consisted of prominent citizens, including one or more Negroes, serving part time and with little or no salary.

With only one exception, the councils were wholly advisory and mediatory, with power to conciliate and make recommendations but not to subpoena witnesses or enforce compliance. While most of the councils had full-time paid staff, they were generally organized only as loosely affiliated departments of the city government. The number of complaints filed with the councils was low considering both the size of the Negro populations and the levels of grievance manifested by the disorders. Only five councils received more than 100 complaints a year. In almost all cases, complaints against private parties were mediated informally by these councils. But complaints against governmental agencies usually were referred for investigation to the agencies against whom the complaints were directed. For example, complaints of police misconduct were accepted by most councils and then referred directly to the police for investigation.

In only two cities did human relations councils attempt to investigate complaints against the police. In neither case did they succeed in completing the investigation.

Where special channels for complaints against the police existed, the result appears to have been similar. In several of the cities, police-community relations units had been established within the police department, in most instances within two years before the disorder. However, complaints about police misconduct generally were forwarded to the police investigative unit, complaint bureau or police chief for investigation.

In all the cities which had a police-community relations unit, during the year preceding the disorder, complaints against policemen had been filed with or forwarded to the police department. In at least two of these cities the police department stated that the complaints had been investigated and that disciplinary action had been taken in several cases. Whether or not these departments in fact did take action on the complaints, the results were never disclosed to the public or to complainants. The grievances on which the complaints were based often appeared to remain alive.


## FEDERAL PROGRAMS

What was the pattern of governmental effort to relieve ghetto conditions and to respond to needs in the cities which experienced disorders in 1967?

We have attempted no comprehensive answer to this large and complex question. Instead, we have surveyed only the key Federal antipoverty programs in Detroit, Newark, and New Haven—cities which received substantial Federal funds and also suffered severe disorders.

Among the large number of Federal programs to aid cities, we have concentrated on five types, which relate to the most serious conditions and which involve sizeable amounts of Federal assistance. We have sought to evaluate these amounts against the proportion of persons reached.

We conclude that:

- While these three cities received substantial amounts of Federal funds in 1967 for manpower, education, housing, welfare and community action programs, the number of persons assisted by those programs in almost all cases constituted only a fraction of those in need.
- In at least 11 of the 15 programs examined (five programs in each of the three cities), the number of people assisted in 1967 was less than half of those in need.
- In one of the 15 programs, the percentage rose as high as 72 percent.
- The median was 33 percent.

## Manpower

Our study included all major manpower and employment programs including basic and remedial education, skill training, on-the-job training, job counseling, and placement.

A 1966 Department of Labor study of 10 slum areas, as well as our own survey of 20 disorder areas, indicates that underemployment may be an even more serious problem for ghetto residents that [*sic*] unemployment. However, our measurement of need for manpower programs is based on unemployment figures alone because underemployment data are not available for the three cities surveyed. The Department of Labor estimates that underemployment rates in major central-city ghettos are a multiple of the unemployment rate.

In Detroit, during the first three quarters of 1967, Federal funds, obligated in the amount of $19.6 million, provided job training opportunities for less than one-half of the unemployed.

During the first 9 months of 1967, the labor force in Detroit totaled

650,000 persons, of whom 200,000 were Negroes. The average unemployment rate for that period was 2.7 percent for whites and 9.6 percent for Negroes. The total average number unemployed during that period was 31,350, of whom 19,200 (61 percent) were Negroes.

During the same period, there were 22 manpower programs (excluding MDTA institutional programs) in various stages of operation in Detroit. Twenty of the programs provided for 13,979 trainees.

In Newark, in the first half of 1967, $2.6 million of Federal funds provided job training opportunities for less than 20 percent of the unemployed. And in New Haven, during the first three quarters of 1967, Federal funds in the amount of $2.1 million provided job training opportunities for less than one-third of the unemployed.

### Education

For purposes of comparing funding to needs, we have limited our examination to two major Federal education programs for the disadvantaged: The Title I program under the Elementary and Secondary Education Act of 1965 (ESEA) and the Adult Basic Education Program. Title I provides assistance to schools having concentrations of educationally disadvantaged children, defined as children from families having annual incomes of less than $3,000 or supported by the Aid to Families with Dependent Children program (AFDC). Title I supports remedial reading, career guidance for potential dropouts, reduced pupil-teacher ratios, special teacher training, educational television and other teaching equipment, and specialized staff for social work, guidance and counseling, psychiatry and medicine. The Adult Basic Education program is designed to teach functionally illiterate adults to read.

In order to measure the total Federal contributions to state and local educational expenditures, we have also included such other Federal programs as Head Start, for disadvantaged preschool children; the larger institutional Manpower Development and Training Programs; the Teacher Corps; library material and supplementary education projects under Titles II and III of ESEA; and vocational education programs.

In Detroit, during the 1967–68 school year, $11.2 million of ESEA Title I funds assist only 31 percent of the eligible students. Adult Basic

Education reaches slightly more than 2 percent of the eligible beneficiaries. Federal contributions to the Detroit public school system add about 10 percent to state and local expenditures.

In Newark, during the 1967–68 school year, $4 million of ESEA Title I funds assist about 72 percent of the eligible students. The number of persons reached by the Adult Basic Education program is only approximately 6 percent of the number of functionally illiterate adults. Federal contributions to the Newark public school system add about 11 percent to state and local expenditures.

In New Haven, during the 1967–68 school year, ESEA Title I funds in the amount of $992,000 assist only 40 percent of the eligible students in the middle and senior high schools. Although all eligible beneficiaries in 14 target elementary schools are aided, none of the eligible beneficiaries in 19 non-target elementary schools is reached. Adult Basic Education reaches less than 4 percent of eligible beneficiaries. Federal contributions to the New Haven public school system add about 7 percent to state and local expenditures.

## Housing

The major Federal programs we have examined which are, at least in part, designed to affect the supply of low-income housing, include urban renewal, low rent public housing, housing for the elderly and handicapped, rent supplements, and FHA below market interest rate mortgage insurance (BMIR).

To measure the extent of need for low-income housing, we have used the number of substandard and overcrowded units. In measuring the size of housing programs, we have included expenditures for years before 1967 because they affected the low-income housing supply available in 1967.

In Detroit, a maximum of 758 low-income housing units have been assisted through these programs since 1956. This amounts to 2 percent of the substandard units and 1.7 percent of the overcrowded units. Yet, since 1960, approximately 8,000 low-income units have been demolished for urban renewal.

Similarly, in Newark, since 1959, a maximum of 3,760 low-income housing units have been assisted through the programs considered. This amounts to 16 percent of the substandard units and 23 percent of the overcrowded units. During the same period, more than 12,000 families, mostly low-income, have been displaced by such public uses as urban renewal, public housing and highways.

In New Haven, since 1952, a maximum of 951 low-income housing units have been assisted through the programs considered. This amounts to 14 percent of the substandard units and 20 percent of the overcrowded units. Yet since 1956, approximately 6,500 housing units, mostly low-income, have been demolished for highway construction and urban renewal.

### Welfare

We have considered four Federally assisted programs which provide monetary benefits to low-income persons: Old Age Assistance, Aid to the Blind, Aid to the Permanently and Totally Disabled, and Aid to Families with Dependent Children (AFDC).

In Detroit, the number of persons reached with $48.2 million of Federal funds through the four welfare programs during fiscal year 1967 was approximately 19 percent of the number of poor persons. In Newark, the number of persons reached with $15 million was approximately 54 percent. In New Haven, the number reached with $3.9 million was approximately 40 percent.

### Community Action Programs

We have considered such community action programs as neighborhood service centers, consumer education, family counseling, low-cost credit services, small business development, legal services, programs for the aged, summer programs, home economics counseling, and cultural programs.

In Detroit, the number of persons reached by $12.6 million of community action funds in 1967 was only about 30 percent of the number of poor persons. Federal funding of these programs averaged approximately $35 for each poor person. In Newark, the number of persons reached by $1.9 million was about 44 percent. Federal funding of these programs averaged approximately $21 for each poor person. In New Haven, the number reached by $2.3 million was approximately 42 percent. Federal funding averaged approximately $72 for each poor person.

## GRIEVANCES

To measure the present attitudes of people in the riot cities as precisely as possible, we are sponsoring two attitude surveys among Negroes and whites in 15 cities and four suburban areas, including four of the 20 cities studied for this chapter. These surveys are to be reported later.

In the interim we have attempted to draw some tentative conclusions based upon our own investigations and the more than 1200 interviews we conducted relatively soon after the disorders.

In almost all the cities surveyed, we found the same major grievance topics among Negro communities—although they varied in importance from city to city. The deepest grievances can be ranked into the following three levels of relative intensity:

*First level of intensity:*
1. Police practices
2. Unemployment and underemployment
3. Inadequate housing

*Second level of intensity:*
4. Inadequate education
5. Poor recreation facilities and programs
6. Ineffectiveness of the political structure and grievance mechanisms

*Third level of intensity:*
7. Disrespectful white attitudes
8. Discriminatory administration of justice
9. Inadequacy of Federal programs
10. Inadequacy of municipal services
11. Discriminatory consumer and credit practices
12. Inadequate welfare programs

Our conclusions for the 20 cities have been generally confirmed by a special interview survey in Detroit sponsored by the Detroit Urban League.

**Police practices** were, in some form, a significant grievance in virtually all cities and were often one of the most serious complaints. Included in this category were complaints about physical or verbal abuse of Negro citizens by police officers, the lack of adequate channels for complaints against police, discriminatory police employment and promotion practices, a general lack of respect for Negroes by police officers, and the failure of police departments to provide adequate protection to Negroes.

**Unemployment and underemployment** were found to be grievances in all 20 cities and also frequently appeared to be one of the most serious complaints. These were expressed in terms of joblessness or inadequate jobs and discriminatory practices by labor unions, local and state governments, state employment services and private employment agencies.

**Housing** grievances were found in almost all of the cities studied and appeared to be among the most serious complaints in a majority of them. These included inadequate enforcement of building and safety codes, discrimination in sales and rentals, and overcrowding.

**The educational system** was a source of grievance in almost all the 20 cities and appeared to be one of the most serious complaints in half of them. These centered on the prevalence of *de facto* segregation, the poor quality of instruction and facilities, deficiences [*sic*] in the curriculum in the public schools (particularly because no Negro history was taught), inadequate representation of Negroes on school boards, and the absence or inadequacy of vocational training.

Grievances concerning **municipal recreation programs** were found in a large majority of the 20 cities and appeared to be one of the most serious complaints in almost half. Inadequate recreational facilities in the ghetto and the lack of organized programs were common complaints.

**The political structure** was a source of grievance in almost all of the cities and was among the most serious complaints in several. There were significant grievances concerning the lack of adequate representation of Negroes in the political structure, the failure of local political structures to respond to legitimate complaints and the absence or obscurity of official grievance channels.

**Hostile or racist attitudes** of whites toward Negroes appeared to be one of the most serious complaints in several cities.

In three-fourths of the cities there were significant grievances growing out of beliefs that the **courts** administer justice on a double, discriminatory standard, and that a presumption of guilt attaches whenever a policeman testifies against a Negro.

Significant grievances concerning **Federal programs** were expressed in a large majority of the 20 cities, but appeared to be one of the most serious complaints in only one. Criticism of the Federal antipoverty programs focused on insufficient participation by the poor, lack of continuity, and inadequate funding. Other significant grievances involved urban renewal, insufficient community participation in planning and decisionmaking, and inadequate employment programs.

**Services provided by municipal governments**—sanitation and garbage removal, health and hospital facilities, and paving and lighting of streets—were sources of complaint in approximately half of the cities, but appeared to be among the most serious grievances in only one.

Grievances concerning **unfair commercial practices** affecting Negro consumers were found in approximately half of the cities, but appeared to be one of the most serious complaints in only two. Beliefs were expressed that Negroes are sold inferior quality goods (particularly meats and produce) at higher prices and are subjected to excessive interest rates and fraudulent commercial practices.

Grievances relating to **the welfare system** were expressed in more than half of the 20 cities, but were not among the most serious complaints in any of the cities. There were complaints related to the inadequacy of welfare payments, "unfair regulations," such as the "man in the house" rule, which governs welfare eligibility, and the sometimes hostile and contemptuous attitude of welfare workers. The Commission's recommendations for reform of the welfare system are based on the necessity of attacking the cycle of poverty and dependency in the ghetto.

## Chart I.—Pervasiveness of Grievances
Grievances Found and Number of Cities Where Mentioned as Significant

1. *Employment and underemployment* (found in at least one of the following forms in 20 cities):

| | |
|---|---|
| Unemployment and underemployment (General lack of full-time jobs) | 19 |
| Union discrimination | 13 |
| Discrimination in hiring by local and state government | 9 |
| Discrimination in placement by state employment service | 6 |
| Discrimination in placement by private employment agencies | 3 |

2. *Police practices* (found in at least one of the following forms in 19 cities):

| | |
|---|---|
| Physical abuse | 15 |
| Verbal abuse | 15 |
| Nonexistent or inadequate channels for the redress of grievances against police | 13 |
| Discrimination in employment and promotion of Negroes | 13 |
| General lack of respect for Negroes, i.e., using derogatory language short of threats | 11 |
| Abuse of Negroes in police custody | 10 |
| Failure to answer ghetto calls promptly where Negro is victim of unlawful act | 8 |

3. *Inadequate housing* (found in at least one of the following forms in 18 cities):

| | |
|---|---|
| Poor housing code enforcement | 13 |
| Discrimination in sales and rentals | 12 |
| Overcrowding | 12 |

4. *Inadequate education* (found in at least one of the following forms in 17 cities):

| | |
|---|---|
| *De facto* segregation | 15 |
| Poor quality of instruction and facilities | 12 |
| Inadequacy of curriculum (e.g., no Negro history) | 10 |
| Inadequate Negro representation on school board | 10 |
| Poor vocational education or none at all | 9 |

5. *Political structure and grievance mechanism* (found in at least one of the following forms in 16 cities):

| | |
|---|---|
| Lack of adequate Negro representation | 15 |
| Lack of response to legitimate grievances of Negroes | 13 |
| Grievance mechanism nonexistent or inadequately publicized | 11 |

6. *Inadequate programs* (found in at least one of the following forms in 16 cities):

| | |
|---|---|
| Poverty programs (OEO) (e.g., insufficient participation of the poor in project planing [*sic*]; lack of continuity in programs; inadequate funding; and unfulfilled promises) | 12 |
| Urban renewal (HUD) (e.g., too little community participation in planning and decisionmaking; programs are not urban renewal but "Negro removal") | 9 |

Employment training (Labor–HEW) (e.g., persons are trained for jobs that are not available in the community)        7

7. *Discriminatory administration of justice* (found in at least one of the following forms in 15 cities):

Discriminatory treatment in the courts        15

Lower courts act as arm of police department rather than as an objective arbiter in truly adversary proceedings        10

Presumption of guilt when policeman testifies against Negro        8

8. *Poor recreation facilities and programs* (found in at least one of the following forms in 15 cities):

Inadequate facilities (parks, playgrounds, athletic fields, gymnasiums, and pools)        15

Lack of organized programs        10

9. *Racist and other disrespectful white attitudes* (found in at least one of the following forms in 15 cities):

Racism and lack of respect for dignity of Negroes        15

General animosity toward Negroes        10

10. *Inadequate and poorly administered welfare programs* (found in at least one of the following forms in 14 cities):

Unfair qualification regulations (e.g., "man in the house" rule)        6

Attitude of welfare workers toward recipients (e.g., manifestations of hostility and contempt for persons on welfare)        6

11. *Inadequate municipal services* (found in at least one of the following forms in 11 cities):

Inadequate sanitation and garbage removal        9

Inadequate health and hospital facilities        6

Inadequate street paving and lighting        6

12. *Discriminatory consumer and credit practices* (found in at least one of the following forms in 11 cities):

Inferior quality goods (especially meats and produce)        11

Overpricing (especially on days welfare checks issued)        8

Exorbitant interest rates (particularly in connection with furniture and appliance sales)        7

Fraudulent practices        6 . . .

PART II

# WHY DID IT HAPPEN?

CHAPTER 4

# THE BASIC CAUSES

―――

We have seen what happened. Why did it happen?

In addressing this question, we shift our focus from the local to the national scene, from the particular events of the summer of 1967 to the factors within the society at large that created a mood for violence among so many urban Negroes.

The record before this Commission reveals that the causes of recent racial disorders are imbedded in a massive tangle of issues and circumstances—social, economic, political, and psychological—which arise out of the historical pattern of Negro-white relations in America.

These factors are both complex and interacting; they vary significantly in their effect from city to city and from year to year; and the consequences of one disorder, generating new grievances and new demands, become the causes of the next. It is this which creates the "thicket of tension, conflicting evidence, and extreme opinions" cited by the President.

Despite these complexities, certain fundamental matters are clear. Of these, the most fundamental is the racial attitude and behavior of white Americans toward black Americans. Race prejudice has shaped our history decisively in the past; it now threatens to do so again. White racism is essentially responsible for the explosive mixture which has been accumulating in our cities since the end of World War II. At the base of this mixture are three of the most bitter fruits of white racial attitudes:

**Pervasive discrimination and segregation.** The first is surely the continuing exclusion of great numbers of Negroes from the benefits of economic progress through discrimination in employment and education and their enforced confinement in segregated housing and schools. The corrosive and degrading effects of this condition and the attitudes that underlie it are the source of the deepest bitterness and lie at the center of the problem of racial disorder.

**Black migration and white exodus.** The second is the massive and growing concentration of impoverished Negroes in our major cities resulting from Negro migration from the rural South, rapid population growth, and the continuing movement of the white middle class to the suburbs. The consequence is a greatly increased burden on the already depleted resources of cities, creating a growing crisis of deteriorating facilities and services and unmet human needs.

**Black ghettos.** Third, in the teeming racial ghettos, segregation and poverty have intersected to destroy opportunity and hope and to enforce failure. . . . These three forces have converged on the inner city in recent years and on the people who inhabit it. At the same time, most whites and many Negroes outside the ghetto have prospered to a degree unparalleled in the history of civilization. Through television—the universal appliance in the ghetto—and the other media of mass communications, this affluence has been endlessly flaunted before the eyes of the Negro poor and the jobless ghetto youth.

As Americans, most Negro citizens carry within themselves two basic aspirations of our society. They seek to share in both the material resources of our system and its intangible benefits—dignity, respect, and acceptance. Outside the ghetto, many have succeeded in achieving a decent standard of life and in developing the inner resources which give life meaning and direction. Within the ghetto, however, it is rare that either aspiration is achieved.

Yet these facts alone—fundamental as they are—cannot be said to have caused the disorders. Other and more immediate factors help explain why these events happened now.

Recently, three powerful ingredients have begun to catalyze the mixture.

**Frustrated hopes.** The expectations aroused by the great judicial and legislative victories of the civil rights movement have led to frustration, hostility, and cynicism in the face of the persistent gap between promise and fulfillment. The dramatic struggle for equal rights in the South has sensitized northern Negroes to the economic inequalities reflected in the deprivations of ghetto life.

**Legitimation of violence.** A climate that tends toward the approval and encouragement of violence as a form of protest has been created by white terrorism directed against nonviolent protest, including instances of abuse and even murder of some civil rights workers in the South, by the open defiance of law and Federal authority by state and local officials resisting desegregation, and by some protest groups engaging in civil disobedience who turn their backs on nonviolence, go beyond the constitutionally protected rights of petition and free assembly and resort to violence to attempt to compel alteration of laws and policies with which they disagree. . . .

**Powerlessness.** Finally, many Negroes have come to believe that they are being exploited politically and economically by the white "power structure." Negroes, like people in poverty everywhere, in fact lack the channels of communication, influence, and appeal that traditionally have been available to ethnic minorities within the city and which enabled them—unburdened by color—to scale the walls of the white ghettos in an earlier era. The frustrations of powerlessness have led some to the conviction that there is no effective alternative to violence as a means of expression and redress, as a way of "moving the system." More generally, the result is alienation and hostility toward the institutions of law and government and the white society which controls them. . . .

These facts have combined to inspire a new mood among Negroes, particularly among the young. Self-esteem and enhanced racial pride are replacing apathy and submission to "the system." Moreover, Negro youth, who make up over half of the ghetto population, share the growing sense of alienation felt by many white youth in our country. Thus, their role in recent civil disorders reflects not only a shared sense of deprivation and victimization by white society but also the rising incidence of disruptive conduct by a segment of American youth throughout the society. . . .

**The police.** It is the convergence of all these factors that makes the role of the police so difficult and so significant. Almost invariably the incident that ignites disorder arises from police action. Harlem, Watts, Newark, and Detroit—all the major outbursts of recent years—were precipitated by arrests of Negroes by white police for minor offenses.

But the police are not merely the spark. In discharge of their obligation to maintain order and insure public safety in the disruptive conditions of ghetto life, they are inevitably involved in sharper and more frequent conflicts with ghetto residents than with the residents of other areas. Thus, to many Negroes, police have come to symbolize white power, white racism, and white repression. And the fact is that many police do reflect and express these white attitudes. The atmosphere of hostility and cynicism is reinforced by a widespread perception among Negroes of the existence of police brutality and corruption and of a "double standard" of justice and protection—one for Negroes and one for whites.

To this point, we have attempted only to identify the prime components of the "explosive mixture." In the chapter that follows we seek to analyze them in the perspective of history. Their meaning, however, is already clear:

In the summer of 1967, we have seen in our cities a chain reaction of racial violence. If we are heedless, none of us shall escape the consequences. . . .

# CHAPTER 6

# THE FORMATION OF THE RACIAL GHETTOS

———

## MAJOR TRENDS IN NEGRO POPULATION

Throughout the 20th century, and particularly in the last three decades, the Negro population of the United States has been steadily moving— from rural areas to urban, from South to North and West.

In 1910, 2.7 million Negroes lived in American cities—28 percent of the nation's Negro population of 9.8 million. Today, about 15 million Negro Americans live in metropolitan areas, or 69 percent of the Negro population of 21.5 million. In 1910, 885,000 Negroes—9 percent— lived outside the South. Now, almost 10 million, about 45 percent, live in the North or West.

These shifts in population have resulted from three basic trends:

- A rapid increase in the size of the Negro population.
- A continuous flow of Negroes from Southern rural areas, partly to large cities in the South, but primarily to large cities in the North and West.
- An increasing concentration of Negroes in large metropolitan areas within racially segregated neighborhoods.

Taken together, these trends have produced large and constantly growing concentrations of Negro population within big cities in all parts of the nation. Because most major civil disorders of recent years occurred in predominantly Negro neighborhoods, we have examined the causes of this concentration. . . .

# THE MIGRATION OF NEGROES FROM THE SOUTH

## THE MAGNITUDE OF THIS MIGRATION

In 1910, 91 percent of the Nation's 9.8 million Negroes lived in the South. Twenty-seven percent of American Negroes lived in cities of 2,500 persons or more, as compared to 49 percent of the Nation's white population.

By 1966, the Negro population had increased to 21.5 million, and two significant geographic shifts had taken place. The proportion of Negroes living in the South had dropped to 55 percent, and about 69 percent of all Negroes lived in metropolitan areas compared to 64 percent for whites. While the total Negro population more than doubled from 1910 to 1966, the number living in cities rose over fivefold (from 2.7 million to 14.8 million) and the number outside the South rose elevenfold (from 885,000 to 9.7 million).

Negro migration from the South began after the Civil War. By the turn of the century, sizable Negro populations lived in many large Northern cities—Philadelphia, for example, had 63,400 Negro residents in 1900. The movement of Negroes out of the rural South accelerated during World War I, when floods and boll weevils hurt farming in the South and the industrial demands of the war created thousands of new jobs for unskilled workers in the North. After the war, the shift to mechanized farming spurred the continuing movement of Negroes from rural Southern areas.

The Depression slowed this migratory flow, but World War II set it in motion again. More recently, continuing mechanization of agriculture and the expansion of industrial employment in Northern and Western cities have served to sustain the movement of Negroes out of the South, although at a slightly lower rate.

| Period | Net Negro Out-migration from the South | Annual Average Rate |
|---|---|---|
| 1910–20 | 454,000 | 45,400 |
| 1920–30 | 749,000 | 74,900 |
| 1930–40 | 348,000 | 34,800 |
| 1940–50 | 1,597,000 | 159,700 |
| 1950–60 | 1,457,000 | 145,700 |
| 1960–66 | 613,000 | 102,500 |

From 1960 to 1963, annual Negro out-migration actually dropped to 78,000 but then rose to over 125,000 from 1963 to 1966.

## IMPORTANT CHARACTERISTICS OF THIS MIGRATION

It is useful to recall that even the latest scale of Negro migration is relatively small when compared to the earlier waves of European immigrants. A total of 8.8 million immigrants entered the United States between 1901 and 1911, and another 5.7 million arrived during the following decade. Even during the years from 1960 through 1966, the 1.8 million immigrants from abroad were almost three times the 613,000 Negroes who departed the South. In these same 6 years, California alone gained over 1.5 million new residents from internal shifts of American population.

Three major routes of Negro migration from the South have developed. One runs north along the Atlantic Seaboard toward Boston, another north from Mississippi toward Chicago, and the third west from Texas and Louisiana toward California. Between 1955 and 1960, 50 percent of the nonwhite migrants to the New York metropolitan area came from North Carolina, South Carolina, Virginia, Georgia, and Alabama; North Carolina alone supplied 20 percent of all New York's nonwhite immigrants. During the same period, almost 60 percent of the nonwhite migrants to Chicago came from Mississippi, Tennessee, Arkansas, Alabama, and Louisiana; Mississippi accounted for almost one-third. During these years, three-fourths of the nonwhite migrants to Los Angeles came from Texas, Louisiana, Mississippi, Arkansas, and Alabama.

The flow of Negroes from the South has caused the Negro population to grow more rapidly in the North and West, as indicated below.

| Period | Total Negro Population Gains (Millions) | | Percent of Gain in North & West |
|---|---|---|---|
| | North & West | South | |
| 1940–50 | 1.859 | 0.321 | 85.2 |
| 1950–60 | 2.741 | 1.086 | 71.6 |
| 1960–66 | 2.119 | 0.517 | 80.4 |

As a result, although a much higher proportion of Negroes still reside in the South, the distribution of Negroes throughout the United States is beginning to approximate that of whites, as the following tables show.

Percent Distribution of the Population by Region—1950, 1960, and 1966

| | Negro | | | White | | |
|---|---|---|---|---|---|---|
| | 1950 | 1960 | 1966 | 1950 | 1960[1] | 1966 |
| United States | 100 | 100 | 100 | 100 | 100 | 100 |
| South | 68 | 60 | 55 | 27 | 27 | 28 |
| North | 28 | 34 | 37 | 59 | 56 | 55 |
| Northeast | 13 | 16 | 17 | 28 | 26 | 26 |
| Northcentral | 15 | 18 | 20 | 31 | 30 | 29 |
| West | 4 | 6 | 8 | 14 | 16 | 17 |

[1] Rounds to 99.

Negroes as a Percentage of the Total Population in the United States and Each Region 1950, 1960, and 1966

| | 1950 | 1960 | 1966 |
|---|---|---|---|
| United States | 10 | 11 | 11 |
| South | 22 | 21 | 20 |
| North | 5 | 7 | 8 |
| West | 3 | 4 | 5 |

Negroes in the North and West are now so numerous that natural increase rather than migration provides the greater part of Negro population gains there. And even though Negro migration has continued at a high level, it comprises a constantly declining proportion of Negro growth in these regions.

| Period: | Percentage of total North and West Negro gain from Southern In-migration |
|---|---|
| 1940–50 | 85.9 |
| 1950–60 | 53.1 |
| 1960–66 | 28.9 |

In other words, we have reached the point where the Negro populations of the North and West will continue to expand significantly even if migration from the South drops substantially.

## FUTURE MIGRATION

Despite accelerating Negro migration from the South, the Negro population there has continued to rise.

| Date | Negro population in the South (millions) | Change from preceding date | |
|---|---|---|---|
| | | Total | Annual average |
| 1940 | 9.9 | | |
| 1950 | 10.2 | 321,000 | 32,100 |
| 1960 | 11.3 | 1,086,000 | 108,600 |
| 1966 | 11.8 | 517,000 | 86,200 |

Nor is it likely to halt. Negro birth rates in the South, as elsewhere, have fallen sharply since 1957, but so far this decline has been offset by the rising Negro population base remaining in the South. From 1950 to 1960, southern Negro births generated an average net increase of 254,000 per year and, from 1960 to 1966, an average of 188,000 per year. Even if Negro birth rates continue to fall they are likely to remain high enough to support significant migration to other regions for some time to come.

The Negro population in the South is becoming increasingly urbanized. In 1950, there were 5.4 million southern rural Negroes; by 1960, 4.8 million. But this decline has been more than offset by increases in the urban population. A rising proportion of interregional migration now consists of persons moving from one city to another. From 1960 to 1966, rural Negro population in the South was far below its peak, but the annual average migration of Negroes from the South was still substantial.

These facts demonstrate that Negro migration from the South, which has maintained a high rate for the past 60 years, will continue unless economic conditions change dramatically in either the South or the North and West. This conclusion is reinforced by the fact that most Southern states in recent decades have also experienced outflows of white population. From 1950 to 1960, 11 of the 17 Southern states (including the District of Columbia) "exported" white population—as compared to 13 which "exported" Negro population. Excluding Florida's net gain by migration of 1.5 million, the other 16 Southern states together had a net loss by migration of 1.46 million whites.

# THE CONCENTRATION OF NEGRO POPULATION IN LARGE CITIES

## WHERE NEGRO URBANIZATION HAS OCCURRED

Statistically, the Negro population in America has become more urbanized, and more metropolitan, than the white population. According to Census Bureau estimates, almost 70 percent of all Negroes in 1966 lived in metropolitan areas, compared to 64 percent of all whites. In the South, more than half the Negro population now lives in cities. Rural Negroes outnumber urban Negroes in only four states: Arkansas, Mississippi, North Carolina, and South Carolina.

Basic data concerning Negro urbanization trends, presented in tables at the conclusion of this chapter, indicate that:

- Almost all Negro population growth is occurring within metropolitan areas, primarily within central cities. From 1950 to 1966, the U.S. Negro population rose 6.5 million. Over 98 percent of that increase took place in metropolitan areas—86 percent within central cities, 12 percent in the urban fringe.
- The vast majority of white population growth is occurring in

suburban portions of metropolitan areas. From 1950 to 1966, 77.8 percent of the white population increase of 35.6 million took place in the suburbs. Central cities received only 2.5 percent of this total white increase. Since 1960, white central-city population has actually declined by 1.3 million.

- As a result, central cities are steadily becoming more heavily Negro, while the urban fringes around them remain almost entirely white. The proportion of Negroes in all central cities rose steadily from 12 percent in 1950, to 17 percent in 1960, to 20 percent in 1966. Meanwhile, metropolitan areas outside of central cities remained 95 percent white from 1950 to 1960 and became 96 percent white by 1966.

- The Negro population is growing faster, both absolutely and relatively, in the larger metropolitan areas than in the smaller ones. From 1950 to 1966, the proportion of nonwhites in the central cities of metropolitan areas with 1 million or more persons doubled, reaching 26 percent, as compared with 20 percent in the central cities of metropolitan areas containing from 250,000 to 1 million persons and 12 percent in the central cities of metropolitan areas containing under 250,000 persons.

- The 12 largest central cities—New York, Chicago, Los Angeles, Philadelphia, Detroit, Baltimore, Houston, Cleveland, Washington, D.C., St. Louis, Milwaukee, and San Francisco— now contain over two-thirds of the Negro population outside the South and almost one-third of the total in the United States. All these cities have experienced rapid increases in Negro population since 1950. In six—Chicago, Detroit, Cleveland, St. Louis, Milwaukee, and San Francisco—the proportion of Negroes at least doubled. In two others—New York and Los Angeles—it probably doubled. In 1968, seven of these cities are over 30 percent Negro, and one, Washington, D.C., is two-thirds Negro.

## FACTORS CAUSING RESIDENTIAL SEGREGATION
## IN METROPOLITAN AREAS

The early pattern of Negro settlement within each metropolitan area followed that of immigrant groups. Migrants converged on the older sections of the central city because the lowest cost housing was located there, friends and relatives were likely to be living there, and the older neighborhoods then often had good public transportation.

But the later phases of Negro settlement and expansion in metropolitan areas diverge sharply from those typical of white immigrants. As the whites were absorbed by the larger society, many left their predominantly ethnic neighborhoods and moved to outlying areas to obtain newer housing and better schools. Some scattered randomly over the suburban area. Others established new ethnic clusters in the suburbs, but even these rarely contained solely members of a single ethnic group. As a result, most middle-class neighborhoods—both in the suburbs and within central cities—have no distinctive ethnic character, except that they are white.

Nowhere has the expansion of America's urban Negro population followed this pattern of dispersal. Thousands of Negro families have attained incomes, living standards, and cultural levels matching or surpassing those of whites who have "upgraded" themselves from distinctly ethnic neighborhoods. Yet most Negro families have remained within predominantly Negro neighborhoods, primarily [sic] because they have been effectively excluded from white residential areas.

Their exclusion has been accomplished through various discriminatory practices, some obvious and overt, others subtle and hidden. Deliberate efforts are sometimes made to discourage Negro families from purchasing or renting homes in all-white neighborhoods. Intimidation and threats of violence have ranged from throwing garbage on lawns and making threatening phone calls to burning crosses in yards and even dynamiting property. More often, real estate agents simply refuse to show homes to Negro buyers.

Many middle-class Negro families, therefore, cease looking for homes beyond all-Negro areas or nearby "changing" neighborhoods. For them, trying to move into all-white neighborhoods is not worth the psychological efforts and costs required.

Another form of discrimination just as significant is white withdrawal from, or refusal to enter, neighborhoods where large numbers of Negroes are moving or already residing. Normal population turnover causes about 20 percent of the residents of average U.S. neighborhoods to move out every year because of income changes, job transfers, shifts in life-cycle position or deaths. This normal turnover rate is even higher in apartment areas. The refusal of whites to move into changing areas when vacancies occur there from normal turnover means that most of these vacancies are eventually occupied by Negroes. An inexorable shift toward heavy Negro occupancy results.

Once this happens, the remaining whites seek to leave, thus confirming the existing belief among whites that complete transformation of a neighborhood is inevitable once Negroes begin to enter. Since the belief itself is one of the major causes of the transformation, it becomes a self-fulfilling prophecy which inhibits the development of racially integrated neighborhoods.

As a result, Negro settlements expand almost entirely through "massive racial transition" at the edges of existing all-Negro neighborhoods, rather than by a gradual dispersion of population throughout the metropolitan area.

Two points are particularly important:

- "Massive transition" requires no panic or flight by the original white residents of a neighborhood into which Negroes begin moving. All it requires is the failure or refusal of other whites to fill the vacancies resulting from normal turnover.
- Thus, efforts to stop massive transition by persuading present white residents to remain will ultimately fail unless whites outside the neighborhood can be persuaded to move in.

It is obviously true that some residential separation of whites and Negroes would occur even without discriminatory practices by whites. This would result from the desires of some Negroes to live in predominantly Negro neighborhoods and from differences in meaningful social variables, such as income and educational levels. But these factors alone would not lead to the almost complete segregation of whites and Negroes which has developed in our metropolitan areas.

## THE EXODUS OF WHITES FROM CENTRAL CITIES

The process of racial transition in central-city neighborhoods has been only one factor among many others causing millions of whites to move out of central cities as the Negro populations there expanded. More basic perhaps have been the rising mobility and affluence of middle-class families and the more attractive living conditions—particularly better schools—in the suburbs.

Whatever the reason, the result is clear. In 1950, 45.5 million whites lived in central cities. If this population had grown from 1950 to 1960 at the same rate as the Nation's white population as a whole, it would have increased by 8 million. It actually rose only 2.2 million, indicating an outflow of 5.8 million.*

From 1960 to 1966, the white outflow appears to have been even more rapid. White population of central cities declined 1.3 million instead of rising 3.6 million—as it would if it had grown at the same rate as the entire white population. In theory, therefore, 4.9 million whites left central cities during these 6 years.

Statistics for all central cities as a group understate the relationship between Negro population growth and white outflow in individual central cities. The fact is, many cities with relatively few Negroes experienced rapid white-population growth, thereby obscuring the size of white outmigration that took place in cities having large increases in Negro population. For example, from 1950 to 1960, the 10 largest cities in the United States had a total Negro population increase of 1.6 million, or 55 percent, while the white population there declined 1.4 million. If the two cities where the white population increased (Los Angeles and Houston) are excluded, the nonwhite population in the remaining eight rose 1.4 million, whereas their white population declined 2.1 million. If the white population in these cities had increased at only half the rate of the white population in the United States as a whole from 1950 to 1960, it would have risen by 1.4 million.

---

* The outflow of whites may be somewhat smaller than the 5.8 million difference between these figures, because the ages of the whites in many central cities are higher than in the Nation as a whole, and therefore the population would have grown somewhat more slowly.

Thus, these eight cities actually experienced a white outmigration of at least 3.5 million, while gaining 1.4 million nonwhites.

## THE EXTENT OF RESIDENTIAL SEGREGATION

The rapid expansion of all-Negro residential areas and large-scale white withdrawal have continued a pattern of residential segregation that has existed in American cities for decades. A recent study* reveals that this pattern is present to a high degree in every large city in America. The authors devised an index to measure the degree of residential segregation. The index indicates for each city the percentage of Negroes who would have to move from the blocks where they now live to other blocks in order to provide a perfectly proportional, unsegregated distribution of population.

According to their findings, the average segregation index for 207 of the largest U.S. cities was 86.2 in 1960. This means that an average of over 86 percent of all Negroes would have had to change blocks to create an unsegregated population distribution. Southern cities had a higher average index (90.9) than cities in the Northeast (79.2), the North Central (87.7), or the West (79.3). Only eight cities had index values below 70, whereas over 50 had values above 91.7.

The degree of residential segregation for all 207 cities has been relatively stable, averaging 85.2 in 1940, 87.3 in 1950, and 86.2 in 1960. Variations within individual regions were only slightly larger. However, a recent Census Bureau study shows that in most of the 12 large cities where special censuses were taken in the mid-1960's, the proportions of Negroes living in neighborhoods of greatest Negro concentration had increased since 1960.

Residential segregation is generally more prevalent with respect to Negroes than for any other minority group, including Puerto Ricans, Orientals, and Mexican-Americans. Moreover, it varies little between central city and suburb. This nearly universal pattern cannot be explained in terms of economic discrimination against all low-income groups. Analysis of 15 representative cities indicates that white upper

* "Negroes in Cities," Karl and Alma Taeuber, Aldine Publishing Co., Chicago (1965).

and middle-income households are far more segregated from Negro upper and middle-income households than from white lower income households.

In summary, the concentration of Negroes in central cities results from a combination of forces. Some of these forces, such as migration and initial settlement patterns in older neighborhoods, are similar to those which affected previous ethnic minorities. Others—particularly discrimination in employment and segregation in housing and schools—are a result of white attitudes based on race and color. These forces continue to shape the future of the central city.

# TABLES

Proportion of Negroes in Each of the 30 Largest Cities,
1950, 1960, and Estimated 1965

|  | 1950 | 1960 | Estimate,[1] 1965 |
|---|---|---|---|
| New York, N.Y. | 10 | 14 | 18 |
| Chicago, Ill | 14 | 23 | 28 |
| Los Angeles, Calif | 9 | 14 | 17 |
| Philadelphia, Pa | 18 | 26 | 31 |
| Detroit, Mich | 16 | 29 | 34 |
| Baltimore, Md | 24 | 35 | 38 |
| Houston, Tex | 21 | 23 | 23 |
| Cleveland, Ohio | 16 | 29 | 34 |
| Washington, D.C. | 35 | 54 | 66 |
| St. Louis, Mo | 18 | 29 | 36 |
| Milwaukee, Wis | 3 | 8 | 11 |
| San Francisco, Calif | 6 | 10 | 12 |
| Boston, Mass | 5 | 9 | 13 |
| Dallas, Tex | 13 | 19 | 21 |
| New Orleans, La | 32 | 37 | 41 |
| Pittsburgh, Pa | 12 | 17 | 20 |
| San Antonio, Tex | 7 | 7 | 8 |
| San Diego, Calif | 5 | 6 | 7 |

| | | | |
|---|---|---|---|
| Seattle, Wash | 3 | 5 | 7 |
| Buffalo, N.Y. | 6 | 13 | 17 |
| Cincinnati, Ohio | 16 | 22 | 24 |
| Memphis, Tenn | 37 | 37 | 40 |
| Denver, Colo | 4 | 6 | 9 |
| Atlanta, Ga | 37 | 38 | 44 |
| Minneapolis, Minn | 1 | 2 | 4 |
| Indianapolis, Ind | 15 | 21 | 23 |
| Kansas City, Mo | 12 | 18 | 22 |
| Columbus, Ohio | 12 | 16 | 18 |
| Phoenix, Ariz | 5 | 5 | 5 |
| Newark, N.J. | 17 | 34 | 47 |

[1] Except for Cleveland, Buffalo. Memphis, and Phoenix, for which a special census has been made in recent years, these are very rough estimations computed on the basis of the change in relative proportions of Negro births and deaths since 1960.

SOURCE: U.S. Department of Commerce, Bureau of the Census, BLS Report No. 332, p. 11.

## Percent of All Negroes in Selected Cities Living in Census Tracts Grouped according to Proportion Negro in 1960 and 1964–66[1]

| | Year | All census tracts | 75 percent or more Negro | 50 to 74 percent Negro | 25 to 49 percent Negro | Less than 25 percent Negro |
|---|---|---|---|---|---|---|
| Cleveland, Ohio. | 1960 | 100 | 72 | 16 | 8 | 4 |
| | 1965 | 100 | 80 | 12 | 4 | 4 |
| Phoenix, Ariz. | 1960 | 100 | 19 | 36 | 24 | 21 |
| | 1965 | 100 | 18 | 23 | 42 | 17 |
| Buffalo, N.Y. | 1960 | 100 | 35 | 47 | 6 | 12 |
| | 1966 | 100 | 69 | 10 | 13 | 8 |
| Louisville, Ky. | 1960 | 100 | 57 | 13 | 17 | 13 |
| | 1964 | 100 | 67 | 13 | 10 | 10 |
| Rochester, N.Y. | 1960 | 100 | 8 | 43 | 17 | 32 |
| | 1964 | 100 | 16 | 45 | 24 | 15 |
| Sacramento, Calif. | 1960 | 100 | 9 | .... | 14 | 77 |
| | 1964 | 100 | 8 | 14 | 28 | 50 |
| Des Moines, Iowa. | 1960 | 100 | .... | 28 | 31 | 41 |
| | 1966 | 100 | .... | 42 | 19 | 39 |

## Percent of All Negroes in Selected Cities Living in Census Tracts Grouped according to Proportion Negro in 1960 and 1964–66[1] *(Continued)*

| | Year | All census tracts | 75 percent or more Negro | 50 to 74 percent Negro | 25 to 49 percent Negro | Less than 25 percent Negro |
|---|---|---|---|---|---|---|
| Providence, R.I. | 1960 | 100 | .... | 23 | 2 | 75 |
| | 1965 | 100 | .... | 16 | 46 | 38 |
| Shreveport, La. | 1960 | 100 | 79 | 10 | 7 | 4 |
| | 1966 | 100 | 90 | .... | 6 | 4 |
| Evansville, Ind. | 1960 | 100 | 34 | 27 | 9 | 30 |
| | 1966 | 100 | 59 | 14 | .... | 27 |
| Little Rock, Ark. | 1960 | 100 | 33 | 33 | 19 | 15 |
| | 1964 | 100 | 41 | 18 | 22 | 19 |
| Raleigh, N.C. | 1960 | 100 | 86 | .... | 7 | 7 |
| | 1966 | 100 | 88 | 4 | 2 | 6 |

[1] Selected cities of 100,000 or more in which a special census was taken in any of the years 1964–66. Ranked according to total population at latest census.

SOURCE: U.S. Department of Commerce, Bureau of the Census, BLS Report No. 332, p.12.

## Percent Distribution of Population by Location, Inside and Outside Metropolitan Areas, 1950, 1960, and 1966

| | Negro | | | White | | |
|---|---|---|---|---|---|---|
| | 1950 | 1960 | 1966 | 1950 | 1960 | 1966 |
| United States | 100 | 100 | 100 | 100 | 100 | 100 |
| Metropolitan areas | 56 | 65 | 69 | 59 | 63 | 64 |
| Central cities | 43 | 51 | 56 | 34 | 30 | 27 |
| Urban fringe | 13 | 13 | 13 | 26 | 33 | 37 |
| Smaller cities, towns, and rural | 44 | 35 | 31 | 41 | 37 | 36 |

SOURCE: U.S. Department of Commerce, Bureau of the Census, BLS Report No. 332, p. 9.

## Negroes as a Percentage of Total Population by Location Inside and Outside Metropolitan Areas and by Size of Metropolitan Areas—1950, 1960 and 1966

| | Percent Negro | | |
|---|---|---|---|
| | 1950 | 1960 | 1966 |
| United States | 10 | 11 | 11 |
| Metropolitan areas | 9 | 11 | 12 |
| Central cities | 12 | 17 | 20 |
| Central cities in metropolitan areas[1] of— | | | |
| 1,000,000 or more | 13 | 19 | [2]26 |
| 250,000 to 1,000,000 | 12 | 15 | [2]20 |
| Under 250,000 | 12 | 12 | [2]12 |
| Urban fringe | 5 | 5 | 4 |
| Smaller cities, towns and rural | 11 | 10 | 10 |

[1] In metropolitan areas of population shown as of 1960.

[2] Percent nonwhite; data for Negroes are not available. The figures used are estimated to be closely comparable to those for Negroes alone, using a check for Negro and nonwhite percentages in earlier years.

SOURCE: U.S. Department of Commerce, Bureau of the Census, BLS Report No. 332, p. 10.

## Population Change by Location, Inside and Outside Metropolitan Areas, 1950–66 (Numbers in Millions)

| | Population | | | | | | Change, 1950–66 | | | |
|---|---|---|---|---|---|---|---|---|---|---|
| | Negro | | | White | | | Negro | | White | |
| | 1950 | 1960 | 1966 | 1950 | 1960 | 1966 | Number | Percent | Number | Percent |
| United States | 15.0 | 18.8 | 21.5 | 135.2 | 158.8 | 170.8 | 6.5 | 43 | 35.6 | 26 |
| Metropolitan areas | 8.4 | 12.2 | 14.8 | 80.3 | 99.7 | 109.0 | 6.4 | 77 | 28.7 | 36 |
| Central cities | 6.5 | 9.7 | 12.1 | 45.5 | 47.7 | 46.4 | 5.6 | 87 | .9 | 2 |
| Urban fringe | 1.9 | 2.5 | 2.7 | 34.8 | 52.0 | 62.5 | .8 | 42 | 27.7 | 79 |
| Small cities, towns, and rural | 6.7 | 6.7 | 6.7 | 54.8 | 59.2 | 61.8 | [1] | 1 | 7.0 | 13 |

[1] Rounds to less than 50,000. Source: U.S. Department of Commerce, Bureau of the Census, BLS Report No. 332, p. 8.

# CHAPTER 7

# UNEMPLOYMENT, FAMILY STRUCTURE AND SOCIAL DISORGANIZATION

## RECENT ECONOMIC TRENDS

The Negro population in our country is as diverse in income, occupation, family composition, and other variables as the white community. Nevertheless, for purposes of analysis, three major Negro economic groups can be identified.

The first and smallest group consists of middle and upper income individuals and households whose educational, occupational, and cultural characteristics are similar to those of middle and upper income white groups.

The second and largest group contains Negroes whose incomes are above the "poverty level" but who have not attained the educational, occupational, or income status typical of middle-class Americans.

The third group has very low educational, occupational, and income attainments and lives below the "poverty level."

A recent compilation of data on American Negroes by the Departments of Labor and Commerce shows that although incomes of both Negroes and whites have been rising rapidly,

- Negro incomes still remain far below those of whites. Negro median family income was only 58 percent of the white median in 1966.
- Negro family income is not keeping pace with white family income growth. In constant 1965 dollars, median nonwhite income in 1947 was $2,174 lower than median white income. By 1966, the gap had grown to $3,036.
- The Negro upper income group is expanding rapidly and achieving sizeable income gains. In 1966, 28 percent of all Negro families received incomes of $7,000 or more, compared with 55 percent of white families. This was 1.6 times the proportion of Negroes receiving comparable incomes in 1960, and four times greater than the proportion receiving such incomes in 1947. Moreover, the proportion of Negroes employed in high-skill, high-status, and well-paying jobs rose faster than comparable proportions among whites from 1960 to 1966.
- As Negro incomes have risen, the size of the lowest income group has grown smaller, and the middle and upper groups have grown larger—both relatively and absolutely.

| Group | Percentage of Negro families | | | Percentage of white families |
|---|---|---|---|---|
| | 1947 | 1960 | 1966 | 1966 |
| $7,000 and over | 7 | 17 | 28 | 55 |
| $3,000 to $6,999 | 29 | 40 | 41 | 33 |
| Under $3,000 | 65 | 44 | 32 | 13 |

- About two-thirds of the lowest income group—or 20 percent of all Negro families—are making no significant economic gains despite continued general prosperity. Half of these hardcore disadvantaged—more than 2 million persons—live in central-city neighborhoods. Recent special censuses in Los Angeles and Cleveland indicate that the incomes of persons living in the worst slum areas have not risen at all during this period, unemployment rates have declined only slightly, the proportion of families with female heads has increased, and housing conditions have worsened even though rents have risen.

Thus, between 2.0 and 2.5 million poor Negroes are living in disadvantaged neighborhoods of central cities in the United States. These persons comprise only slightly more than 1 percent of the Nation's total population, but they make up about 16 to 20 percent of the total Negro population of all central cities, and a much higher proportion in certain cities.

# UNEMPLOYMENT AND UNDEREMPLOYMENT

## THE CRITICAL SIGNIFICANCE OF EMPLOYMENT

The capacity to obtain and hold a "good job" is the traditional test of participation in American society. Steady employment with adequate compensation provides both purchasing power and social status. It develops the capabilities, confidence, and self-esteem an individual needs to be a responsible citizen, and provides a basis for a stable family life. . . .

. . . For the Negro American it is already, and will continue to be, the master problem. It is the measure of white bona fides. It is the measure of Negro competence, and also of the competence of American society. Most importantly, the linkage between problems of employment and the range of social pathology that afflicts the Negro community is unmistakable. Employment not only controls the present for the Negro American but, in a most profound way, it is creating the future as well.

For residents of disadvantaged Negro neighborhoods, obtaining good jobs is vastly more difficult than for most workers in society. For decades, social, economic, and psychological disadvantages surrounding the urban Negro poor have impaired their work capacities and opportunities. The result is a cycle of failure—the employment disabilities of one generation breed those of the next.

## NEGRO UNEMPLOYMENT

Unemployment rates among Negroes have declined from a post-Korean War high of 12.6 percent in 1958 to 8.2 percent in 1967. Among married Negro men, the unemployment rate for 1967 was down to 3.2 percent.*

Notwithstanding this decline, unemployment rates for Negroes are still double those for whites in every category, including married men, as they have been throughout the postwar period. Moreover, since 1954, even during the current unprecedented period of sustained economic growth, unemployment among Negroes has been continuously above the 6 percent "recession" level widely regarded as a sign of serious economic weakness when prevalent for the entire work force.

While the Negro unemployment rate remains high in relation to the white rate, the number of additional jobs needed to lower this to the level of white unemployment is surprisingly small. In 1967, approximately 3 million persons were unemployed during an average week, of whom about 638,000, or 21 percent, were nonwhites. When corrected for undercounting, total nonwhite unemployment was approximately 712,000 or 8 percent of the nonwhite labor force. To reduce the unemployment rate to 3.4 percent, the rate prevalent among whites, jobs must be found for 57.5 percent of these unemployed persons. This amounts to nearly 409,000 jobs, or about 27 percent of the net number of new jobs added to the economy in the year 1967 alone and only slightly more than one-half of 1 percent of all jobs in the United States in 1967.

## THE LOW-STATUS AND LOW-PAYING NATURE OF MANY NEGRO JOBS

Even more important perhaps than unemployment is the related problem of the undesirable nature of many jobs open to Negroes. Negro workers are concentrated in the lowest skilled and lowest paying occupations. These jobs often involve substandard wages, great instability and uncertainty of tenure, extremely low status in the eyes of both employer and employee, little or no chance for meaningful advance-

---

* Adjusted for Census Bureau undercounting.

ment, and unpleasant or exhausting duties. Negro men in particular are more than three times as likely as whites to be in unskilled or service jobs which pay far less than most:

| Type of occupation | Percentage of male workers in each type of occupation, 1966 | | Median earnings of all male civilians in each occupation, 1965 |
|---|---|---|---|
| | White | Nonwhite | |
| Professional, technical, and managerial | 27 | 9 | $7,603[1] |
| Clerical and sales | 14 | 9 | 5,532[1] |
| Craftsmen and foremen | 20 | 12 | 6,270 |
| Operatives | 20 | 27 | 5,046 |
| Service workers | 6 | 16 | 3,436 |
| Nonfarm laborers | 6 | 20 | 2,410 |
| Farmers and farm workers | 7 | 8 | 1,669[1] |

[1] Average of two categories from normal Census Bureau categories as combined in data presented in The Social and Economic Conditions of Negroes in the United States (BLS No. 332).

This concentration in the least desirable jobs can be viewed another way by calculating the changes which would occur if Negro men were employed in various occupations in the same proportions as the male labor force as a whole (not solely the white labor force).

| Type of occupation | Number of male nonwhite workers, 1966 | | | |
|---|---|---|---|---|
| | As actually distributed[1] | If distributed the same as all male workers | Difference | |
| | | | Number | Percent |
| Professional, technical, and managerial | 415,000 | 1,173,000 | +758,000 | +183 |
| Clerical and sales | 415,000 | 628,000 | +213,000 | +51 |
| Craftsmen and foremen | 553,000 | 894,000 | +341,000 | +62 |
| Operatives | 1,244,000 | 964,000 | −280,000 | −23 |
| Service workers | 737,000 | 326,000 | −411,000 | −56 |
| Nonfarm laborers | 922,000 | 340,000 | −582,000 | −63 |
| Farmers and farm workers | 369,000 | 330,000 | −39,000 | −11 |

[1] Estimates based upon percentages set forth in BLS No. 332, p. 41.

Thus, upgrading the employment of Negro men to make their occupational distribution identical with that of the labor force as a whole would have an immense impact upon the nature of their occupations. About 1.3 million nonwhite men—or 28 percent of those employed in 1966—would move up the employment ladder into one of the higher status and higher paying categories. The effect of such a shift upon the incomes of Negro men would be very great. Using the 1966 job distribution, the shift indicated above would produce about $4.8 billion more earned income for nonwhite men alone if they received the 1965 median income in each occupation. This would be a rise of approximately 30 percent in the earnings actually received by all nonwhite men in 1965 (not counting any sources of income other than wages and salaries).

Of course, the kind of "instant upgrading" visualized in these calculations does not represent a practical alternative for national policy. The economy cannot drastically reduce the total number of low-status jobs it now contains, or shift large numbers of people upward in occupation in any short period. Therefore, major upgrading in the employment status of Negro men must come through a faster relative expansion of higher level jobs than lower level jobs (which has been occurring for several decades), an improvement in the skills of nonwhite workers so they can obtain a high proportion of those added better jobs, and a drastic reduction of discriminatory hiring and promotion practices in all enterprises, both private and public.

Nevertheless, this hypothetical example clearly shows that the concentration of male Negro employment at the lowest end of the occupational scale is greatly depressing the incomes of U.S. Negroes in general. In fact, this is the single most important source of poverty among Negroes. It is even more important than unemployment, as can be shown by a second hypothetical calculation. In 1966, there were about 724,000 unemployed nonwhites in the United States on the average, including adults and teenagers, and allowing for the Census Bureau undercount of Negroes. If every one of these persons had been employed and had received the median amount earned by nonwhite males in 1966 ($3,864), this would have added a total of $2.8 billion to nonwhite income as a whole. If only enough of these persons had been employed at that wage to reduce nonwhite unemployment from 7.3 percent to 3.3 percent—the rate among whites in 1966—then the income gain for nonwhites would have totaled about $1.5 billion. But if nonwhite unemployment remained at 7.3 percent, and nonwhite men were upgraded so that they had the same occupational distribution and incomes as all men in the labor force considered together, this would have produced about $4.8 billion in additional income, as noted above (using 1965 earnings for calculation). Thus the potential income gains from upgrading the male nonwhite labor force are much larger than those from reducing nonwhite unemployment.

This conclusion underlines the difficulty of improving the economic status of Negro men. It is far easier to create new jobs than either to create new jobs with relatively high status and earning power, or to upgrade existing employed or partly employed workers into such better quality employment. Yet only such upgrading will eliminate the fundamental basis of poverty and deprivation among Negro families.

Access to good-quality jobs clearly affects the willingness of Negro men actively to seek work. In riot cities surveyed by the Commission with the largest percentage of Negroes in skilled and semiskilled jobs, Negro men participated in the labor force to the same extent as, or greater than, white men. Conversely, where most Negro men were heavily concentrated in menial jobs, they participated less in the labor force than white men.

Even given similar employment, Negro workers with the same education as white workers are paid less. This disparity doubtless results to some extent from inferior training in segregated schools, and also from the fact that large numbers of Negroes are only now entering certain occupations for the first time. However, the differentials are so large and so universal at all educational levels that they clearly reflect the patterns of discrimination which characterize hiring and promotion practices in many segments of the economy. For example, in 1966, among persons who had completed high school, the median income of Negroes was only 73 percent that of whites. Even among persons with an eighth-grade education, Negro median income was only 80 percent of white median income.

At the same time, a higher proportion of Negro women than white women participates in the labor force at nearly all ages except 16 to 19. For instance, in 1966, 55 percent of nonwhite women from 25 to 34 years of age were employed, compared to only 38 percent of white women in the same age group. The fact that almost half of all adult Negro women work reflects the fact that so many Negro males have unsteady and low-paying jobs. Yet even though Negro women are often better able to find work than Negro men, the unemployment rate among adult nonwhite women (20 years old and over) in 1967 was 7.1 percent, compared to the 4.3 percent rate among adult non-white men. . . .

## SUBEMPLOYMENT IN DISADVANTAGED NEGRO NEIGBORHOODS [*SIC*]

In disadvantaged areas, employment conditions for Negroes are in a chronic state of crisis. Surveys in low-income neighborhoods of nine large cities made by the Department of Labor late in 1966 revealed that the rate of unemployment there was 9.3 percent, compared to 7.3 percent for Negroes generally and 3.3 percent for whites. Moreover, a high proportion of the persons living in these areas were "underemployed," that is, they were either part-time workers looking for fulltime employment, or full-time workers earning less than $3000 per year, or had dropped out of the labor force. The Department of Labor estimated that this underemployment is 2½ times greater than the number of unemployed in these areas. Therefore, the "subemployment rate," including both the unemployed and the underemployed, was about 32.7 percent in the nine areas surveyed, or 8.8 times greater than the overall unemployment rate for all U.S. workers. Since underemployment also exists outside disadvantaged neighborhoods, comparing the full subemployment rate in these areas with the unemployment rate for the Nation as a whole is not entirely valid. However, it provides some measure of the enormous disparity between employment conditions in most of the Nation and those prevalent in disadvantaged Negro areas in our large cities. . . .

# THE MAGNITUDE OF POVERTY IN DISADVANTAGED NEIGHBORHOODS

[The first paragraph in this section is intentionally omitted.]

"Poverty" in the affluent society is more than absolute deprivation. Many of the poor in the United States would be well off in other societies. Relative deprivation—inequality—is a more useful concept of poverty with respect to the Negro in America because it encompasses social and political exclusions as well as economic inequality. Because of the lack of data of this type, we have had to focus our analysis on a measure of poverty which is both economic and absolute—the Social Security Administration's "poverty level'" concept. It is clear, however, that broader measures of poverty would substantiate the conclusions that follow.

In 1966, there were 29.7 million persons in the United States—15.3 percent of the Nation's population—with incomes below the "poverty level," as defined by the Social Security Administration. Of these, 20.3 million were white (68.3 percent), and 9.3 million nonwhite (31.7 percent). Thus, about 11.9 percent of the Nation's whites and 40.6 percent of its nonwhites were poor under the Social Security definition.

The location of the Nation's poor is best shown from 1964 data as indicated by the following table:

| Group | Percentage of those in poverty in each group living in— | | | |
| | Metropolitan areas | | | |
| | In central cities | Outside central cities | Other areas | Total |
|---|---|---|---|---|
| Whites | 23.8 | 21.8 | 54.4 | 100 |
| Nonwhites | 41.7 | 10.8 | 47.5 | 100 |
| Total | 29.4 | 18.4 | 52.2 | 100 |

SOURCE: Social Security Administration.

---

* $3335 per year for an urban family of four.

The following facts concerning poverty are relevant to an understanding of the problems faced by people living in disadvantaged neighborhoods.*

- In central cities 30.7 percent of nonwhite families of two or more persons lived in poverty compared to only 8.8 percent of whites.
- Of the 10.1 million poor persons in central cities in 1964, about 4.4 million of these (43.6 percent) were nonwhites, and 5.7 million (56.4 percent) were whites. The poor whites were much older on the average than the poor nonwhites. The proportion of poor persons 65 years old or older was 23.2 percent among whites, but only 6.8 percent among nonwhites.
- Poverty was more than twice as prevalent among nonwhite families with female heads than among those with male heads, 57 percent compared to 21 percent. In central cities, 26 percent of all nonwhite families of two or more persons had female heads, as compared to 12 percent of white families.
- Among nonwhite families headed by a female, and having children under 6, the incidence of poverty was 81 percent. Moreover, there were 243,000 such families living in poverty in central cities—or over 9 percent of all nonwhite families in those cities.
- Among all children living in poverty within central cities, nonwhites outnumbered whites by over 400,000. The number of poor nonwhite children equalled or surpassed the number of white poor children in every age group.

**Number of Children Living in Poverty (Millions)**

| Age group | White | Nonwhite | Percent of total nonwhite |
|-----------|-------|----------|---------------------------|
| Under 6   | 0.9   | 1.0      | 53                        |
| 6 to 15   | 1.0   | 1.3      | 57                        |
| 16 to 21  | 0.4   | 0.4      | 50                        |
| Total     | 2.3   | 2.7      | 54                        |

* Source: Social Security Administration; based on 1964 data.

Two stark facts emerge:

- 54 percent of all poor children in central cities in 1964 were nonwhites.
- Of the 4.4 million nonwhites living in poverty within central cities in 1964, 52 percent were children under 16 and 61 percent were under 21.

Since 1964, the number of nonwhite families living in poverty within central cities has remained about the same; hence, these poverty conditions are probably still prevalent in central cities in terms of absolute numbers of persons, although the proportion of persons in poverty may have dropped slightly. . . .*

## NOTE: CALCULATIONS OF NONWHITE SUBEMPLOYMENT IN DISADVANTAGED AREAS OF ALL CENTRAL CITIES, 1967

In 1967, total unemployment in the United States was distributed as follows, by age and color:

| Group | Nonwhite | White | Total |
|---|---|---|---|
| Adult men (20 and over) | 193,000 | 866,000 | 1,059,000 |
| Adult women (20 and over) | 241,000 | 837,000 | 1,078,000 |
| Teenagers (16–19) | 204,000 | 635,000 | 839,000 |
| Total | 638,000 | 2,338,000 | 2,976,000 |

Adjustments for the Census Bureau undercount of nonwhite males in the labor force amounting to 7.5 percent for the teenage group, 18

---

* For the Nation as a whole, the proportion of nonwhite families living in poverty, dropped from 39 percent to 35 percent from 1964 to 1966 (defining "family" somewhat diffently from the definition used in the data above). The number of such families declined from 1.9 million to 1.7 million. However, the number and proportion of all nonwhites living in central cities rose in the same period. As a result, the number of nonwhite families living in so-called "poverty areas" of large cities actually rose from 1,561,000 in 1960 to 1,588,000 in 1966.

percent for the adult male group and approximately 10 percent for adult females result in the following revised total employment:

| Group | Nonwhite | White | Total |
|---|---|---|---|
| Adult men | 228,000 | 866,000 | 1,094,000 |
| Adult women | 265,000 | 837,000 | 1,102,000 |
| Teenagers | 219,000 | 635,000 | 854,000 |
| Total | 712,000 | 2,338,000 | 3,050,000 |

These figures cover the entire United States. To provide an estimate of the number of unemployed in disadvantaged neighborhoods within central cities, it is necessary to discover what proportion of the non-white unemployed are in central cities and what proportion of those in central cities are within the most disadvantaged neighborhoods. The Department of Labor survey in nine large central cities covering the first 9 months of 1967 showed that these cities contained 27.3 percent of the total nonwhite labor force in the United States, and 26.4 percent of total nonwhite unemployment. Hence, it is reasonable to assume that nonwhite unemployment is concentrated in central cities to about the same degree as the nonwhite labor force. In turn, the nonwhite labor force is located in central cities in about the same proportion as the nonwhite population, or 57.1 percent in 1967. Thus central-city unemployment among nonwhites was presumably about 57.1 percent of the national figures:

**Nonwhite Unemployment in All Central Cities**

| | [Rounded] |
|---|---|
| Adult men | 130,000 |
| Adult women | 151,000 |
| Teenagers | 125,000 |
| Total | 406,000 |

Within large central cities, about 62 percent of all nonwhite families lived in certain Census Tracts which have been designated "poverty areas." These tracts ranked lowest in United States cities over 250,000 persons in size, according to an index of "deprivation" based upon family income, children in broken homes, persons with low educational attainment, males in unskilled jobs, and substandard housing. On the assumption that conditions in these poverty areas are comparable to those in the nine disadvantaged areas surveyed by the Department of Labor in 1966, the number of unemployed nonwhites in disadvanagted [*sic*] areas of central cities is as follows:*

**Nonwhite Unemployment in Disadvantaged Areas of All Central Cities, 1967**

| Adult men | 102,000 |
|-----------|---------|
| Adult women | 118,000 |
| Teenagers | 98,000 |
| Total | 318,000 |

The number of underemployed nonwhites in these areas was about 2.5 times larger than the number of unemployed. But we have already accounted for some underemployment in the adjustment for undercounting—so we will assume nonwhite underemployment was 2.25 times adjusted unemployment for all three age and sex groups. The resulting rough estimates are as follows:

**Nonwhite Subemployment in Disadvantaged Areas of All Central Cities, 1967**

| Group | Unemployment | Underemployment | Total subemployment |
|-------|--------------|-----------------|---------------------|
| Adult men | 102,000 | 230,000 | 332,000 |
| Adult women | 118,000 | 266,000 | 384,000 |
| Teenagers | 98,000 | 220,000 | 318,000 |
| Total | 318,000 | 716,000 | 1,034,000 |

* The number of nonwhite unemployed in the more disadvantaged areas was 26 percent higher than it would have been had it been proportional to the total population residing there. Therefore, the proportion of central city nonwhite unemployed in poverty areas is assumed to equal 78.1 percent (62 percent times 1.26).

# CHAPTER 8

# CONDITIONS OF LIFE IN THE RACIAL GHETTO

———

The conditions of life in the racial ghetto are strikingly different from those to which most Americans are accustomed—especially white, middle-class Americans. We believe it important to describe these conditions and their effect on the lives of people who cannot escape from the ghetto.*

## CRIME AND INSECURITY

Nothing is more fundamental to the quality of life in any area than the sense of personal security of its residents, and nothing affects this more than crime.

In general, crime rates in large cities are much higher than in other areas of our country. Within such cities, crime rates are higher in disadvantaged Negro areas than anywhere else.

The most widely used measure of crime is the number of "index

———

* We have not attempted here to describe conditions relating to the fundamental problems of housing, education, and welfare, which are treated in detail in later chapters.

crimes" (homicide, forcible rape, aggravated assault, robbery, burglary, grand larceny, and auto theft) in relation to population. In 1966, 1,754 such crimes were reported to police for every 100,000 Americans. In cities over 250,000, the rate was 3,153, and in cities over 1 million, it was 3,630—or more than double the national average. In suburban areas alone, including suburban cities, the rate was only 1,300, or just over one-third the rate in the largest cities.

Within larger cities, personal and property insecurity has consistently been highest in the older neighborhoods encircling the downtown business district. In most cities, crime rates for many decades have been higher in these inner areas than anywhere, except in downtown areas themselves, where they are inflated by the small number of residents.

High crime rates have persisted in these inner areas even though the ethnic character of their residents continually changed. Poor immigrants used these areas as "entry ports," then usually moved on to more desirable neighborhoods as soon as they acquired enough resources. Many "entry port" areas have now become racial ghettos.

The difference between crime rates in these disadvantaged neighborhoods and in other parts of the city is usually startling, as a comparison of crime rates in five police districts in Chicago for 1965 illustrates. These five include one high-income, all-white district at the periphery of the city, two very low-income, virtually all-Negro districts near the city core with numerous public housing projects, and two predominantly white districts, one with mainly lower middle-income families, the other containing a mixture of very high-income and relatively low-income households. The table shows crime rates against persons and against property in these five districts, plus the number of patrolmen assigned to them per 100,000 residents, as follows:

Incidence of Index Crimes and Patrolmen Assignments per
100,000 Residents in 5 Chicago Police Districts, 1965

| Number | High-income white district | Low middle-income white district | Mixed high- and low-income white district | Very low income Negro district No. 1 | Very low income Negro district No. 2 |
|---|---|---|---|---|---|
| Index crimes against persons | 80 | 440 | 338 | 1,615 | 2,820 |
| Index crimes against property | 1,038 | 1,750 | 2,080 | 2,508 | 2,630 |
| Patrolmen assigned | 93 | 133 | 115 | 243 | 291 |

These data indicate that:

- Variations in the crime rate against persons within the city are extremely large. One very low income Negro district had 35 times as many serious crimes against persons per 100,000 residents as did the high-income white district.
- Variations in the crime rate against property are much smaller. The highest rate was only 2.5 times larger than the lowest.
- The lower the income in an area, the higher the crime rate there. Yet low-income Negro areas have significantly higher crime rates than low-income white areas. This reflects the high degree of social disorganization in Negro areas described in the previous chapter, as well as the fact that poor Negroes as a group have lower incomes than poor whites as a group.
- The presence of more police patrolmen per 100,000 residents does not necessarily offset high crime in certain parts of the city. Although the Chicago Police Department had assigned over three times as many patrolmen per 100,000 residents to the highest crime areas shown as to the lowest, crime rates in the highest crime area for offenses against both persons and property combined were 4.9 times as high as in the lowest crime area.

Because most middle-class Americans live in neighborhoods similar to the more crime-free district described above, they have little comprehension of the sense of insecurity that characterizes the ghetto resident. Moreover, official statistics normally greatly understate actual crime rates because the vast majority of crimes are not reported to the police. For example, studies conducted for the President's Crime Commission in Washington, D.C., Boston, and Chicago, showed that three to six times as many crimes were actually committed against persons and homes as were reported to the police.

Two facts are crucial to a understanding of the effects of high crime rates in racial ghettos; most of these crimes are committed by a small minority of the residents, and the principal victims are the residents themselves. Throughout the United States, the great majority of crimes committed by Negroes involve other Negroes as victims. A special tabulation made by the Chicago Police Department for the President's Crime Commission indicated that over 85 percent of the crimes committed against persons by Negroes between September, 1965, and March, 1966, involved Negro victims.

As a result, the majority of law-abiding citizens who live in disadvantaged Negro areas face much higher probabilities of being victimized than residents of most higher income areas, including almost all suburbs. For nonwhites, the probability of suffering from any index crime except larceny is 78 percent higher than for whites. The probability of being raped is 3.7 times higher among nonwhite women, and the probability of being robbed is 3.5 times higher for nonwhites in general.

The problems associated with high crime rates generate widespread hostility toward the police in these neighborhoods for reasons described elsewhere in this Report. Thus, crime not only creates an atmosphere of insecurity and fear throughout Negro neighborhoods but also causes continuing attrition of the relationship between Negro residents and police. This bears a direct relationship to civil disorder. . . .

# HEALTH AND SANITATION CONDITIONS

The residents of the racial ghetto are significantly less healthy than most other Americans. They suffer from higher mortality rates, higher incidence of major diseases, and lower availability and utilization of medical services. They also experience higher admission rates to mental hospitals.

These conditions result from a number of factors.

## POVERTY

From the standpoint of health, poverty means deficient diets, lack of medical care, inadequate shelter and clothing and often lack of awareness of potential health needs. As a result, almost 30 percent of all persons with family incomes less than $2,000 per year suffer from chronic health conditions that adversely affect their employment—as compared with less than 8 percent of the families with incomes of $7,000 or more.

Poor families have the greatest need for financial assistance in meeting medical expenses. Only about 34 percent of families with incomes of less than $2,000 per year use health insurance benefits, as compared to nearly 90 percent of those with incomes of $7,000 or more.*

These factors are aggravated for Negroes when compared to whites for the simple reason that the proportion of persons in the United States who are poor is 3.5 times as high among Negroes (41 percent in 1966) as among whites (12 percent in 1966).

---

* Public programs of various kinds have been providing significant financial assistance for medical care in recent years. In 1964, over $1.1 billion was paid out by various governments for such aid. About 52 percent of medical vendor payments came from Federal Government agencies, 33 percent from states, and 12 percent from local governments. The biggest contributions were made by the Old Age Assistance Program and the Medical Assistance for the Aged Program. The enactment of Medicare in 1965 has significantly added to this flow of public assistance for medical aid. However, it is too early to evaluate the results upon health conditions among the poor.

## MATERNAL MORTALITY

Mortality rates for nonwhite mothers are four times as high as those for white mothers. There has been a sharp decline in such rates since 1940, when 774 nonwhite and 320 white mothers died for each 100,000 live births. In 1965, only 84 nonwhite and 21 white mothers died per 100,000 live births—but the gap between nonwhites and whites actually increased.

## INFANT MORTALITY

Mortality rates among nonwhite babies are 58 percent higher than among whites for those under 1 month old and almost three times as high among those from 1 month to 1 year old. This is true in spite of a large drop in infant mortality rates in both groups since 1940.

Number of Infants Who Died per 1,000 Live Births

| Year | Less than 1 month old | | 1 month to 1 year old | |
|------|-------|----------|-------|----------|
|      | White | Nonwhite | White | Nonwhite |
| 1940 | 27.2  | 39.7     | 16.0  | 34.1     |
| 1950 | 19.4  | 27.5     | 7.4   | 17.0     |
| 1960 | 17.2  | 26.9     | 5.7   | 16.4     |
| 1965 | 16.1  | 25.4     | 5.4   | 14.9     |

## LIFE EXPECTANCY

To some extent because of infant mortality rates, life expectancy at birth was 6.9 years longer for whites (71.0 years) than for nonwhites (64.1 years) in 1965. Even in the prime working ages, life expectancy is significantly lower among nonwhites than among whites. In 1965, white persons 25 years old could expect to live an average of 48.6 more years, whereas nonwhites 25 years old could expect to live another 43.3 years, or 11 percent less. Similar but smaller discrepancies existed at all ages from 25 through 55; some actually increased slightly between 1960 and 1965.

## LOWER UTILIZATION OF HEALTH SERVICES

A fact that also contributes to poorer health conditions in the ghetto is that Negro families with incomes similar to those of whites spend less on medical services and visit medical specialists less often.

Percent of Family Expenditures Spent for Medical Care, 1960–61

| Income group | White | Nonwhite | Ratio, white to nonwhite |
|---|---|---|---|
| Under $3,000 | 9 | 5 | 1.8:1 |
| $3,000 to $7,499 | 7 | 5 | 1.4:1 |
| $7,500 and over | 6 | 4 | 1.5:1 |

Since the lowest income group contains a much larger proportion of nonwhite families than white families, the overall discrepancy in medical care spending between these two groups is very significant, as shown by the following table:

Health Expenses per Person per Year for the
Period from July to December 1962

| Income by racial group | Expenses | | | | | |
|---|---|---|---|---|---|---|
| | Total | Hospital | Doctor | Dental | Medical | Other medical |
| Under $2,000 per family per year: | | | | | | |
| White | $130 | $33 | $41 | $11 | $32 | $13 |
| Nonwhite | 63 | 15 | 23 | 5 | 16 | 5 |
| $10,000 and more per family per year: | | | | | | |
| White | 179 | 34 | 61 | 37 | 31 | 16 |
| Nonwhite | 133 | 34 | 50 | 19 | 23 | 8 |

These data indicate that nonwhite families in the lower income group spent less than half as much per person on medical services as white families with similar incomes. This discrepancy sharply declines but is still significant in the higher income group, where total nonwhite medical expenditures per person equal, on the average, 74.3 percent of white expenditures.

Negroes spend less on medical care for several reasons. Negro households generally are larger, requiring greater nonmedical expenses for each household and leaving less money for meeting medical expenses. Thus, lower expenditures per person would result even if expenditures per household were the same. Negroes also often pay more for other basic necessities such as food and consumer durables, as discussed in the next part of this chapter. In addition, fewer doctors, dentists, and medical facilities are conveniently available to Negroes than to most whites—a result both of geographic concentration of doctors in higher income areas in large cities and of discrimination against Negroes by doctors and hospitals. A survey in Cleveland indicated that there were 0.45 physcians [sic] per 1,000 people in poor neighborhoods, compared to 1.13 per 1,000 in nonpoverty areas. The result nationally is fewer visits to physicians and dentists.

**Percent of Population Making One or More Visits to Indicated Type of Medical Specialist from July 1963 to June 1964**

| Type of medical specialist | Family incomes of $2,000–$3,999 | | Family incomes of $7,000–$9,999 | |
|---|---|---|---|---|
| | White | Nonwhite | White | Nonwhite |
| Physician | 64 | 56 | 70 | 64 |
| Dentist | 31 | 20 | 52 | 33 |

Although widespread use of health insurance has led many hospitals to adopt nondiscriminatory policies, some private hospitals still refuse to admit Negro patients or to accept doctors with Negro patients. And many individual doctors still discriminate against Negro patients. As a result, Negroes are more likely to be treated in hospital clinics than whites and they are less likely to receive personalized service. This conclusion is confirmed by the following data:

**Percent of All Visits to Physicians from July 1963
to June 1964, Made in Indicated Ways**

| Type of visit to physician | Family Incomes of $2,000–$3,000 | | Family Incomes of $7,000–$9,999 | |
|---|---|---|---|---|
| | White | Nonwhite | White | Nonwhite |
| In physician's office | 68 | 56 | 73 | 66 |
| Hospital clinic | 17 | 35 | 7 | 16 |
| Other (mainly telephone) | 15 | 9 | 20 | 18 |
| Total | 100 | 100 | 100 | 100 |

## ENVIRONMENTAL FACTORS

Environmental conditions in disadvantaged Negro neighborhoods create further reasons for poor health conditions there. The level of sanitation is strikingly below that which is prevalent in most higher income areas. One simple reason is that residents often lack proper storage facilities for food—adequate refrigerators, freezers, even garbage cans, which are sometimes stolen as fast as landlords can replace them.

In areas where garbage collection and other sanitation services are grossly inadequate—commonly in the poorer parts of our large cities—rats proliferate. It is estimated that in 1965, there were over 14,000 cases of ratbite in the United States, mostly in such neighborhoods. . . .

. . .  * * *  There is no known study comparing sanitation services between slum and non-slum areas. The experts agree, however, that there are more services in the slums on a quantitative basis, although perhaps not on a per capita basis. In New York, for example, garbage pickups are supposedly scheduled for about six times a week in slums, compared to three times a week in other areas of the city; the comparable figures in Chicago are two to three times a week versus once a week.

The point, therefore, is not the relative quantitative level of services but the peculiarly intense needs of ghetto areas for sanitation services. This high demand is the product of numerous factors including: (1) higher population density; (2) lack of well managed buildings and adequate garbage services provided by landlords, number of receptacles, carrying to curbside, number of electric garbage disposals; (3) high relocation rates of tenants and businesses, producing heavy volume of bulk refuse left on streets and in buildings; (4) different uses of the streets—as outdoor living rooms in summer, recreation areas—producing high visibility and sensitivity to garbage problems; (5) large numbers of abandoned cars; (6) severe rodent and pest problems; (7) traffic congestion blocking garbage collection; and (8) obstructed street cleaning and snow removal on crowded, car-choked streets. Each of these elements adds to the problem and suggests a different possible line of attack.

## EXPLOITATION OF DISADVANTAGED CONSUMERS BY RETAIL MERCHANTS

Much of the violence in recent civil disorders has been directed at stores and other commercial establishments in disadvantaged Negro areas. In some cases, rioters focused on stores operated by white merchants who, they apparently believed, had been charging exorbitant prices or selling inferior goods. Not all the violence against these stores can be attributed to "revenge" for such practices. Yet it is clear that many residents of disadvantaged Negro neighborhoods believe they suffer constant abuses by local merchants.

Significant grievances concerning unfair commercial practices affecting Negro consumers were found in 11 of the 20 cities studied by the Commission. The fact that most of the merchants who operate stores in Negro areas are white undoubtedly contributes to the conclusion among Negroes that they are exploited by white society.

It is difficult to assess the precise degree and extent of exploitation. No systematic and reliable survey comparing consumer pricing and credit practices in all-Negro and other neighborhoods has ever been conducted on a nationwide basis. Differences in prices and credit practices between white middle-income areas and Negro low-income areas to some extent reflect differences in the real costs of serving these two markets (such as differential losses from pilferage in supermarkets), but the exact extent of these cost differences has never been estimated accurately. Finally, an examination of exploitative consumer practices must consider the particular structure and functions of the low-income consumer durables market.

## INSTALLMENT BUYING

This complex situation can best be understood by first considering certain basic facts:

- Various cultural factors generate constant pressure on low-income families to buy many relatively expensive durable goods and display them in their homes. This pressure comes in part from continuous exposure to commercial advertising, especially on television. In January, 1967, over 88 percent of all Negro households had TV sets. A 1961 study of 464 low-income families in New York City showed that 95 percent of these relatively poor families had TV sets.

- Many poor families have extremely low incomes, bad previous credit records, unstable sources of income or other attributes which make it virtually impossible for them to buy merchandise from established large national or local retail firms. These families lack enough savings to pay cash, and they cannot meet the standard credit requirements of established general merchants because they are too likely to fall behind in their payments.

- Poor families in urban areas are far less mobile than others. A 1967 Chicago study of low-income Negro households indicated their low automobile ownership compelled them to patronize neighborhood merchants. These merchants typically provided smaller selection, poorer services and higher prices than big national outlets. The 1961 New York study also indicated that families who shopped outside their own neighborhoods were far less likely to pay exorbitant prices.

- Most low-income families are uneducated concerning the nature of credit purchase contracts, the legal rights and obligations of both buyers and sellers, sources of advice for consumers who are having difficulties with merchants and the operation of the courts concerned with these matters. In contrast, merchants engaged in selling goods to them are very well informed.
- In most states, the laws governing relations between consumers and merchants in effect offer protection only to informed, sophisticated parties with understanding of each other's rights and obligations. Consequently, these laws are little suited to protect the rights of most low-income consumers.

In this situation, exploitative practices flourish. Ghetto residents who want to buy relatively expensive goods cannot do so from standard retail outlets and are thus restricted to local stores. Forced to use credit, they have little understanding of the pitfalls of credit buying. But because they have unstable incomes and frequently fail to make payments, the cost to the merchants of serving them is significantly above that of serving middle-income consumers. Consequently, a special kind of merchant appears to sell them goods on terms designed to cover the high cost of doing business in ghetto neighborhoods.

Whether they actually gain higher profits, these merchants charge higher prices than those in other parts of the city to cover the greater credit risks and other higher operating costs inherent in neighborhood outlets. A recent study conducted by the Federal Trade Commission in Washington, D.C., illustrates this conclusion dramatically. The FTC identified a number of stores specializing in selling furniture and appliances to low-income households. About 92 percent of the sales of these stores were credit sales involving installment purchases, as compared to 27 percent of the sales in general retail outlets handling the same merchandise.

The median income annually of a sample of 486 customers of these stores was about $4,200, but one-third had annual incomes below $3,600, about 6 percent were receiving welfare payments, and another 76 percent were employed in the lowest paying occupations (service workers, operatives, laborers and domestics), as compared to 36 percent of the total labor force in Washington in those occupations.

Definitely catering to a low-income group, these stores charged significantly higher prices than general merchandise outlets in the Washington area. According to testimony by Paul Rand Dixon, Chairman of the FTC, an item selling wholesale at $100 would retail on the average for $165 in a general merchandise store and for $250 in a low-income specialty store. Thus, the customers of these outlets were paying an average price premium of about 52 percent.

While higher prices are not necessarily exploitative in themselves, many merchants in ghetto neighborhoods take advantage of their superior knowledge of credit buying by engaging in various exploitative tactics—high-pressure salesmanship, "bait advertising," misrepresentation of prices, substitution of used goods for promised new ones, failure to notify consumers of legal actions against them, refusal to repair or replace substandard goods, exorbitant prices or credit charges, and use of shoddy merchandise. Such tactics affect a great many low-income consumers. In the New York study, 60 percent of all households had suffered from consumer problems (some of which were purely their own fault). About 23 percent had experienced serious exploitation. Another 20 percent, many of whom were also exploited, had experienced repossession, garnishment, or threat of garnishment.

## GARNISHMENT

Garnishment practices in many states allow creditors to deprive individuals of their wages through court action, without hearing or trial. In about 20 states, the wages of an employee can be diverted to a creditor merely upon the latter's deposition, with no advance hearing where the employee can defend himself. He often receives no prior notice of such action and is usually unaware of the law's operation and too poor to hire legal defense. Moreover, consumers may find themselves still owing money on a sales contract even after the creditor has repossessed the goods. The New York study cited earlier in this chapter indicated that 20 percent of a sample of low-income families had been subjected to legal action regarding consumer purchases. And the Federal Trade Commission study in Washington, D.C., showed that, on the average, retailers specializing in credit sales of furniture and appliances to low-income consumers resorted to court action once for every $2,200 of sales. Since their average sale was for $207, this amounted to using the courts to collect from one of every 11 customers. In contrast, department stores in the same area used court action against approximately one of every 14,500 customers.*

## VARIATIONS IN FOOD PRICES

Residents of low-income Negro neighborhoods frequently claim that they pay higher prices for food in local markets than wealthier white suburbanites and receive inferior quality meat and produce. Statistically reliable information comparing prices and quality in these two kinds of areas is generally unavailable. The U.S. Bureau of Labor Statistics, studying food prices in six cities in 1966, compared prices of a standard list of 18 items in low-income areas and higher income areas in each city. In a total of 180 stores, including independent and chain stores, and for items of the same type sold in the same types of stores, there were no significant differences in prices between low-income and high-income areas. However, stores in low-income areas were more likely to be small independents (which had somewhat higher prices), to sell low-quality produce and meat at any given price, and to be patronized by people who typically bought smaller sized packages which are more expensive per unit of measure. In other words, many low-income consumers in fact pay higher prices, although the situation varies greatly from place to place.

Although these findings must be considered inconclusive, there are significant reasons to believe that poor households generally pay higher prices for the food they buy and receive lower quality food. Low-income consumers buy more food at local groceries because they are less mobile. Prices in these small stores are significantly higher than in major supermarkets because they cannot achieve economies of scale and because real operating costs are higher in low-income Negro areas than in outlying suburbs. For instance, inventory "shrinkage" from pilfering and other causes is normally under 2 percent of sales but can run twice as much in high-crime areas. Managers seek to make up for these added costs by charging higher prices for food or by substituting lower grades.

---

* Assuming their sales also averaged $207 per customer.

These practices do not necessarily involve exploitation, but they are often perceived as exploitative and unfair by those who are aware of the price and quality differences involved but unaware of operating costs. In addition, it is probable that genuinely exploitative pricing practices exist in some areas. In either case, differential food prices constitute another factor convincing urban Negroes in low-income neighborhoods that whites discriminate against them.

# PART III

# WHAT CAN BE DONE?

# CHAPTER 11

# POLICE AND THE COMMUNITY

---

## INTRODUCTION

We have cited deep hostility between police and ghetto communities as a primary cause of the disorders surveyed by the Commission. In Newark, Detroit, Watts, and Harlem—in practically every city that has experienced racial disruption since the summer of 1964, abrasive relationships between police and Negroes and other minority groups have been a major source of grievance, tension and, ultimately, disorder.

In a fundamental sense, however, it is wrong to define the problem solely as hostility to police. In many ways, the policeman only symbolizes much deeper problems.

The policeman in the ghetto is a symbol not only of law, but of the entire system of law enforcement and criminal justice.

As such, he becomes the tangible target for grievances against shortcomings throughout that system: Against assembly-line justice in teeming lower courts; against wide disparities in sentences; against antiquated correctional facilities; against the basic inequities imposed by the system on the poor—to whom, for example, the option of bail means only jail.

The policeman in the ghetto is a symbol of increasingly bitter social debate over law enforcement.

One side, disturbed and perplexed by sharp rises in crime and urban violence, exerts extreme pressure on police for tougher law enforcement. Another group, inflamed against police as agents of repression, tends toward defiance of what it regards as order maintained at the expense of justice.

The policeman in the ghetto is the most visible symbol, finally, of a society from which many ghetto Negroes are increasingly alienated.

At the same time, police responsibilities in the ghetto are even greater than elsewhere in the community since the other institutions of social control have so little authority: The schools, because so many are segregated, old and inferior; religion, which has become irrelevant to those who have lost faith as they lost hope; career aspirations, which for many young Negroes are totally lacking; the family, because its bonds are so often snapped. It is the policeman who must deal with the consequences of this institutional vacuum and is then resented for the presence and the measures this effort demands.

Alone, the policeman in the ghetto cannot solve these problems. His role is already one of the most difficult in our society. He must deal daily with a range of problems and people that test his patience, ingenuity, character, and courage in ways that few of us are ever tested. Without positive leadership, goals, operational guidance, and public support, the individual policeman can only feel victimized. Nor are these problems the responsibility only of police administrators; they are deep enough to tax the courage, intelligence and leadership of mayors, city officials, and community leaders. As Dr. Kenneth B. Clark told the Commission:

> This society knows * * * that if human beings are confined in ghetto compounds of our cities and are subjected to criminally inferior education, pervasive economic and job discrimination, committed to houses unfit for human habitation, subjected to unspeakable conditions of municipal services, such as sanitation, that such human beings are not likely to be responsive to appeals to be lawful, to be respectful, to be concerned with property of others.

And yet, precisely because the policeman in the ghetto is a symbol—precisely because he symbolizes so much—it is of critical importance that the police and society take every possible step to allay grievances that flow from a sense of injustice and increased tension and turmoil.

In this work, the police bear a major responsibility for making needed changes. In the first instance, they have the prime responsibility for safeguarding the minimum goal of any civilized society: Security of life and property. To do so, they are given society's maximum power: Discretion in the use of force. Second, it is axiomatic that effective law enforcement requires the support of the community. Such support will not be present when a substantial segment of the community feels threatened by the police and regards the police as an occupying force.

At the same time, public officials also have a clear duty to help the police make any necessary changes to minimize so far as possible the risk of further disorders.

We see five basic problem areas:

- The need for change in police operations in the ghetto, to insure proper conduct by individual officers and to eliminate abrasive practices.
- The need for more adequate police protection of ghetto residents, to eliminate the present high sense of insecurity to person and property.
- The need for effective mechanisms for resolving citizen grievances against the police.
- The need for policy guidelines to assist police in areas where police conduct can create tension.
- The need to develop community support for law enforcement.

Our discussion of each of these problem areas is followed by specific recommendations which relate directly to achieving more effective law enforcement and to the prevention and control of civil disorders.*

---

* We wish to acknowledge our indebtedness to and reliance upon the extensive work done by the President's Commission of Law Enforcement and Administration of Justice (the "Crime Commission"). The reports, studies, surveys, and analyses of the Crime Commission have contributed to many of our conclusions and recommendations.

# POLICE CONDUCT AND PATROL PRACTICES

In an earlier era, third-degree interrogations were widespread, indiscriminate arrests on suspicion were generally accepted and "alley justice" dispensed with the nightstick was common.

Today, many disturbances studied by the Commission began with a police incident. But these incidents were not, for the most part, the crude acts of an earlier time. They were routine police actions such as stopping a motorist or raiding an illegal business. Indeed, many of the serious disturbances took place in cities whose police are among the best led, best organized, best trained and most professional in the country.

Yet some activities of even the most professional police department may heighten tension and enhance the potential for civil disorder. An increase in complaints of police misconduct, for example, may in fact be a reflection of professionalism; the department may simply be using law enforcement methods which increase the total volume of police contacts with the public. The number of charges of police misconduct may be greater simply because the volume of police-citizen contacts is higher.

Here we examine two aspects of police activities that have great tension-creating potential. Our objective is to provide recommendations to assist city and police officials in developing practices which can allay rather than contribute to tension.

## POLICE CONDUCT

Negroes firmly believe that police brutality and harassment occur repeatedly in Negro neighborhoods. This belief is unquestionably one of the major reasons for intense Negro resentment against the police.

The extent of this belief is suggested by attitude surveys. In 1964, a New York Times study of Harlem showed that 43 percent of those questioned believed in the existence of police "brutality."* In 1965, a

---

* The "brutality" referred to in this and other surveys is often not precisely defined and covers conduct ranging from use of insulting language to excessive and unjustified use of force.

nationwide Gallup poll found that 35 percent of Negro men believed there was police brutality in their areas; 7 percent of white men thought so. In 1966, a survey conducted for the Senate Subcommittee on Executive Reorganization found that 60 percent of Watts Negroes aged 15 to 19 believed there was some police brutality. Half said they had witnessed such conduct. A University of California at Los Angeles study of the Watts area found that 79 percent of the Negro males believed police lack respect for, or use insulting language to, Negroes, and 74 percent believed police use unnecessary force in making arrests. In 1967, an Urban League study of the Detroit riot area found that 82 percent believed there was some form of police brutality.

The true extent of excessive and unjustified use of force is difficult to determine. One survey done for the Crime Commission suggests that when police-citizen contacts are systematically observed, the vast majority are handled without antagonism or incident. Of 5,339 police-citizen contacts observed in slum precincts in three large cities, in the opinion of the observer only 20—about three-tenths of 1 percent—involved excessive or unnecessary force. And although almost all of those subjected to such force were poor, more than half were white. Verbal discourtesy was more common—15 percent of all such contacts began with a "brusque or nasty command" on the part of the officer. Again, however, the objects of such commands were more likely to be white than Negro.

Such "observer" surveys may not fully reflect the normal pattern of police conduct. The Crime Commission Task Force concluded that although the study gave "no basis for stating the extent to which police officers used force, it did confirm that such conduct still exists in the cities where observations were made." Our investigations confirm this conclusion.

Physical abuse is only one source of aggravation in the ghetto. In nearly every city surveyed, the Commission heard complaints of harassment of interracial couples, dispersal of social street gatherings and the stopping of Negroes on foot or in cars without objective basis. These, together with contemptuous and degrading verbal abuse, have great impact in the ghetto. As one Commission witness said, these strip the Negro of the one thing that he may have left—his dignity, "the question of being a man."

Some conduct—breaking up of street groups, indiscriminate stops and searches—is frequently directed at youths, creating special tensions in the ghetto where the average age is generally under 21. Ghetto youths, often without work and with homes that may be nearly uninhabitable, particularly in the summer, commonly spend much time on the street. Characteristically, they are not only hostile to police but eager to demonstrate their own masculinity and courage. The police, therefore, are often subject to taunts and provocations, testing their self-control and, probably, for some, reinforcing their hostility to Negroes in general. Because youths commit a large and increasing proportion of crime, police are under growing pressure from their supervisors—and from the community—to deal with them forcefully. "Harassment of youths" may therefore be viewed by some police departments—and members even of the Negro community—as a proper crime prevention technique.

In a number of cities, the Commission heard complaints of abuse from Negro adults of all social and economic classes. Particular resentment is aroused by harassing Negro men in the company of white women—often their light-skinned Negro wives.

"Harassment" or discourtesy may not be the result of malicious or discriminatory intent of police officers. Many officers simply fail to understand the effects of their actions because of their limited knowledge of the Negro community. Calling a Negro teenager by his first name may [arouse] resentment because many whites still refuse to extend to adult Negroes the courtesy of the title, "Mister." A patrolman may take the arm of a person he is leading to the police car. Negroes are more likely to resent this than whites because the action implies that they are on the verge of flight and may degrade them in the eyes of friends or onlookers.

In assessing the impact of police misconduct, we emphasize that the improper acts of a relatively few officers may create severe tensions between the department and the entire Negro community. Whatever the actual extent of such conduct, we concur in the Crime Commission's conclusion that:

> * * * all such behavior is obviously and totally reprehensible,
> and when it is directed against minority-group citizens, it

is particularly likely to lead, for quite obvious reasons, to bitterness in the community.

## POLICE PATROL PRACTICES

Although police administrators may take steps to eliminate misconduct by individual police officers, many departments have adopted patrol practices which in the words of one commentator, have "* * * replaced harassment by individual patrolmen with harassment by entire departments."

These practices, sometimes known as "aggressive preventive patrol," take a number of forms, but invariably they involve a large number of police-citizen contacts initiated by police rather than in response to a call for help or service. One such practice utilizes a roving task force which moves into high-crime districts without prior notice and conducts intensive, often indiscriminate, street stops and searches. A number of obviously suspicious persons are stopped. But so also are persons whom the beat patrolman would know are respected members of the community. Such task forces are often deliberately moved from place to place making it impossible for its members to know the people with whom they come in contact.

In some cities, aggressive patrol is not limited to special task forces. The beat patrolman himself is expected to participate and to file a minimum number of "stop-and-frisk" or field interrogation reports for each tour of duty. This pressure to produce, or a lack of familiarity with the neighborhood and its people, may lead to widespread use of these techniques without adequate differentiation between genuinely suspicious behavior and behavior which is suspicious to a particular officer merely because it is unfamiliar.

Police administrators, pressed by public concern about crime, have instituted such patrol practices often without weighing their tension-creating effects and the resulting relationship to civil disorder.

Motorization of police is another aspect of patrol that has affected law enforcement in the ghetto. The patrolman comes to see the city through a windshield and hear about it over a police radio. To him, the area increasingly comes to consist only of lawbreakers. To the ghetto resident, the policeman comes increasingly to be only an enforcer.

Loss of contact between the police officer and the community he serves adversely affects law enforcement. If an officer has never met, does not know and cannot understand the language and habits of the people in the area he patrols, he cannot do an effective police job. His ability to detect truly suspicious behavior is impaired. He deprives himself of important sources of information. He fails to know those persons with an "equity" in the community—homeowners, small businessmen, professional men, persons who are anxious to support proper law enforcement—and thus sacrifices the contributions they can make to maintaining community order.

## RECOMMENDATIONS

Police misconduct—whether described as brutality, harassment, verbal abuse or discourtesy—cannot be tolerated even if it is infrequent. It contributes directly to the risk of civil disorder. It is inconsistent with the basic responsibility and function of a police force in a democracy. Police departments must have rules prohibiting such misconduct and enforce them vigorously. Police commanders must be aware of what takes place in the field and take firm steps to correct abuses. We consider this matter further in the section on policy guidelines.

Elimination of misconduct also requires care in selecting police for ghetto areas, for there the police responsibility is particularly sensitive, demanding and often dangerous. The highest caliber of personnel is required if police are to overcome feelings within the ghetto community of inadequate protection and unfair, discriminatory treatment. Despite this need, data from Commission investigators and from the Crime Commission disclose that often a department's worst, not its best, are assigned to minority group neighborhoods. As Prof. Albert Reiss, director of the Center for Research on Social Organization, University of Michigan, testified before the Commission:

> I think we confront in modern urban police departments
> in large cities much of what we encounter in our schools in
> these cities. The slum police precinct is like the slum schools.
> It gets, with few exceptions, the worst in the system.

Referring to extensive studies in one city, Professor Reiss concluded:

> In predominantly Negro precincts, over three-fourths of the white policemen expressed prejudice or highly prejudiced attitudes towards Negroes. Only one percent of the officers expressed attitudes which could be described as sympathetic towards Negroes. Indeed, close to one-half of all the police officers in predominantly Negro high-crime-rate areas showed extreme prejudice against Negroes. What do I mean by extreme racial prejudice? I mean that they describe Negroes in terms that are not people terms. They describe them in terms of the animal kingdom. * * *

Although some prejudice was displayed in only 8 percent of police-citizen encounters:

> The cost of such prejudiced behavior I suggest is much higher than my statistics suggest. Over a period of time, a substantial proportion of citizens, particularly in high-crime-rate areas, may experience at least one encounter with a police officer where prejudice is shown.

To insure assignment of well-qualified police to ghetto areas, the Commission recommends:

- Officers with bad reputations among residents in minority areas should be immediately reassigned to other areas. This will serve the interests of both the police and the community.
- Screening procedures should be developed to ensure that officers with superior ability, sensitivity and the common sense necessary for enlightened law enforcement are assigned to minority group areas. We believe that, with proper training in ghetto problems and conditions, and with proper standards for recruitment of new officers, in the long run most policemen can meet these standards.
- Incentives, such as bonuses or credits for promotion, should be developed wherever necessary to attract outstanding officers for ghetto positions.

The recommendations we have proposed are designed to help insure proper police conduct in minority areas. Yet there is another facet of the problem: Negro perceptions of police misconduct. Even if those perceptions are exaggerated, they do exist. If outstanding officers are assigned to ghetto areas, if acts of misconduct, however infrequent, result in proper—and visible—disciplinary action and if these corrective practices are made part of known policy, we believe the community will soon learn to reject unfounded claims of misconduct.

Problems stemming from police patrol cannot, perhaps, be so easily resolved. But there are two considerations which can help to allay such problems. The first relates to law enforcement philosophy behind the use of techniques like aggressive patrol. Many police officials believe strongly that there are law enforcement gains from such techniques. However, these techniques also have law enforcement liabilities. Their employment therefore should not be merely automatic but the product of a deliberate balancing of pluses and minuses by command personnel.

We know that advice of this sort is easier to give than to act on. The factors involved are difficult to weigh. Gains cannot be measured solely in the number of arrests. Losses in police protection cannot be accepted solely because of some vague gain in diminished community tension. The kind of thorough, objective assessment of patrol practices and search for innovation we need will require the best efforts of research and development units within police departments, augmented if necessary by outside research assistance. The Federal Government can also play a major role in funding and conducting such research.

The second consideration concerning patrol is execution. There is more crime in the ghetto than in other areas. If the aggressive patrol clearly relates to the control of crime, the residents of the ghetto are likely to endorse the practice. What may arouse hostility is not the fact of aggressive patrol but its indiscriminate use so that it comes to be regarded not as crime control but as a new method of racial harassment. All patrol practices must be carefully reviewed to insure they are properly carried out by individual officers.

New patrol practices must be designed to increase the patrolman's knowledge of the ghetto. Although motorized patrols are essential, means should be devised to get the patrolman out of the car and into the neighborhood and keeping him on the same beat long enough to get to know the people and understand the conditions. This will require training the patrolman to convince him of the desirability of such practices. There must be continuing administrative supervision. In practice as well as theory, all aspects of patrol must be lawful and conform to policy guidelines. Unless carried out with courtesy and with understanding of the community, even the most enlightened patrol practices may degenerate into what residents will come to regard as harassment. Finally, this concept of patrol should be publicly explained so that ghetto residents understand it and know what to expect.

## THE PROBLEM OF POLICE PROTECTION

The strength of ghetto feelings about hostile police conduct may even be exceeded by the conviction that ghetto neighborhoods are not given adequate police protection.

This belief is founded on two basic types of complaint. The first is that the police maintain a much less rigorous standard of law enforcement in the ghetto, tolerating there illegal activities like drug addiction, prostitution, and street violence that they would not tolerate elsewhere. The second is that police treat complaints and calls for help from Negro areas much less urgently than from white areas. These perceptions are widespread. As David Hardy, of the staff of the *New York Daily News*, testified:

> To put it simply, for decades little if any law enforcement has prevailed among Negroes in America, particularly those in the ghettos. If a black man kills another black man, the law is generally enforced at its minimum. Violence of every type runs rampant in a ghetto.

A Crime Commission study found that Negroes in Philadelphia and San Diego are convinced that the police apply a different standard of law enforcement in the ghettos. Another Crime Commission study found that about one white person in two believes police provide very good protection in his community; for Negroes, the figure is one in five. Other surveys have reported that Negroes in Harlem and south central Los Angeles mention inadequate protection more often than brutality or harassment as a reason for their resentment toward the police.

The report of a New Haven community group summarizes the complaints:

> The problem of the adequacy of current police protection ranked with "police misconduct" as the most serious sore points in police-community relations.
>
> * * * When calls for help are registered, it is all too frequent that police respond too slowly or not at all.
>
> * * * When they do come, [they] arrive with many more men and cars than are necessary * * * brandishing guns and adding to the confusion.*

There is evidence to suggest that the lack of protection does not necessarily result from different basic police attitudes but rather from a relative lack of police personnel for ghetto areas, considering the volume of calls for police. As a consequence, the police work according to priorities. Because of the need for attention to major crimes, little, if any, attention can be accorded to reports of a suspicious person, for example, or a noisy party or a drunk. And attention even to major crimes may sometimes be routine or skeptical.

Ghetto residents, however, see a dual standard of law enforcement. Particularly because many work in other areas of the city and have seen the nature of police responsiveness there, they are keenly aware of the difference. They come to believe that an assault on a white victim produces one reaction and an assault on a Negro quite another. The police, heavily engaged in the ghetto, might assert that they cannot cover serious offenses and minor complaints at the same time—that they cannot be two places at once. The ghetto resident, however, often concludes that the police respond neither to serious offenses nor to minor complaints.

---

* "In Search of Fair and Adequate Law Enforcement," report of the Hill-Dwight Citizens Commission on Police Community Relations, June 1967, pp. 12–13.

Recent studies have documented the inadequacies of police response in some ghetto areas. A Yale Law Journal study of Hartford, Conn., found that:

> [T]he residents of a large area in the center of the Negro ghetto are victims of over one-third of the daylight residential burglaries in the city. Yet during the daytime, only one of Hartford's 18 patrol cars and none of its 11 foot patrolmen is assigned to this area. Sections in the white part of town about the same size as the central ghetto area receive slightly more intensive daytime patrol even though the citizens in the ghetto area summon the police about six times as often because of criminal acts.*

In a United States Commission on Civil Rights study, a review of police communications records in Cleveland disclosed that police took almost four times as long to respond to calls concerning robbery from the Negro district as for the district where response was next slowest. The response time for some other crimes was at least twice as long.

**The Commission recommends:**

- Police departments should have a clear and enforced policy that the standard of law enforcement in ghetto areas is the same as in other communities; complaints and appeals from the ghetto should be treated with the same urgency and importance as those from white neighborhoods.
- Because a basic problem in furnishing protection to the ghetto is the shortage of manpower, police departments should review existing deployment of field personnel to ensure the most efficient use of manpower. The Police Task Force of the Crime Commission stressed the need "to distribute patrol officers in accordance with the actual need for their presence." Communities may have to pay for more and better policing for the entire community as well as for the ghetto.

---

* "Program Budgeting for Police Departments," 76 Yale L.J. 822 (1967).

In allocating manpower to the ghetto, enforcement emphasis should be given to crimes that threaten life and property. Stress on social gambling or loitering, when more serious crimes are neglected, not only diverts manpower but fosters distrust and tension in the ghetto community.

# THE PROBLEM OF GRIEVANCE MECHANISMS

A third source of Negro hostility to police is the almost total lack of effective channels for redress of complaints against police conduct. In Milwaukee, Wis., and Plainfield, N.J., for example, ghetto residents complained that police reject complaints out of hand. In New Haven, a Negro citizens' group characterized a police review board as worthless. In Detroit, the Michigan Civil Rights Commission found that, despite well-intentioned leadership, no real sanctions are imposed on offending officers. In Newark, the mayor referred complaints to the FBI, which had very limited jurisdiction over them. In many of the cities surveyed by the Commission, Negro complaints focused on the continued presence in the ghetto of officers regarded as notorious for prejudice and brutality.

The 1967 Report of the Civil Rights Commission also states that a major issue in the Negro community is inadequate investigation of complaints against the police. It even reports threats of criminal actions designed to discourage complainants. A survey for the Crime Commission found substantial evidence that policemen in some cities have little fear of punishment for using unnecessary force because they appear to have a degree of immunity from their departments.

## RECOMMENDATIONS

Objective evaluation, analysis and innovation on this subject are vitally necessary. Yet attention has been largely and, unfortunately, diverted by protracted debate over the desirability of "civilian review boards." Research conducted by the Crime Commission and others shows that the benefits and liabilities of such boards have probably both been exaggerated.

In the context of civil disorder, appearances and reality are of almost equal importance in the handling of citizen complaints against the police. It is not enough that there are adequate machinery and procedures for handling complaints; it is also necessary that citizens believe these procedures are adequate. Some citizens will never trust an agency against which they have a grievance. Some irresponsible citizens will attempt to provoke distrust of every agency. Hence, some police administrators have been tempted to throw up their hands and do nothing on the ground that whatever they do will be misunderstood. These sentiments may be understandable, but the police should appreciate that Negro citizens also want to throw up their hands. For they believe that the "police stick together," that they will cover up for each other, that no officer ever receives more than token punishment for misconduct and that even such expensive legal steps as false arrest or civil damage suits are foredoomed because "it is the officer's word against mine."

We believe that an internal review board—in which the police department itself receives and acts on complaints—regardless of its efficiency and fairness, can rarely generate the necessary community confidence or protect the police against unfounded charges. We also believe, as did the Crime Commission, that police should not be the only municipal agency subject to outside scrutiny and review. Incompetence and mistreatment by any public servant should be equally subject to review by an independent agency.

The Crime Commission Police Task Force reviewed the various external grievance procedures attempted or suggested in this country and abroad. Without attempting to recommend a specific procedure, our Commission believes that police departments should be subject to external review. We discussed this problem in Chapter 10, The Community Response. Here, we highlight what we believe to be the basic elements of an effective system.

**The Commission recommends:**
- Making a complaint should be easy. It should be possible to file a grievance without excessive formality. If forms are used, they should be easily available and their use explained in widely distributed pamphlets. In large cities, it should not be necessary

to go to a central headquarters office to file a complaint, but it should also be possible to file a complaint at neighborhood locations. Police officers on the beat, community service aides or other municipal employees in the community should be empowered to receive complaints.

- A specialized agency, with adequate funds and staff, should be created separate from other municipal agencies, to handle, investigate and to make recommendations on citizen complaints.

- The procedure should have a built-in conciliation process to attempt to resolve complaints without the need for full investigation and processing.

- The complaining party should be able to participate in the investigation and in any hearings, with right of representation by counsel, so that the complaint is fully investigated and findings made on the merits. He should be promptly and fully informed of the outcome. The results of the investigation should be made public.

- Since many citizen complaints concern departmental policies rather than individual conduct, information concerning complaints of this sort should be forwarded to the departmental unit which formulates or reviews policy and procedures. Information concerning all complaints should be forwarded to appropriate training units so that any deficiencies correctable by training can be eliminated.

Although we advocate an external agency as a means of resolving grievances, we believe that the basic need is to adopt procedures which will gain the respect and confidence of the entire community. This need can, in the end, be met only by sustained direction through the line of command, thorough investigation of complaints, and prompt, visible disciplinary action where justified.

## THE NEED FOR POLICY GUIDELINES

How a policeman handles day-to-day contacts with citizens will, to a large extent, shape the relationships between the police and the community. These contacts involve considerable discretion. Improper exercise of such discretion can needlessly create tension and contribute to community grievances.

Formally, the police officer has no discretion; his task is to enforce all laws at all times. Formally, the officer's only basic enforcement option is to make an arrest or to do nothing. Formally, when a citizen resists arrest, the officer's only recourse is to apply such reasonable force as he can bring with his hands, nightstick and revolver.

Informally—and in reality—the officer faces an entirely different situation. He has and must have a great deal of discretion; there are not enough police or jails to permit the levels of surveillance that would be necessary to enforce all laws all the time—levels which the public would, in any event, regard as intolerable.

Patrick V. Murphy, now Director of Public Safety in the District of Columbia, told the Commission:

> The police, of course, exercise very broad discretion, and although in many states the law says or implies that all laws must be enforced and although the manuals of many police departments state every officer is responsible for the enforcement of all laws, as a practical matter it is impossible for the police to enforce all laws and, as a result, they exercise very broad discretion. * * * [B]y failing to understand the fact that they do exercise important discretion every day, some police do not perceive just how they maintain the peace in different ways in different sections of a city.

The formal remedies of law, further, are inappropriate for many common problems. A family quarrel or a street fight, followed by an arrest, would give the parties a record and, typically, a suspended sentence; it would not solve the problem. And the appropriate legal grounds for making an arrest are often not present, for the officer has not witnessed the incident nor does he have a sworn complaint from someone who has. Pacifying the dispute may well be the best approach, but many officers lack the training or experience to do so effectively. If the parties resist pacification or arrest, the officer, alone on the street, must either back down or use force—sometimes lethal.

Crime Commission studies and our police survey show that guidance for the exercise of discretion in many situations is often not available to the policeman. There are guidelines for wearing uniforms—but not for how to intervene in a domestic dispute; for the cleaning of a revolver—but not for when to fire it; for use of departmental property—but not for whether to break up a sidewalk gathering; for handling stray dogs—but not for handling field interrogations.

## RECOMMENDATIONS

Contacts between citizens and the police in the ghetto require discretion and judgment which should be based upon carefully-drawn, written departmental policy. The Report of the Crime Commission and the Police Task Force Report considered this problem in detail and recommended subjects for policy guidelines.

**The Commission recommends** the establishment of guidelines covering, at a minimum:

- The issuance of orders to citizens regarding their movements or activities—for example, when, if ever, should a policeman order a social street gathering to break up or move on.
- The handling of minor disputes—between husband and wife, merchant and customer or landlord and tenant. Guidelines should cover resources available in the community—family courts, probation departments, counseling services, welfare agencies—to which citizens can be referred.
- The decision whether to arrest in a specific situation involving a specific crime—for example, when police should arrest persons engaged in crimes such as social gambling, vagrancy and loitering and other crimes which do not involve victims. The use of alternatives to arrest, such as a summons, should also be considered.
- The selection and use of investigating methods. Problems concerning use of field interrogations and "stop-and-frisk" techniques are especially critical. Crime Commission studies and evidence before this Commission demonstrate that these techniques have the potential for becoming a major source of friction between police and minority groups. Their

constitutionality is presently under review in the United States Supreme Court. We also recognize that police regard them as important methods of preventing and investigating crime. Although we do not advocate use or adoption of any particular investigative method, we believe that any such method should be covered by guidelines drafted to minimize friction with the community.

- Safeguarding the constitutional right of free expression, such as rights of persons engaging in lawful demonstrations, the need to protect lawful demonstrators and how to handle spontaneous demonstrations.
- The circumstances under which the various forms of physical force—including lethal force—can and should be applied. Recognition of this need was demonstrated by the regulations recently adopted by the City of New York further implementing the state law governing police use of firearms.
- The proper manner of address for contacts with any citizen.

. . . Guidelines, no matter how carefully drafted, will have little effect unless the department enforces them. This primarily requires command supervision and commitment to the guidelines. It also requires:

- A strong internal investigative unit to enforce compliance. Such a unit should not only enforce the guidelines on a case-by-case basis against individual officers but should also develop procedures to deter and prevent violations. The Crime Commission discussed the various methods available.
- A fair and effective means to handle citizen complaints.

Finally, provision should be made for periodic review of the guidelines, to ensure that changes are made to take account of current court rulings and new laws.

# COMMUNITY SUPPORT FOR
# LAW ENFORCEMENT

A fifth major reason for police-community hostility—particularly obvious since the recent disorders—is the general breakdown of communication between police and the ghetto. The contacts that do occur are primarily adversary contacts.

In the section on police patrol practices, we discussed one basic aspect of this problem. Here we consider how police forces have tried, with varying degrees of success, to deal with three issues underlying relations with ghetto communities.

## RECRUITMENT, ASSIGNMENT, AND
## PROMOTION OF NEGROES

The Crime Commission Police Task Force found that for police in a Negro community, to be predominantly white can serve as a dangerous irritant; a feeling may develop that the community is not being policed to maintain civil peace but to maintain the status quo. It further found that contact with Negro officers can help to avoid stereotypes and prejudices in the minds of white officers. Negro officers also can increase departmental insight into ghetto problems and provide information necessary for early anticipation of the tensions and grievances that can lead to disorders. Commission witnesses confirm these conclusions.

There is evidence that Negro officers also can be particularly effective in controlling any disorders that do break out. In studying the relative performance of Army and National Guard forces in the Detroit disorder, we concluded that the higher percentage of Negroes in the Army forces contributed substantially to their better performance. As a result, last August, we recommended an increase in the percentage of Negroes in the National Guard. The need for increased Negro participation in police departments is equally acute.

Despite this need—and despite recent efforts to hire more Negro police, the proportion of Negroes on police forces still falls far below the proportion of Negroes in the total population. Of 28 departments which reported information of this kind in a Commission survey of police departments, the percentage of Negro sworn personnel ranged from less than 1 percent to 21 percent. The median figure for Negro sworn personnel on the force was 6 percent; the median figures for the Negro population was approximately 24 percent. In no case was the proportion of Negroes in the police department equal to the proportion in the population.* A 1962 survey of the United States Civil Rights Commission, as reported in the Crime Commission Police Task Force Report, shows correspondingly low figures for other cities.

There are even more marked disproportions of Negro supervisory personnel. Our survey showed the following ratios:

- One in every 26 Negroes is a sergeant; the white ratio is one in 12.
- One in every 114 Negroes is a lieutenant; the white ratio is one in 26.
- One in every 235 Negroes is a captain or above; the white ratio is one in 53.

Public Safety Director Murphy, testifying before the Commission, described the problem and at least one of its causes:

> I think one of the serious problems facing the police in the nation today is the lack of adequate representation of Negroes in police departments. I think the police have not recruited enough Negroes in the past and are not recruiting enough of them today. I think we would be less than honest if we didn't admit that Negroes have been kept out of police departments in the past for reasons of racial discrimination.

In a number of cities, particularly larger ones, police officials are not only willing but anxious to appoint Negro officers. There are obstacles other than discrimination. While these obstacles cannot

---

* The data from this survey can be found in Table A at the end of this chapter, p. 214.

readily be measured, they can be identified. One is the relatively high standards for police employment. Another is pay; better qualified Negroes are often more attracted by other, better paying positions. Another obstacle is the bad image of police in the Negro community. There also are obstacles to promotion apart from discrimination, such as the more limited educational background of some Negro officers.

## RECOMMENDATIONS

**The Commission recommends:**
- Police departments should intensify their efforts to recruit more Negroes. The Police Task Force of the Crime Commission discussed a number of ways to do this and the problems involved. The Department of Defense program to help police departments recruit returning servicemen should be fully utilized. An Army report of Negro participation in the National Guard and Army reserves may also provide useful information.
- In order to increase the number of Negroes in supervisory positions, police departments should review promotion policies to ensure that Negroes have full opportunity to be rapidly and fairly promoted.
- Negro officers should be so assigned as to ensure that the police department is fully and visibly integrated. Some cities have adopted a policy of assigning one white and one Negro officer to patrol cars, especially in ghetto areas. These assignments result in better understanding, tempered judgment and increased ability to separate the truly suspect from the unfamiliar.

Recruiting more Negro officers, alone, will not solve the problems of lack of communication and hostility toward police. A Negro's understanding of the ghetto is not enough to make him a good officer. He must also meet the same high standards as white officers and pass the same screening process. These requirements help create a dilemma noted by the Crime Commission. The need to develop better relations with minority group communities requires recruitment of police from these groups—groups handicapped by lack of educational opportunities and achievement. To require that police recruits have a high school diploma sets a standard too low in terms of the need for recruiting college graduates and perhaps too high in terms of the need for recruiting members of minority groups. . . .

**The Commission recommends:**

- The community service officer program should be adopted. Use of this program to increase the number of Negroes in police departments will help to establish needed channels of communication with the Negro community; will permit the police to perform better their community service functions, especially in the minority group neighborhoods; and will also create a number of badly needed jobs for Negro youths.

The standards of selection for such community service officers or aides should be drawn to insure that the great majority of young Negro males are eligible to participate in the program. As stated in the Crime Commission Task Force Report, selection should not be based on inflexible educational requirements, but instead "* * * should be made on an individual basis with priority being given to applicants with promising aspirations, honesty, intelligence, a desire and a tested capacity to advance his education and an understanding of the neighborhood and its problems." An arrest record or a minor conviction record should not in itself be a bar to employment.

**The Commission recommends:**

- The Federal Government should launch a program to establish community service officers or aides in cities with populations over 50,000. Eligible police departments should be reimbursed for 90 percent of the costs of employing one aide for every 10 full-time police officers.

We emphasize, however, that recruitment of community service aides must complement, not replace, efforts to recruit more Negroes as police officers.

## COMMUNITY SERVICE FUNCTIONS

Because police run almost the only 24-hour-a-day, 7-day-a-week emergency service, they find it very hard not to become involved in a host of nonpolice services. Complaints about a wide range of matters, from noisy neighbors and deteriorated streets to building code violations, at best are only peripheral to police work. Because these are often not police matters and because police increasingly face serious shortages of manpower and money, police administrators have resisted becoming involved in such matters. This resistance, coupled with centralization and motorization of the police, has resulted in the police becoming more distant from the people they serve.

## RECOMMENDATIONS

The Commission believes that police cannot, and should not, resist becoming involved in community service matters. There will be benefits for law enforcement no less than for public order.

First, police, because of their "front line position" in dealing with ghetto problems, will be better able to identify problems in the community that may lead to disorder. Second, they will be better able to handle incidents requiring police intervention, particularly marital disputes that have a potential for violence. How well the police handle domestic disturbances affects the incidence of serious crimes, including assaults and homicides. Third, willing performance of such work can gain police the respect and support of the community. Finally, development of nonadversary contacts can provide the police with a vital source of information and intelligence concerning the communities they serve.

A variety of methods have been devised to improve police performance of this service function. We comment on two of special interest. The first is the New York Police Department's experimental "Family Crisis Intervention" program to develop better police response to mar-

---

* We join in the Crime Commission's caveat that police should not become involved in service tasks which involve neither policing nor community help (such as tax collection, licensing, and dog-pound duties).

ital disputes; if results develop as expected, this may serve as a model for other departments.

Second, neighborhood service centers have been opened in some cities. These centers typically are established in tense, high-crime areas, in easily accessible locations such as store-fronts or public housing projects. Staffed by a civilian city employee as well as a police officer, their task is to provide information and service—putting a citizen in touch with the right agency, furnishing general advice. This gives the beat patrolman somewhere to refer a marital dispute. It gives the local resident a clear, simple contact with official advice. It gives the police in general the opportunity to provide services, not merely to enforce the law. The needed additional manpower for such centers could be provided by the community service aides recommended earlier or by continuing to employ experienced policemen who have reached the age of retirement.

## COMMUNITY RELATIONS PROGRAMS

Many police departments have established programs to deal specifically with police-community relations. The Crime Commission recommended a number of such programs, and Federal funds have been made available for putting them into operation. Although of great potential benefit, the results thus far have been disappointing. This is true partly because the changes in attitude sought by such programs can only be achieved over time. But there are other reasons, as was shown by Detroit's experience with police-community meetings: Minimum participation by ghetto residents; infrequent meetings; lack of patrolmen involvement; lack of attention to youth programs; lack of coordination by police leadership, either within the department or with other city programs.

More significantly, both the Detroit evaluation and studies carried on for the Commission show that too often these are not community-relations programs but public-relations programs, designed to improve the department's image in the community. In one major city covered by the Commission's study, the department's plan for citizen observers of police work failed because people believed that the citizen observer was allowed to see only what the police thought he should see. Similarly, the police chief's "open house," an opportunity for discussion, was considered useless by many who regarded him as unsympathetic and unresponsive.

Moreover, it is clear that these programs have little support among rank and file officers. In Detroit, more than a year after instructions were sent out to establish such programs, several precincts still had failed to do so. Other cities have had similar experiences. On the command level, there is often little interest. Programs are not integrated into the departments; units do not receive adequate budgetary support.

Nevertheless, some programs have been successful. In Atlanta, a Crime Prevention Bureau has within 2 years established a good relationship with the community, particularly with the young people. It has concentrated on social services, persuading almost 600 dropouts to return to school, assisting some 250 hardship cases with food and work, arranging for dances and hydrant showers during the summer, working quickly and closely with families of missing persons. The result is a close rapport with the community—and recruits for the department. Baltimore and Winston-Salem are reported to have equally successful programs.

## RECOMMENDATIONS

Community relations programs and training can be important in increasing communication and decreasing hostility between the police and the ghetto. Community relations programs can also be used by police to explain new patrol practices, law enforcement programs, and other police efforts to reduce crime. Police have a right to expect ghetto leaders to work responsibly to reduce crime. Community relations programs offer a way to create and foster these efforts.

We believe that community relations is an integral part of all law enforcement. But it cannot be made so by part-time effort, peripheral status or cliche methods.

One way to bolster community relations is to expand police department award systems. Traditionally, special awards, promotional credit, bonuses, and selection for special assignments are based on heroic acts and arrest activity. Award systems should take equal cognizance of the work of officers who improve relations with alienated members of the community and by so doing minimize the potential for disorder.

However, we see no easy solution to police-community relations and misunderstandings, and we are aware that no single procedure or program will suffice. Improving community relations is a full-time assignment for every commander and every officer—an assignment that must include the development of an attitude, a tone, throughout the force that conforms with the ultimate responsibility of every policeman: Public service.

See TABLE A

TABLE A
Nonwhite Personnel in Selected Police Departments

| Name of department | Number[5] police officers | Number[5] Nonwhite police officers | Number sergeants[5] | | Number lieutenants[5] | | Number captains[5] | | Number above captain[5] | |
|---|---|---|---|---|---|---|---|---|---|---|
| | | | Non-white | White | Non-white | White | Non-white | White | Non-white | White |
| Atlanta, Ga | 968 | 98 | 2 | 12 | 3 | 56 | 0 | 15 | 0 | 6 |
| Baltimore, Md | 3,046 | 208 | 7 | 389 | 3 | 105 | 1 | 17 | 1 | 21 |
| Boston, Mass | 2,508 | 49 | 1 | 228 | 0 | 80 | 0 | 20 | 0 | 12 |
| Buffalo, N.Y. | 1,375 | 37 | 1 | 60 | 1 | 93 | 0 | 24 | 0 | 32 |
| Chicago, Ill | 11,091 | 1,842 | 87 | 1,067 | 2 | 266 | 1 | 73 | 6 | 66 |
| Cincinnati, Ohio | 891 | 54 | 2 | 68 | 2 | 34 | 0 | 13 | 0 | 7 |
| Cleveland, Ohio | 2,216 | 165 | 6 | 155 | 0 | 78 | 0 | 26 | 0 | 17 |
| Dayton, Ohio | 417 | 16 | 1 | 58 | 0 | 13 | 0 | 6 | 0 | 4 |
| Detroit, Mich | 4,326 | 227 | 9 | 339 | 2 | 156 | 0 | 0 | 1 | 62 |
| Hartford, Conn | 342 | 38 | 0 | 32 | 1 | 16 | 0 | 9 | 0 | 2 |
| Kansas City, Mo | 927 | 51 | 7 | 158 | 0 | 36 | 0 | 11 | 1 | 14 |
| Louisville, Ky | 562 | 35 | 1 | 42 | 1 | 29 | 0 | 10 | 1 | 7 |
| Memphis, Tenn | 869 | 46 | 0 | 0 | 4 | 192 | 0 | 45 | 0 | 44 |
| Michigan State Police | 1,502 | 1 | 0 | 135 | 0 | 24 | 0 | 19 | 0 | 3 |
| New Haven, Conn | 446 | 31 | 0 | 20 | 0 | 16 | 0 | 12 | 0 | 6 |
| New Orleans, La | 1,308 | 54 | 7 | 107 | 1 | 51 | 0 | 27 | 0 | 10 |

| | | | | | | | | | | |
|---|---|---|---|---|---|---|---|---|---|---|
| New York, N.Y. | 27,610 | 1,485 | 65 | 1,785 | 20 | 925 | 2 | 273 | 3 | 157 |
| New Jersey State Police | 1,224 | 5 | 0 | 187 | 0 | 43 | 0 | 17 | 0 | 4 |
| Newark, N.J. | 1,869 | 184 | 5 | 97 | 3 | 95 | 1 | 22 | 0 | 0 |
| Oakland, Calif | 658 | 27 | 1 | 95 | 0 | 25 | 1 | 10 | 0 | 3 |
| Oklahoma City, Okla | 438 | 16 | 0 | 32 | 1 | 19 | 0 | 11 | 0 | 6 |
| Philadelphia, Pa | 6,890 | 1,377 | 26 | 314 | 8 | 139 | 3 | 46 | 0 | 23 |
| Phoenix, Ariz | 707 | 7 | 0 | 88 | 1 | 22 | 0 | 10 | 0 | 4 |
| Pittsburgh, Pa | 1,558 | 109 | 3 | 137 | 3 | 47 | 0 | 4 | 1 | 6 |
| St. Louis, Mo | 2,042 | 224 | 21 | 201 | 3 | 46 | 4 | 17 | 0 | 11 |
| San Francisco, Calif | 1,754 | 102 | 0 | 217 | 0 | 66 | 0 | 15 | 0 | 10 |
| Tampa, Fla | 511 | 17 | 0 | 50 | 0 | 12 | 0 | 13 | 0 | 8 |
| Washington, D.C. | 2,721 | 559 | 19 | 216 | 3 | 107 | 3 | 37 | 0 | 31 |
| TOTAL | 80,621 | 7,046 | 271 | 6,289 | 62 | 2,791 | 16 | 802 | 14 | 576 |

| Name of department | Percent nonwhite population | Percent nonwhite police officers | Ratio: Sergeants to officers | | Ratio: Lieutenants to officers | | Ratio: Captains to officers | | Ratio: Above captain to officers | |
|---|---|---|---|---|---|---|---|---|---|---|
| | | | Non-white | White | Non-white | White | Non-white | White | Non-white | White |
| Atlanta, Ga | [1]38 | 10 | 1:49 | 1:73 | 1:33 | 1:16 | 0:98 | 1:58 | 0:98 | 1:14 |
| Baltimore, Md | [1]41 | 7 | 1:30 | 1:7 | 1:69 | 1:27 | 1:208 | 1:167 | 1:208 | 1:135 |
| Boston, Mass | [1]11 | 2 | 1:49 | 1:11 | 0:49 | 1:31 | 0:49 | 1:123 | 0:49 | 1:205 |
| Buffalo, N.Y. | [1]18 | 3 | 1:37 | 1:22 | 1:37 | 1:14 | 0:37 | 1:56 | 0:37 | 1:42 |
| Chicago, Ill | [1]27 | 17 | 1:21 | 1:9 | 1:921 | 1:35 | 1:1842 | 1:127 | 1:307 | 1:140 |
| Cincinnati, Ohio | [1]28 | 6 | 1:27 | 1:12 | 1:27 | 1:25 | 0:54 | 1:64 | 0:54 | 1:120 |
| Cleveland, Ohio | [1]34 | 7 | 1:28 | 1:13 | 0:165 | 1:26 | 0:165 | 1:79 | 0:165 | 1:121 |
| Dayton, Ohio | [1]26 | 4 | 1:16 | 1:7 | 0:16 | 1:30 | 0:16 | 1:67 | 0:16 | 1:100 |
| Detroit, Mich | [1]39 | 5 | 1:25 | 1:12 | 1:114 | 1:26 | No such rank | | 1:227 | 1:66 |
| Hartford, Conn | [2]20 | 11 | 0:38 | 1:10 | 1:38 | 1:20 | 0:38 | 1:34 | 0:38 | 1:152 |
| Kansas City, Mo | [1]20 | 6 | 1:7 | 1:6 | 0:51 | 1:24 | 0:51 | 1:80 | 1:51 | 1:63 |
| Louisville, Ky | [1]21 | 6 | 1:35 | 1:13 | 1:35 | 1:18 | 0:35 | 1:53 | 1:35 | 1:75 |
| Memphis, Tenn | [1]38 | 5 | No such rank | | 1:12 | 1:4 | 0:46 | 1:18 | 0:46 | 1:19 |
| Mich. St. Pol | [3]9 | ([4]) | 0:1 | 1:11 | 0:1 | 1:63 | 0:1 | 1:79 | 0:1 | 1:500 |
| New Haven, Conn | [2]19 | 7 | 0:31 | 1:21 | 0:31 | 1:26 | 0:31 | 1:35 | 0:31 | 1:69 |
| New Orleans, La | [1]41 | 4 | 1:8 | 1:12 | 1:54 | 1:25 | 0:54 | 1:46 | 0:54 | 1:125 |

| | | | | | | | | | | |
|---|---|---|---|---|---|---|---|---|---|---|
| New York, N.Y. | [1]6 | 5 | 1:23 | 1:15 | 1:74 | 1:28 | 1:743 | 1:96 | 1:495 | 1:166 |
| New Jersey State Police | [3]9 | ([4]) | 0:5 | 1:7 | 0:5 | 1:28 | 0:5 | 1:72 | 0:5 | 1:305 |
| Newark, N.J. | [1]40 | 10 | 1:37 | 1:17 | 1:61 | 1:18 | 1:184 | 1:77 | None listed | |
| Oakland, Calif | [3]31 | 4 | 1:27 | 1:7 | 0:27 | 1:25 | 1:27 | 1:63 | 0:27 | 1:210 |
| Oklahoma City, Okla | [1]15 | 4 | 0:16 | 1:13 | 1:16 | 1:22 | 0:16 | 1:38 | 0:16 | 1:70 |
| Philadelphia, Pa | [1]29 | 20 | 1:53 | 1:18 | 1:172 | 1:40 | 1:459 | 1:120 | 0:1377 | 1:240 |
| Phoenix, Ariz | [1]8 | 1 | 0:7 | 1:8 | 1:7 | 1:32 | 0:7 | 1:70 | 0:7 | 1:175 |
| Pittsburgh, Pa | [1]19 | 7 | 1:36 | 1:11 | 1:36 | 1:31 | 0:109 | 1:362 | 1:109 | 1:242 |
| St. Louis, Mo | [1]37 | 11 | 1:11 | 1:9 | 1:75 | 1:40 | 1:56 | 1:107 | 0:224 | 1:165 |
| San Francisco, Calif | [1]14 | 6 | 0:102 | 1:8 | 0:102 | 1:25 | 0:102 | 1:110 | 0:102 | 1:165 |
| Tampa, Fla | [1]17 | 3 | 0:17 | 1:10 | 0:17 | 1:41 | 0:17 | 1:38 | 0:17 | 1:62 |
| Washington, D.C. | [1]63 | 21 | 1:29 | 1:10 | 1:186 | 1:20 | 1:186 | 1:58 | 0:559 | 1:70 |

[1] Percent Negro population figures, 1965 estimates by the Center for Research in Marketing, Cong. Quarterly, Weekly Report, No. 36, Sept 8, 1967.

[2] Percent Negro population figures, 1966 estimates, Office of Economic Opportunity.

[3] Percent Negro population figures for States of Michigan and New Jersey, 1960 Census figures.

[4] Less than ½ of 1 percent.

[5] All police data from a survey conducted for the Commission by the International Association of Chiefs of Police in October 1967.

# CHAPTER 12

# CONTROL OF DISORDER

---

## INTRODUCTION

To analyze the complex social causes of disorder, to plumb the impact of generations of deprivation, to work for broad and sensitive efforts at prevention are vital tasks, but they are slow and difficult. When, in the meantime, civil disorder breaks out, three simple principles emerge.

First: Preserving civil peace is the first responsibility of government.

Individuals cannot be permitted to endanger the public peace and safety, and public officials have a duty to make it clear that all just and necessary means to protect both will be used. Our society is founded on the rule of law. That rule must prevail; without it, we will lack not only order but the environment essential to social and economic progress.

Second: In maintaining the rule of law, we must be careful not to sacrifice it in the name of order.

In our concern over civil disorder, we must not mistake lawful protest for illegal activities. The guardians of the law are also subject to the law they serve. As the FBI states in its riot manual for law enforcement officers:

> A peaceful or lawful demonstration should not be looked
> upon with disapproval by a police agency; rather, it should

be considered as a safety valve possibly serving to prevent a riot. The police agency should not countenance violations of law. However, a police agency does not have the right to deny the demonstrator his constitutional rights.

Third: Maintaining civil order is the responsibility of the entire community.

Not even the most professional and devoted law enforcement agency alone can quell civil disorder any more than it alone can prevent civil disorder. A thin blue line is too thin. Maintaining civil peace is the responsibility of the entire community, particularly public officials. The guidance, assistance and support of the mayor can be decisive.

This does not deny the very great responsibility which is and should be borne by the police. . . . In this chapter, . . . the Commission considers ways by which the police—with the leadership and support of the civil authorities—can suppress and restrain potentially major disorders in their initial phases.*

---

\* In arriving at these assessments and recommendations, the Commission has relied heavily on information and advice supplied by the many police, military and other leading authorities. In addition to the studies conducted for the Commission by the International Association of Chiefs of Police, a number of outstanding authorities worked closely with the Commission staff and provided invaluable assistance. In particular, we wish to thank John Ingersoll, Chief of Police of Charlotte, North Carolina, and former Director of Field Services of the International Association of Chiefs of Police; Daryl F. Gates, Deputy Chief of Police, Los Angeles Police Department, who was one of the commanders in the field during the Watts riot; and Major General George M. Gelston, Adjutant General of Maryland and former Police Commissioner of Baltimore.

In addition to the testimony and reports received on the cities studied by the Commission which had experienced disorders, the Commission drew upon the valuable information and material furnished by the Boston, Chicago, Cincinnati, Kansas City, Los Angeles, New York City and Oakland Police Departments. Valuable guidance also was provided by Colonel Orlando W. Wilson, until recently Superintendent of Police of Chicago and formerly Dean of the School of Criminology, University of California.

The Commission also was assisted by material made available by the Federal Bureau of Investigation and its pamphlet, "Prevention and Control of Mobs and Riots," related reports by the Crime Commission and information supplied by the Office of Public Safety, Agency for International Development. The Commission also received the active cooperation and assistance of the Department of Defense

# THE INITIAL INCIDENT

Last summer, almost 150 cities experienced some form of civil disorder. Most remained minor disturbances, effectively controlled by the local police and civil authorities. In some cities similar incidents led to serious disorder. Why?

Testimony and evidence studied by the Commission point to the preeminent role of police reaction to the initial incident. How the police and the community respond to and deal with such incidents may well determine whether they remain relatively minor police problems—or balloon into major disorders.

## INITIAL POLICE RESPONSE

When police receive word of an accident, fight or similar incident, a patrolman is routinely sent to the scene. He is called on to exercise technical and professional skills at which he is practiced—investigation, individual control and perhaps arrest. Infrequently, he may have to call for assistance. In any event, his judgments, while important, normally have an impact only on the immediate participants.

In the densely populated ghetto, however, particularly when summer heat drives many residents into the streets, even the most routine incident may call for far more than a technical assessment. The responding officer's initial judgment here is critical in two respects. First, it will guide his own conduct. Second, it will guide the response of his superiors. What orders, if any, should they give him? What help should they send if he asks for help? An assessment of this sort may be difficult for the best-informed officer. What makes it even more difficult is that police often do not know what to expect when they respond to incidents in ghetto areas where virtually all the 1967 disorders occurred.

The average police officer has little knowledge or understanding of

---

and in particular from the special Army task force established in the Office of the Deputy Chief of Staff for Military Operations to study and make recommendations relative to the role of the Army and National Guard in controlling civil disorders.

the underlying tensions and grievances that exist in the ghetto. Yet this information is vital if the police officer is to decide correctly what police or other control measures should be taken to deal with the incident. The task is to find ways to inform his judgment to the maximum extent possible.

While good judgment cannot be institutionalized, some broad considerations can be offered.

## THE BASIC FACTORS

Five factors, often inseparable, recurred in the major disorders of last summer: (1) crowded ghetto living conditions, worsened by summer heat; (2) youth on the streets; (3) hostility to police; (4) delay in appropriate police response, and (5) persistent rumors and inadequate information.

On hot summer nights, the front steps and the street become a refuge from the stifling tenements of the ghetto. Detroit's 12th Street, New Haven's Congress Street and the grim public housing blocks of Newark illustrate how ghetto streets come alive with people, especially on summer nights and weekends, when many of the disorders of 1967 began. The people on the streets invariably include a very high proportion of youth.

It takes little to attract a crowd in this setting. Making an arrest is a routine matter to many police officers. In the ghetto, it can draw a crowd instantly—quick to misunderstand, quick to characterize the police action as unfair, quick to abandon curiosity for anger.

Crowded ghetto living conditions and youth on the streets—the first two factors—cannot be remedied by the police. But the police must take these conditions into account in assessing even the most routine ghetto incident. Every police officer responding to a call in tense, heavily-populated areas must be sensitive to tension situations. Here more than in any other type of police duty, the individual officer must exercise good judgment and common sense. The Chicago Police Department issued the following training bulletin to all its personnel:

> Preventing civil disorders is always easier than suppressing them. The police officer, by disciplining his emotions, rec-

ognizing the rights of all citizens and conducting himself in the manner his office demands can do much to prevent a tension situation from erupting into a serious disturbance.*

There are, however, steps police can take to eliminate or minimize the effects of the remaining three factors.

In the preceding chapter, we have already discussed the factor of hostility to police. As for delay, sufficient manpower is a prerequisite for controlling potentially dangerous crowds; the speed with which it arrives may well determine whether the situation can be controlled. In the summer of 1967, we believe that delay in mobilizing help permitted several incidents to develop into dangerous disorders, in the end requiring far more control personnel and creating increased hazards to life and property.

Rumors significantly aggravated tension and disorder in more than 65 percent of the disorders studied by the Commission. Sometimes, as in Tampa and New Haven, rumor served as the spark which turned an incident into a civil disorder. Elsewhere, notably Detroit and Newark, even where they were not precipitating or motivating factors, inflaming rumors made the job of police and community leaders far more difficult. Experience also has shown that the harmful effect of rumors can be offset if police, public officials and community leaders quickly and effectively circulate the facts.

An innovative method is that of a "Rumor Central"—an office responsible for the collection, evaluation and countering of rumors which could lead to civil disorder. To be most effective, such units might be located outside police departments. In any event, they should work closely with police and other public officials.

In addition to the problem of rumors incident to disorders, the police are often handicapped by the lack of adequate, reliable information. An effective police intelligence unit trained and equipped to gather, evaluate, analyze, and disseminate information is needed to rectify this deficiency.

---

* Training Bulletin—Tension Situations, 24 April 1967, The Chicago Police Department.

# CONTROL CAPABILITIES

Whenever an initial incident erupts into a major crowd control problem, most police departments are confronted with a difficult manpower problem. A police department normally has only a fraction—something around 13 percent—of its uniformed force on duty during the peak 4 p.m. to midnight watch, when nearly all the riots studied by the Commission began. For example, a city like Cincinnati, with a population of about 500,000 and an area of 77 square miles, would normally have fewer than 100 uniformed policemen available if trouble broke out. A city like Peoria, Illinois, with a population of about 100,000, would have fewer than 25 uniformed patrolmen on hand.*

Dispersal is also a factor. Normal police operations require personnel to be distributed over the entire geographical area of a city. When disorder breaks out, the task of mobilizing all available manpower is enormous. The police administrator must weigh the need for police to control the riot against the risks of leaving vital areas of the city without police protection.

It is apparent that most American cities would not have enough policemen quickly available to assure control in the event of a sudden large disorder. A high premium must hence be placed on the capability to prevent disorders—or to contain them before they develop into serious proportions.

---

* The majority of American cities between 50,000 and 100,000 population have less than 100 policemen. Of those with over 100,000 population, 71 percent have less than 500 policemen. Only 19 cities have more than 1000. As suggested by the cited figure of 13 percent manpower available, these figures are deceptively reassuring. Considering three shifts, days off, vacations and sick leave, five men are required to keep one police post manned 24 hours a day. In addition, manpower for regular police services like administration, records and detective work must be taken into account.

## TRAINING

Despite the obvious importance of well-trained police in controlling disorder, the Commission survey of the capabilities of selected police departments disclosed serious deficiencies. For example, riot-control training is primarily given to recruits. This averaged 18 hours for the departments surveyed, ranging from 62 hours to only 2. Little additional training is provided for command-level officers. In contrast, the National Guard now receives a minimum of 32 hours of riot-control training under new U.S. Army regulations, and National Guard officers receive 16 hours of command training for disorder situations.

The deficiencies in police training for disorders are magnified by the fact that standard police training and operations differ radically from training needed for the control of riots. Traditional training and emphasis have been on the individual policeman. His routine duties involve isolated incidents and dealings with small numbers of people at one time. The nature of his work—riding or walking mostly alone or in pairs—means that he has considerable individual discretion.

The control of civil disturbances, on the other hand, requires large numbers of disciplined personnel, comparable to soldiers in a military unit, organized and trained to work as a team under a highly unified command and control system. Thus, when a civil disturbance occurs, a police department must suddenly shift into a new type of organization with different operational procedures. The individual officer must stop acting independently and begin to perform as a member of a closely supervised, disciplined team. Our survey disclosed that training in practically all departments is limited to the individual.

Last year's disorders demonstrated that the control problems encountered were different from those for which riot-control training had been designed. Violence often involved small groups and hit-and-run tactics. Except in the later stages of the largest disorders, the crowds included large numbers of spectators not active in looting or destruction. Since they were mostly residents of the area, dispersal alone was futile. As a result, training in conventional riot-control formations and tactics, designed primarily to control and disperse mobs, was often inapplicable and ineffective.

Few departments have the resources and expertise to provide adequate and relevant training for control of serious disorders. . . .

## DISCIPLINE AND COMMAND

As the Riot Profiles in the opening chapter of the Report have shown, discipline of the control force is a crucial factor. Officers at the scene of a ghetto disorder are likely to suffer vilification, and to be the targets for rocks or bottles. Nevertheless, police discipline must be sufficiently strong so that an individual officer is not provoked into unilateral action. He must develop sufficient confidence in himself and his fellow officers to avoid panic or the indiscriminate [*sic*]—and inflammatory— use of force that has sometimes occurred in the heat of disorders. Discipline of this sort depends on the leadership of seasoned commanders and the presence in the field of sufficient supervisory officers to make major decisions.

The ability of police commanders to maintain command and control of units at the scene of disorder is severely handicapped by deficiencies in police communications. Police departments usually can communicate with their personnel only through radios in police vehicles. Once the officer leaves his police car or motorcycle, he loses communication with his superiors and is outside their effective control.

The military has field communications systems which make it possible to achieve effective command and control. The Nation's police departments do not. . . .

## POLICE TACTICS

There are no all-purpose control tactics. Last summer's disorders demonstrated repeatedly that tactics which are effective in one situation may be totally ineffective in another. The cardinal requirement is to have enough men and control equipment available to carry out effectively whatever tactics are necessary and appropriate according to the dictates of sound judgment. . . .

# THE USE OF FORCE

## JUSTIFICATION OF DEADLY FORCE

There are at least three serious problems involved in the use of deadly weapons in a civil disorder. The first is the risk of killing or wounding innocent persons—bystanders or passersby who may in fact be hundreds of feet away when a shot is fired.

The second is the justification for the use of deadly force against looting or vandalism. Are bullets the correct response to offenses of this sort? Maj. Gen. George Gelston* told the Commission: "* * * I am not going to order a man killed for stealing a six-pack of beer or a television set." Instead, he said, a nonlethal tear gas can stop any looting.

The third problem is that the use of excessive force—even the inappropriate display of weapons—may be inflammatory and lead to even worse disorder. As the FBI riot-control manual states:

> The basic rule, when applying force, is to use only the minimum force necessary to effectively control the situation. Unwarranted application of force will incite the mob to further violence, as well as kindle seeds of resentment for police that, in turn, could cause a riot to recur. Ill-advised or excessive application of force will not only result in charges of police brutality but also may prolong the disturbance.

Such counsel with respect to disorders accords with the clearly established legal and social principle of minimum use of force by police.

The major difficulty in dealing with all these problems, however, is the limited choice still presented to police in mass disorders: to use too much force or too little. The police who faced the New York riot of 1863 were equipped with two weapons—a wooden stick and a gun. For the most part, the police faced with urban disorders last summer had to rely on two weapons—a wooden stick and a gun.

Our police departments today require a middle range of phys-

---

* Adjutant General of Maryland, commander of National Guard forces in Cambridge, Md., last summer, and former Police Commissioner of Baltimore.

ical force with which to restrain and control illegal behavior more humanely and more effectively.

## ALTERNATIVES TO DEADLY FORCE

The dilemma regarding force has endured for more than a century for two reasons. One is that police are inhibited from using even the new tools which have been developed. The second is that the improvement and perfection of these tools are proceeding far too slowly.

. . . [F]ear of public reaction and other policy considerations have tended to inhibit police use of nonlethal chemical agents in civil disorders. The U.S. Army, on the other hand, relies heavily on the use of CS, a chemical agent, for controlling riots. The Army has found it to be both much more effective and safer than the more traditional tear gas, CN. The use of CS is prescribed in the standard military sequence of force prior to the employment of any lethal firearms. Moreover, new developments now make it possible to use chemical agents selectively against individuals and small groups with minimum danger to innocent persons. Thus, the understandable concern of many police and public officials as to the wisdom of using massive amounts of gas in densely populated areas need no longer prove a barrier.

The value and effectiveness of chemical agents in restoring law and order, with minimum danger to lives and property, is also attested to by the FBI's riot-control manual: "Chemical agents * * * can negate the numerical superiority the mob has over the police force. They are the most effective and most humane means of achieving temporary neutralization of a mob with a minimum of personal injury."

**The Commission recommends** that, in suppressing disorder, the police, whenever possible, follow the example of the U.S. Army in requiring the use of chemical agents before the use of deadly weapons.

The experience of many police forces has demonstrated, however, that the value and community acceptance of new nonlethal methods may be jeopardized if police officers employ them in an indiscriminate way. In some of the cities we studied, reports of improper use of some chemical weapons by individual police officers have led to charges that these weapons are brutalizing or demeaning. To assure public confidence and prevent misuse, police administrators should issue clear guidelines on where and how police may employ such control measures.

The Commission has received many suggestions for other nonlethal control equipment. Distinctive marking dyes or odors and the filming of rioters have been recommended both to deter and positively identify persons guilty of illegal acts. Sticky tapes, adhesive blobs, and liquid foam are advocated to immobilize or block rioters. Intensely bright lights and loud distressing sounds capable of creating temporary disability may prove to be useful. Technology will provide still other tools.

There is need for additional experience and evaluation before the police and the public and be reasonably assured that these control innovations meet the performance and safety standards required for use in civilian communities. The Commission believes, however, that the urgent need for nonlethal alternatives requires immediate attention and Federal support. . . .

## COMMUNITY ASSISTANCE IN DISORDER CONTROL

Commission studies have shown that in a number of instances both police and other responsible civil authorities were forced to make decisions without adequate facts in an atmosphere charged by rumor.

Police administrators consulted by the Commission emphasized the importance of employing trained police intelligence officers to collect, evaluate, and disseminate information. The use of undercover police officers, reliable informants and the assignment of police personnel to provide fast, accurate, on-the-scene reports, were all cited as essential.

During the early stage of a disorder when lawlessness is still relatively restricted, the cooperation and assistance of Negro leaders and other community residents with a common interest in the maintenance of order can be extremely valuable. They can provide the police with the kind of pertinent, reliable information essential for decisionmaking during the disorder. Many agencies and organizations in the area, public and private, have valuable contacts and channels of communication. These also can serve as important information resources.

In some cities, "counterrioters" have played an important role in dampening disturbance. Volunteers have assisted in restoring order by patrolling their neighborhoods and trying independently to persuade others to go home. Sometimes local authorities have actively recruited ghetto residents to perform these missions. The Commission believes that mayors and police chiefs should recognize and assess carefully the potential benefit such efforts can sometimes provide, restoring the peace in a way that will earn public support and confidence.

The larger question, however—whether police should withdraw from the disorder area and let community leaders or forces seek to cool the rioting—raises a number of critical issues. The first and most important is whether by so doing the police are abdicating their basic responsibility to maintain order and protect lives and property.

Some police administrators are deeply convinced that it is a dereliction of duty for police to delegate complete authority to individuals or groups who lack legal responsibility. In their judgment, such action creates the danger of vigilante groups. The Commission shares this concern; a sanctioned control group could use its position to intimidate or terrorize.

Also, those who come forward to discourage rioting may have no influence with the rioters. If they fail, they may well blame officials, creating new enforcement problems.

The Commission believes that only the mayor—who has the ultimate responsibility for the welfare and safety of the community—can, with the advice of the police administrator, make the critical judgment.


## THE ROLE OF PUBLIC OFFICIALS

The Commission believes incidents are less likely to escalate into larger violence if ghetto residents know they have effective political channels of protest. We discussed formal grievance outlets at length in the preceding chapters. Here we are particularly concerned with the role of the mayor or city manager and police chief.

Civil disorders are fundamental governmental problems, not simply police matters. As the chief elected official, the mayor must take ultimate responsibility for all governmental action in times of disorder. To make this meaningful, he must have the corresponding authority and control. He must become fully involved in disorder planning and operations. He must understand the nature of the problems posed by a disorder, the strategy of response and field operations.

In some cities, mayors have taken the view that disorders were entirely police matters. This represents a failure to accept a fundamental responsibility. The unwillingness of a mayor to become personally involved and to negotiate grievances with local residents may cut off a vital outlet for peaceful protest.

Similarly, police chiefs should understand this responsibility and involve the mayor in their planning activities and operations. Only regular participation by the mayor in police problems, in cold winters as well as hot summers, will educate both the mayor and the police to the mutually reinforcing nature of their relationship.

Parallel responsibilities exist at the state level. Governors and other civilian officials with responsibility over state law enforcement activities, such as attorneys general, have an obligation to supervise planning and operations for civil disorders.

One of the most important responsibilities of local officials is to maintain close personal contact with the ghetto. The importance of creating channels of communication with ministers, with community organizations, with Negro leaders including young activists and militants cannot be overestimated. Given such contacts, officials become more sensitive to ghetto reactions to particular episodes and frictions. They also create acquaintanceships which can be used to help alleviate tensions that might otherwise heighten.

As the Riot Profiles indicate, in a number of the disorders studied by the Commission, efforts were made to respond to grievances. In some instances, Negro leaders took the initiative. In others, mayors and state officials did so. In New Brunswick, for example, discussion alleviated tension and led to a peaceful settlement. Often the determination of civilian officials, especially the mayor, to seek out these opportunities may be decisive in avoiding violence.

Having determined that it will try to resolve its problems by political means, the city must then decide with whom to negotiate—often a difficult question. Large meetings open to the general public or small meetings limited to established, older Negro leaders were rarely found to be effective. City officials are often faced with a fragmented Negro community. If they have failed to keep open broad channels of communication, city officials will have great difficulty identifying leaders with sufficient influence to get through to those on the streets.

Even after contacts are made, negotiations may be extremely difficult. Younger, militant leaders are often distrustful of city government, fearful of compromising their militancy or their leadership by allying themselves too closely with "the power structure," particularly when that structure may have nothing to deliver.

Civil disorders require the maximum coordination of the activities of all governmental agencies. Such cooperation can only be brought about by the chief executive. Examples are joint operations by the police and fire departments, mutual assistance agreements with neighboring communities and state and Federal assistance. . . .

## DANGER OF OVERREACTION

Emergencies are anticipated in police planning. They range from natural threats like floods and storms to man-made incidents like the recent disorders. Until 1964, most civil disorders were regarded as difficult but basically manageable police problems of an essentially local nature. The events of the last few summers, however, particularly the events of 1967, have radically changed this view. Disturbances in densely populated, predominantly Negro areas which might earlier have been labeled brawls became characterized as "riots," with racial overtones. A national climate of tension and fear developed, particularly in cities with large Negro populations.

Were relatively minor incidents inflated or escalated into serious disturbances? Did such inflation result from overly aggressive law enforcement action? Did it stem from unwarranted fears on the part of the ghetto community? Precise answers are impossible. What can be said, however, is that there was widespread misunderstanding and exaggeration of what did occur.

The most notable example is the belief widely held across the country last summer that riot cities were paralyzed by sniper fire. Of 23 cities surveyed by the Commission, there had been reports of sniping in at least 15. What is probable, although the evidence is fragmentary, is that there was at least some sniping. What is certain is that the amount of sniping attributed to rioters—by law enforcement officials as well as the press—was highly exaggerated.

According to the best information available to the Commission, most reported sniping incidents were demonstrated to be gunfire by either police or National Guardsmen.

The climate of fear and expectation of violence created by such exaggerated, sometimes totally erroneous, reports demonstrates the serious risks of over-reaction and excessive use of force. In particular, the Commission is deeply concerned that, in their anxiety to control disorders, some law enforcement agencies may resort to indiscriminate, repressive use of force against wholly innocent elements of the Negro community. The injustice of such conduct—and its abrasive effects—would be incalculable.

Elected officials, police and National Guard officials must take effective steps to prevent false assessments and the tragic consequences that could follow. This will require improved communications. It will require reliable intelligence about ghetto problems and incidents. It will require, equally, assurance of steadfast discipline among control personnel.

# FUNDING OF RECOMMENDATIONS FOR PREVENTION AND CONTROL OF DISORDER

Many of the recommendations in this and the preceding chapter will be costly. Studies of police practices, intensified recruitment of Negro officers, increased planning and training for disorder control—all would impose heavy financial burdens on communities already hard-pressed by the increasing costs of their present systems of criminal justice.

**The Commission recommends** that the Federal Government bear a part of this burden.

Federal funding need not and should not in any way infringe on the principle of local law enforcement authority. The Federal Government already finances a variety of law enforcement assistance programs without such infringement. The Department of Justice provides direct grants for research, planning and demonstration through the Office of Law Enforcement Assistance, and the FBI conducts training programs for state and local police officers. The Department of Health, Education, and Welfare administers juvenile delinquency control programs and educational grants for law enforcement studies. The Department of Labor helps pay for police cadet training programs. The Office of Economic Opportunity assists in police-community relations activities. We commend and endorse these efforts. But we believe more Federal financial assistance is needed.

Such assistance should take two forms. First, in this chapter [and] the preceding one . . . , we specifically recommend Federal funding for certain programs—community service officers, development of portable communications equipment, a national clearinghouse for training information and nonlethal weapons development.

Second, we also believe that more Federal support is necessary to help local communities improve the overall quality of their criminal justice systems. With the Crime Commission, we believe that the Federal Government "* * * can make a dramatic new contribution to the national effort against crime by greatly expanding its support of the agencies of justice in the states and in the cities."

These remarks are in no way intended to excuse local governments from their financial responsibilities. Improved law enforcement at the local level, including increased capacity to prevent and control civil disorders, is possible only if local citizens are willing to put their tax money where their desires are. But this Commission believes that not even the most devoted and willing community can succeed by acting alone. Only the Federal Government is in a position to provide expertise, conduct and evaluate comprehensive test programs, and pay for the large capital investment necessary to develop experimental programs and new equipment.

The Crime Commission outlined a broad program of Federal funding, advice and assistance to meet major criminal justice needs. It estimated that in the next decade, several hundred million dollars could be profitably spent each year on this program. The increased demands imposed on law enforcement agencies by the recent disorders have intensified the urgency and increased the cost of such a program.

Nevertheless, 14 months have now passed since the Crime Commission's exhaustive study and recommendations; 13 months have passed since the President first urged the Congress to enact such a program; that urgent request was renewed by the President in his Public Safety Message on February 7, 1968. No final action has yet been taken. It should be taken—and taken promptly. Because law enforcement is a local responsibility, whatever legislation is adopted should permit direct grants to municipal governments. Funding should be at least as high as that requested by the President in his Message.

# CHAPTER 15

# THE NEWS MEDIA
# AND THE DISORDERS

_____

## INTRODUCTION

The President's charge to the Commission asked specifically: "What effect do the mass media have on the riots?"

The question is far reaching, and a sure answer is beyond the range of presently available scientific techniques. Our conclusions and recommendations are based upon subjective as well as objective factors; interviews as well as statistics; isolated examples as well as general trends.

Freedom of the press is not the issue. A free press is indispensable to the preservation of the other freedoms this Nation cherishes. The recommendations in this chapter have thus been developed under the strong conviction that only a press unhindered by government can contribute to freedom.

To answer the President's question, the Commission:

- Directed its field survey teams to question government officials, law enforcement agents, media personnel, and ordinary citizens about their attitudes and reactions to reporting of the riots.
- Arranged for interviews of media representatives about their coverage of the riots.

- Conducted special interviews with ghetto residents about their response to coverage.
- Arranged for a quantitative analysis of the content of television programs and newspaper reporting in 15 riot cities during the period of the disorder and the days immediately before and after.
- From November 10–12, 1967, sponsored and participated in a conference of representatives from all levels of the newspaper, news magazine, and broadcasting industries at Poughkeepsie, N.Y.

Finally, of course, the Commissioners read newspapers, listened to the radio, watched television, and thus formed their own impressions of media coverage. All of these data, impressions, and attitudes provide the foundation for our conclusions.

The Commission also determined, very early, that the answer to the President's question did not lie solely in the performance of the press and broadcasters in reporting the riots proper. Our analysis had to consider also the overall treatment by the media of the Negro ghettos, community relations, racial attitudes, urban and rural poverty—day by day and month by month, year in and year out.

On this basis, we have reached three conclusions:

First, that despite instances of sensationalism, inaccuracies, and distortions, newspapers, radio, and television, on the whole, made a real effort to give a balanced, factual account of the 1967 disorders.

Second, that despite this effort, the portrayal of the violence that occurred last summer failed to reflect accurately its scale and character. The overall effect was, we believe, an exaggeration of both mood and event.

Third, and ultimately most important, we believe that the media have thus far failed to report adequately on the causes and consequences of civil disorders and the underlying problems of race relations.

With these comments as a perspective, we discuss first the coverage of last summer's disturbances. We will then summarize our concerns with overall coverage of race relations.

## COVERAGE OF THE 1967 DISTURBANCES

We have found a significant imbalance between what actually happened in our cities and what the newspaper, radio, and television coverage of the riots told us happened. The Commission, in studying last summer's disturbances, visited many of the cities and interviewed participants and observers. We found that the disorders, as serious as they were, were less destructive, less widespread, and less of a black-white confrontation than most people believed.

Lacking other sources of information, we formed our original impressions and beliefs from what we saw on television, heard on the radio, and read in newspapers and magazines. We are deeply concerned that millions of other Americans, who must rely on the mass media, likewise formed incorrect impressions and judgments about what went on in many American cities last summer.

As we started to probe the reasons for this imbalance between reality and impression, we first believed that the media had sensationalized the disturbances, consistently overplaying violence and giving disproportionate amounts of time to emotional events and militant leaders. To test this theory, we commissioned a systematic, quantitative analysis, covering the content of newspaper and television reporting in 15 cities where disorders occurred. The results of this analysis do not support our early belief. Of 955 television sequences of riot and racial news examined, 837 could be classified for predominant atmosphere as either "emotional," "calm," or "normal." Of these, 494 were classified as calm, 262 as emotional, and 81 as normal. Only a small proportion of all scenes analyzed showed actual mob action, people looting, sniping, setting fires, or being injured, or killed. Moderate Negro leaders were shown more frequently than militant leaders on television news broadcasts.

Of 3,779 newspaper articles analyzed, more focused on legislation which should be sought and planning which should be done to control ongoing riots and prevent future riots than on any other topic. The findings of this analysis are explained in detail later in this chapter. They make it clear that the imbalance between actual events and the portrayal of those events in the press and on the air cannot be attributed solely to sensationalism in reporting and presentation.

We have, however, identified several factors which, it seems to us, did work to create incorrect and exaggerated impressions about the scope and intensity of the disorders.

First, despite the overall statistical picture, there were instances of gross flaws in presenting news of the 1967 riots. Some newspapers printed scare headlines unsupported by the mild stories that followed. All media reported rumors that had no basis in fact. Some newsmen staged riot events for the cameras. Examples are included in the next section.

Second, the press obtained much factual information about the scale of the disorders—property damage, personal injury, and deaths—from local officials, who often were inexperienced in dealing with civil disorders and not always able to sort out fact from rumor in the confusion. At the height of the Detroit riot, some news reports of property damage put the figure in excess of $500 million.[*] Subsequent investigation shows it to be $40 to $45 million.[†] The initial estimates were not the independent judgment of reporters or editors. They came from beleaguered government officials. But the news media gave currency to these errors. Reporters uncritically accepted, and editors uncritically published, the inflated figures, leaving an indelible impression of damage up to more than 10 times greater than actually occurred.

Third, the coverage of the disorders—particularly on television—tended to define the events as black-white confrontations. In fact, almost all of the deaths, injuries, and property damage occurred in all-Negro neighborhoods, and thus the disorders were not "race riots" as that term is generally understood.

Closely linked to these problems is the phenomenon of cumulative effect. As the summer of 1967 progressed, we think Americans often began to associate more or less neutral sights and sounds (like a squad car with flashing red lights, a burning building, a suspect in police

---

[*] As recently as Feb. 9, 1968, an Associated Press dispatch from Philadelphia said "damage exceeded $1 billion" in Detroit.
[†] Michigan State Insurance Commission estimate, December 1967. See also "Meeting the Insurance Crisis of Our Cities," a report by the President's National Advisory Panel on Insurance in Riot-Affected Areas, January 1968.

custody) with racial disorders, so that the appearance of any particular item, itself hardly inflammatory, set off a whole sequence of association with riot events. Moreover, the summer's news was not seen and heard in isolation. Events of these past few years—the Watts riot, other disorders, and the growing momentum of the civil rights movement— conditioned the responses of readers and viewers and heightened their reactions. What the public saw and read last summer thus produced emotional reactions and left vivid impressions not wholly attributable to the material itself.

Fear and apprehension of racial unrest and violence are deeply rooted in American society. They color and intensify reactions to news of racial trouble and threats of racial conflict. Those who report and disseminate news must be conscious of the background of anxieties and apprehension against which their stories are projected. This does not mean that the media should manage the news or tell less than the truth. Indeed, we believe that it would be imprudent and even dangerous to downplay coverage in the hope that censored reporting of inflammatory incidents somehow will diminish violence. Once a disturbance occurs, the word will spread independently of newspapers and television. To attempt to ignore these events or portray them as something other than what they are can only diminish confidence in the media and increase the effectiveness of those who monger rumors and the fears of those who listen.

But to be complete, the coverage must be representative. We suggest that the main failure of the media last summer was that the totality of its coverage was not as representative as it should have been to be accurate. We believe that to live up to their own professed standards, the media simply must exercise a higher degree of care and a greater level of sophistication than they have yet shown in this area—higher, perhaps, than the level ordinarily acceptable with other stories.

This is not "just another story." It should not be treated like one. Admittedly, some of what disturbs us about riot coverage last summer stems from circumstances beyond media control. But many of the inaccuracies of fact, tone, and mood were due to the failure of reporters and editors to ask tough enough questions about official reports and to apply the most rigorous standards possible in evaluating and presenting the news. Reporters and editors must be sure that descriptions and pictures of violence, and emotional or inflammatory sequences or articles, even though "true" in isolation, are really representative and do not convey an impression at odds with the overall reality of events. The media too often did not achieve this level of sophisticated, skeptical, careful news judgment during last summer's riots.

## THE MEDIA AND RACE RELATIONS

Our second and fundamental criticism is that the news media have failed to analyze and report adequately on racial problems in the United States and, as a related matter, to meet the Negro's legitimate expectations in journalism. By and large, news organizations have failed to communicate to both their black and white audiences a sense of the problems America faces and the sources of potential solutions. The media report and write from the standpoint of a white man's world. The ills of the ghetto, the difficulties of life there, the Negro's burning sense of grievance, are seldom conveyed. Slights and indignities are part of the Negro's daily life, and many of them come from what he now calls the "white press"—a press that repeatedly, if unconsciously, reflects the biases, the paternalism, the indifference of white America. This may be understandable, but it is not excusable in an institution that has the mission to inform and educate the whole of our society.

Our criticisms, important as they are, do not lead us to conclude that the media are a cause of riots, any more than they are the cause of other phenomena which they report. It is true that newspaper and television reporting helped shape people's attitudes toward riots. In some cities, people who watched television reports and read newspaper accounts of riots in other cities later rioted themselves. But the causal chain weakens when we recall that in other cities, people in very much the same circumstances watched the same programs and read the same newspaper stories but did not riot themselves.

The news media are not the sole source of information and certainly not the only influence on public attitudes. People obtained their information and formed their opinions about the 1967 disorders from the multiplicity of sources that condition the public's thinking on all events. Personal experience, conversations with others, the local and long-distance telephone are all important as sources of information and ideas and contribute to the totality of attitudes about riots.

No doubt, in some cases, the knowledge or the sight on a television screen of what had gone on elsewhere lowered inhibitions, kindled outrage or awakened desires for excitement or loot—or simply passed the word. Many ghetto residents we interviewed thought so themselves. By the same token, the news reports of riots must have conditioned the response of officials and police to disturbances in their own cities. The reaction of the authorities in Detroit was almost certainly affected in some part by what they saw or read of Newark a week earlier. The Commission believes that none of these private or official reactions was decisive in determining the course of the disorders. Even if they had been more significant than we think, however, we cannot envision a system of governmental restraints that could successfully eliminate these effects. And an effort to formulate and impose such restraints would be inconsistent with fundamental traditions in our society.

These failings of the media must be corrected and the improvement must come from within the media. A society that values and relies on a free press as intensely as ours is entitled to demand in return responsibility from the press and conscientious attention by the press to its own deficiencies. The Commission has seen evidence that many of those who supervise, edit, and report for the news media are becoming increasingly aware of and concerned about their performance in this field. With that concern, and with more experience, will come more sophisticated and responsible coverage. But much more must be done, and it must be done soon.

The Commission has a number of recommendations designed to stimulate and accelerate efforts toward self-improvement. And we propose a privately organized, privately funded Institute of Urban Communications as a means for drawing these recommendations together and promoting their implementation. . . .

# NEWS COVERAGE OF CIVIL DISORDERS—SUMMER 1967

[The Method of Analysis portion within this section is intentionally omitted.]

## CONCLUSIONS ABOUT CONTENT*

### Television

1. Content analysis of television film footage shows that the tone of the coverage studied was more "calm" and "factual" than "emotional" and "rumor-laden." Researchers viewed every one of the 955 television sequences and found that twice as many "calm" sequences as "emotional" ones were shown. The amount and location of coverage were relatively limited, considering the magnitude of the events. The analysis reveals a dominant, positive emphasis on control of the riot and on activities in the aftermath of the riot (53.8 percent of all scenes broadcast), rather than on scenes of actual mob action, or people looting, sniping, setting fires, or being injured or killed (4.8 percent of scenes shown). According to participants in our Poughkeepsie conference, coverage frequently was of the post-riot or interview variety because newsmen arrived at the scene after the actual violence had subsided. Overall, both network and local television coverage was cautious and restrained.

2. Television newscasts during the periods of actual disorder in 1967 tended to emphasize law enforcement activities, thereby overshadowing underlying grievances and tensions. This conclusion is based on the relatively high frequency with which television showed and described law enforcement agents, police, National Guardsmen, and army troops performing control functions.

---

* What follows is a summary of the major conclusions drawn from the content analysis conducted for the Commission.

Television coverage tended to give the impression that the riots were confrontations between Negroes and whites rather than responses by Negroes to underlying slum problems. The control agents were predominantly white. The ratio of white male adults* to Negro male adults shown on television is high (1:2) considering that the riots took place in predominantly Negro neighborhoods. And some interviews with whites involved landlords or proprietors who lost property or suffered business losses because of the disturbances and thus held strongly antagonistic attitudes.

The content analysis shows that by far the most frequent "actor" appearances on television were Negro male adults, white male adults, law enforcement agents, and public officials. We cannot tell from a content analysis whether there was any preconceived editorial policy of portraying the riots as racial confrontations requiring the intervention of enforcement agents. But the content analysis does present a visual three-way alignment of Negroes, white bystanders, and public officials or enforcement agents. This alignment tended to create an impression that the riots were predominantly racial confrontations involving clashes between black and white citizens.

3. About one-third of all riot-related sequences for network and local television appeared on the first day following the outbreak of rioting, regardless of the course of development of the riot itself. After the first day there was, except in Detroit, a very sharp decline in the amount of television time devoted to the disturbance. In Detroit, where the riot started slowly and did not flare out of control until the evening of July 24, 48 hours after it started, the number of riot-related sequences shown increased until July 26 and then showed the same sharp dropoff as noted after the first day of rioting in the other cities.† These findings tend to controvert the impression that the riot

---

* The white male adult category in this computation does *not* include law enforcement agents or public officials.

† Detroit news outlets substantially refrained from publicizing the riot during the early part of Sunday, the first day of rioting.

intensifies television coverage, thus in turn intensifying the riot. The content analysis indicates that whether or not the riot was getting worse, television coverage of the riot decreased sharply after the first day.

4. The Commission made a special effort to analyze television coverage of Negro leaders. To do this, Negro leaders were divided into three categories: (a) celebrities or public figures, who did not claim any organizational following (e.g., social scientist Dr. Kenneth B. Clark, comedian Dick Gregory); (b) "moderate" Negro leaders, who claim a political or organizational following; and (c) "militant" Negro leaders who claim a political or organizational following. During the riot periods surveyed, Negro leaders appeared infrequently on network news broadcasts and were about equally divided among celebrity or public figures, moderate leaders, and militant leaders. On local television, Negro leaders appeared more often. Of the three categories, "moderate" Negro leaders were shown on local stations more than twice as often as Negro leaders identified primarily as celebrities or public figures and three times more frequently than militant leaders.

## Newspapers

1. Like television coverage, newspaper coverage of civil disturbances in the summer of 1967 was more calm, factual, and restrained than outwardly emotional or inflammatory. During the period of the riot there were many stories dealing exclusively with nonriot racial news. Considering the magnitude of the events, the amount of coverage was limited. Most stories were played down or put on inside pages. Researchers found that almost all the articles analyzed (3,045 of 3,770) tended to focus on one of 16 identifiable subjects. Of this group, 502 articles (16.5 percent) focused primarily on legislation which should be sought and planning which could be done to control ongoing riots and prevent future riots. The second largest category consisted of 471 articles (15.5 percent) focusing on containment or control of riot action. Newspaper coverage of the disorders reflects efforts at caution and restraint.

2. Newspapers tended to characterize and portray last summer's riots in national terms rather than as local phenomena and problems, especially when rioting was taking place in the newspaper's own city. During the actual disorders, the newspapers in each city studied tended to print many stories dealing with disorders or racial troubles in other cities. About 40 percent of the riot or racial stories in each local newspaper during the period of rioting in that city came from the wire services. Furthermore, most newspaper editors appear to have given more headline attention to riots occurring elsewhere than to those at home during the time of trouble in their own cities.

## ACCURACY OF THE COVERAGE

We have tested the accuracy of coverage by means of interviews with local media representatives, city and police officials, and residents of the ghettos. To provide a broad base, we used three separate sources for interview data: The Commission's field survey teams, special field teams, and the findings of a special research study.

As is to be expected, almost everyone had his own version of "the truth," but it is noteworthy that some editors and reporters themselves, in retrospect, have expressed concern about the accuracy of their own coverage. For example, one newspaper editor said at the Commission's Poughkeepsie Conference:

> We used things in our leads and headlines during the riot I wish we could have back now, because they were wrong and they were bad mistakes * * *
> We used the words "sniper kings" and "nests of snipers." We found out when we were able to get our people into those areas and get them out from under the cars that these sniper kings and these nests of snipers were the constituted authorities shooting at each other, most of them. There was just one confirmed sniper in the entire eight-day riot and he was * * * drunk and he had a pistol, and he was firing from a window.

Television industry representatives at the conference stressed their concern about "live" coverage of disorders and said they try, whenever possible, to view and edit taped or filmed sequences before broadcasting them. Conference participants admitted that live television coverage via helicopter of the 1965 Watts riot had been inflammatory, and network news executives expressed doubts that television would ever again present live coverage of a civil disorder.

Most errors involved mistakes of fact, exaggeration of events, overplaying of particular stories, or prominently displayed speculation about unfounded rumors of potential trouble. This is not only a local problem; because of the wire services and networks, it is a national one. An experienced riot reporter told the Commission that initial wire service reports of a disturbance tend to be inflated. The reason, he said, is that they are written by local bureau men who in most cases have not seen a civil disorder before. When out-of-town reporters with knowledge in the field or the wire services' own riot specialists arrive on the scene, the situation is put into a more accurate context.

Some examples of exaggeration and mistakes about facts are cataloged here. These examples are by no means exhaustive. They represent only a few of the incidents discovered by the Commission and, no doubt, are but a small part of the total number of such inaccuracies. But the Commission believes that they are representative of the kinds of errors likely to occur when, in addition to the confusion inherent in civil disorder situations, reporters are rushed and harried or editors are superficial and careless. We present these as examples of mistakes that we hope will be avoided in the future.

In particular, we believe newsmen should be wary of how they play rumors of impending trouble. Whether a rumor is reliable and significant enough to deserve coverage is an editorial decision. But the failure of many headlined rumors to be borne out last summer suggests that these editorial decisions often are not as carefully made as the sensitivity of the subject requires.

- In Detroit, a radio station broadcast a rumor, based on a telephone tip, that Negroes planned to invade suburbia one night later; if plans existed, they never materialized.

- In Cincinnati, several outlets ran a story about white youths arrested for possessing a bazooka; only a few reports mentioned that the weapon was inoperable.
- In Tampa, a newspaper repeatedly indulged in speculation about impending trouble. When the state attorney ruled the fatal shooting of a Negro youth justifiable homicide, the paper's news columns reported: "There were fears today that the ruling would stir new race problems for Tampa tonight." The day before, the paper quoted one "top lawman" as telling reporters "he now fears that Negro residents in the Central Avenue Project and in the West Tampa trouble spots feel they are in competition and are trying to see which can cause the most unrest—which area can become the center of attraction."
- A West Coast newspaper put out an edition headlined: "Rioting Erupts in Washington, D.C. / Negroes Hurl Bottles, Rocks at Police Near White House." The story did not support the headline. It reported what was actually the fact: that a number of teenage Negroes broke store windows and threw bottles and stones at police and firemen near downtown Washington, a mile or more from the White House. On the other hand, the same paper did not report unfounded local rumors of sniping when other news media did.

Television presents a different problem with respect to accuracy. In contrast to what some of its critics have charged, television sometimes may have leaned over too far backward in seeking balance and restraint. By stressing interviews, many with whites in predominantly Negro neighborhoods, and by emphasizing control scenes rather than riotous action, television news broadcasts may have given a distorted picture of what the disorders were all about.

The media—especially television—also have failed to present and analyze to a sufficient extent the basic reasons for the disorders. There have, after the disorders, been some brilliant exceptions.*

---

* As examples, less than a month after the Detroit riot, the Detroit Free Press published the results of a landmark survey of local Negro attitudes and grievances. Newsweek magazine's November 20, 1967, special issue on "The Negro American— What Must Be Done" made a significant contribution to public understanding.

As the content analysis findings suggest, however, coverage during the riot period itself gives far more emphasis to control of rioters and black-white confrontation than to the underlying causes of the disturbances.

## GHETTO REACTIONS TO THE MEDIA COVERAGE

The Commission was particularly interested in public reaction to media coverage; specifically, what people in the ghetto look at and read and how it affects them. The Commission has drawn upon reports from special teams of researchers who visited various cities where outbreaks occurred last summer. Members of these teams interviewed ghetto dwellers and middle-class Negroes on their responses to news media. In addition, we have used information from a statistical study of the mass media in the Negro ghetto in Pittsburgh.*

These interviews and surveys, though by no means a complete study of the subject, lead to four broad conclusions about ghetto and, to a lesser degree, middle-class Negro reactions to the media.

Most Negroes distrust what they refer to as the "white press." As one interviewer reported:

> The average black person couldn't give less of a damn about
> what the media say. The intelligent black person is resentful
> at what he considers to be a totally false portrayal of what
> goes on in the ghetto. Most black people see the newspapers
> as mouthpieces of the "power structure."

These comments are echoed in most interview reports the Commission has read. Distrust and dislike of the media among ghetto Negroes encompass all the media, though in general, the newspapers are mistrusted more than the television. This is not because television is thought to be more sensitive or responsive to Negro needs and aspirations but because ghetto residents believe that television at least lets them see the actual events for themselves. Even so, many

---

* The Commission is indebted, in this regard, to M. Thomas Allen for his document on Mass Media Use Patterns and Functions in the Negro Ghetto in Pittsburgh.

Negroes, particularly teenagers, told researchers that they noted a pronounced discrepancy between what they saw in the riots and what television broadcast.

Persons interviewed offered three chief reasons for their attitude. First, they believe, as suggested in the quotation above, that the media are instruments of the white power structure. They think that these white interests guide the entire white community, from the journalists' friends and neighbors to city officials, police officers, and department store owners. Publishers and editors, if not white reporters, they feel, support and defend these interests with enthusiasm and dedication.

Second, many people in the ghettos apparently believe that newsmen rely on the police for most of their information about what is happening during a disorder and tend to report much more of what the officials are doing and saying than what Negro citizens or leaders in the city are doing and saying. Editors and reporters at the Poughkeepsie conference acknowledged that the police and city officials are their main—and sometimes their only—source of information. It was also noted that most reporters who cover civil disturbances tend to arrive with the police and stay close to them—often for safety and often because they learn where the action is at the same time as the authorities—and thus buttress the ghetto impression that police and press work together and toward the same ends (an impression that may come as a surprise to many within the ranks of police and press).

Third, Negro residents in several cities surveyed cited as specific examples of media unfairness what they considered the failure of the media:

- To report the many examples of Negroes helping law enforcement officers and assisting in the treatment of the wounded during disorders.
- To report adequately about false arrests.
- To report instances of excessive force by the National Guard.
- To explore and interpret the background conditions leading to disturbances.
- To expose, except in Detroit, what they regarded as instances of police brutality.

- To report on white vigilante groups which allegedly came into some disorder areas and molested innocent Negro residents.

Some of these problems are insoluble. But more firsthand reporting in the diffuse and fragmented riot area should temper easy reliance on police information and announcements. There is a special need for news media to cover "positive" news stories in the ghetto before and after riots with concern and enthusiasm.

A multitude of news and information sources other than the established news media are relied upon in the ghetto. One of our studies found that 79 percent of a total of 567 ghetto residents interviewed in seven cities* first heard about the outbreak in their own city by word of mouth. Telephone and word of mouth exchanges on the streets, in churches, stores, pool halls, and bars, provide more information—and rumors—about events of direct concern to ghetto residents than the more conventional news media.

Among the established media, television and radio are far more popular in the ghetto than newspapers. Radios there, apparently, are ordinarily listened to less for news than for music and other programs. One survey showed that an overwhelmingly large number of Negro children and teenagers (like their white counterparts) listen to the radio for music alone, interspersed by disc jockey chatter. In other age groups, the response of most people about what they listen to on the radio was "anything," leading to the conclusion that radio in the ghetto is basically a background accompaniment.

But the fact that radio is such a constant background accompaniment can make it an important influence on people's attitudes, and perhaps on their actions once trouble develops. This is true for several reasons. News presented on local "rock" stations seldom constitutes much more than terse headline items which may startle or frighten but seldom inform. Radio disc jockeys and those who preside over the popular "talk shows" keep a steady patter of information going over the air. When a city is beset by civil strife, this patter can both inform transistor radio-carrying young people where the action is, and terrify their elders and much of the white community. "Burn, baby, burn,"

---

* Detroit, Newark, Atlanta, Tampa, New Haven, Cincinnati, Milwaukee.

the slogan of the Watts riot, was inadvertently originated by a radio disc jockey.

Thus, radio can be an instrument of trouble and tension in a community threatened or inundated with civil disorder. It can also do much to minimize fear by putting fast-paced events into proper perspective. We have found commendable instances, for example, in Detroit, Milwaukee, and New Brunswick, of radio stations and personalities using their air time and influence to try to calm potential rioters. In the next section, we recommend procedures for meetings and consultations for advance planning among those who will cover civil disorders. It is important that radio personnel, and especially disc jockeys and talk show hosts, be included in such preplanning.

Television is the formal news source most relied upon in the ghetto. According to one report, more than 75 percent of the sample turned to television for national and international news, and a larger percentage of the sample (86 percent) regularly watched television from 5 to 7 p.m., the dinner hours when the evening news programs are broadcast.

The significance of broadcasting in news dissemination is seen in Census Bureau estimates that in June 1967, 87.7 percent of nonwhite households and 94.8 percent of white households had television sets.

When ghetto residents do turn to newspapers, most read tabloids, if available, far more frequently than standard size newspapers and rely on the tabloids primarily for light features, racing charts, comic strips, fashion news and display advertising.

## CONDUCT OF PRESS REPRESENTATIVES

Most newsmen appear to be aware and concerned that their very physical presence can exacerbate a small disturbance, but some have conducted themselves with a startling lack of common sense. News organizations, particularly television networks, have taken substantial steps to minimize the effect of the physical presence of their employees at a news event. Networks have issued internal instructions calling for use of unmarked cars and small cameras and tape recorders, and most stations instruct their cameramen to film without artificial light whenever possible. Still, some newsmen have done things "for the sake of the story" that could have contributed to tension.

Reports have come to the Commission's attention of individual newsmen staging events, coaxing youths to throw rocks and interrupt traffic, and otherwise acting irresponsibly at the incipient stages of a disturbance. Such acts are the responsibility of the news organization as well as of its individual reporter.

Two examples occurred in Newark. Television cameramen, according to officials, crowded into and in front of police headquarters, interfering with law enforcement operations and "making a general nuisance of themselves." In a separate incident, a New York newspaper photographer covering the Newark riot repeatedly urged and finally convinced a Negro boy to throw a rock for the camera. Crowding may occasionally be unavoidable; staging of events is not.

We believe every effort should be made to eliminate this sort of conduct. This requires the implementation of thoughtful, stringent staff guidelines for reporters and editors. Such guidelines, carefully formulated, widely disseminated, and strictly enforced, underlie the self-policing activities of some news organizations already, but they must be universally adopted if they are to be effective in curbing journalistic irresponsibility.

The Commission has studied the internal guidelines in use last summer at the Associated Press, United Press International, the Washington Post and the Columbia Broadcasting System. Many other news organizations, large and small, have similar guidelines. In general, the guidelines urge extreme care to ensure that reporting is thorough and balanced and that words and statistics used are appropriate and accurate. The AP guidelines call for broad investigation into the immediate and underlying causes of an incident. The CBS guidelines demand as much caution as possible to avoid the danger of camera equipment and lights exacerbating the disturbance.

Internal guidelines can, and all those studied do, go beyond problems of physical presence at a disturbance to the substantive aspects of searching out, reporting, and writing the story. But the content of the guidelines is probably less important than the fact that the subject has been thoughtfully considered and hammered out within the organization, and an approach developed that is designed to meet the organization's particular needs and solve its particular problems.

We recommend that every news organization that does not now

have some form of guidelines—or suspects that those it has are not working effectively—designate top editors to (a) meet with its reporters who have covered or might be assigned to riots, (b) discuss in detail the problems and procedures which exist or are expected and (c) formulate and disseminate directives based on the discussions. Regardless of the specific provisions, the vital step is for every news-gathering organization to adopt and implement at least some minimal form of internal control.

# A RECOMMENDATION TO IMPROVE RIOT COVERAGE

## A NEED FOR BETTER COMMUNICATION

A recurrent problem in the coverage of last summer's disorders was friction and lack of cooperation between police officers and working reporters. Many experienced and capable journalists complained that policemen and their commanding officers were at best apathetic and at worst overtly hostile toward reporters attempting to cover a disturbance. Policemen, on the other hand, charged that many reporters seemed to forget that the task of the police is to restore order.

After considering available evidence on the subject, the Commission is convinced that these conditions reflect an absence of advance communication and planning among the people involved. We do not suggest that familiarity with the other's problems will beget total amity and cooperation. The interests of the media and the police are sometimes necessarily at variance. But we do believe that communication is a vital step toward removing the obstacles produced by ignorance, confusion, and misunderstanding of what each group is actually trying to do.

## MUTUAL ORIENTATION

What is needed first is a series of discussions, perhaps a combination of informal gatherings and seminar-type workshops. They should encompass all ranks of the police, all levels of media employees, and a cross-section of city officials. At first these would be get-acquainted sessions—to air complaints and discuss common problems. Working reporters should get to know the police who would be likely to draw duty in a disorder. Police and city officials should use the sessions for frank and candid briefings on the problems the city might face and official plans for dealing with disturbances.

Later sessions might consider procedures to facilitate the physical movement of personnel and speed the flow of accurate and complete news. Such arrangements might involve nothing more than a procedure for designating specific locations at which police officers would be available to escort a reporter into a dangerous area. In addition, policemen and reporters working together might devise better methods of identification, communication, and training.

Such procedures are infinitely variable and depend on the initiative, needs, and desires of those involved. If there is no existing institution or procedure for convening such meetings, we urge the mayor or city manager to do so in every city where experience suggests the possibility of future trouble. To allay any apprehension that discussions with officials might lead to restraints on the freedom to seek out and report the news, participants in these meetings should stipulate beforehand that freedom of access to all areas for reporters will be preserved.

## DESIGNATION OF INFORMATION OFFICERS

It is desirable to designate and prepare a number of police officers to act as media information officers. There should be enough of these so that, in the event of a disturbance, a reporter will not have to seek far to find a policeman ready and able to give him information and answer questions. Officers should be of high enough rank within the police department to have ready access to information.

## CREATION OF AN INFORMATION CENTER

A nerve center for reliable police and official government information should be planned and ready for activation when a disturbance reaches a predetermined point of intensity. Such a center might be located at police headquarters or city hall. It should be directed by an experienced, high-ranking information specialist with close ties to police officials. It is imperative, of course, that all officials keep a steady flow of accurate information coming into the center. Ideally, rooms would be set aside for taping and filming interviews with public officials. Local television stations might cut costs and relieve congestion by pooling some equipment at this central facility. An information center should not be thought of as replacing other news sources inside and outside the disturbance area. If anything, our studies suggest that reporters are already too closely tied to police and officials as news sources in a disorder. An information center should not be permitted to intensify this dependence. Properly conceived, however, a center can supplement on-the-spot reporting and supply news about official action.

## OUT-OF-TOWN REPORTERS

Much of the difficulty last summer apparently revolved around relations between local law enforcement officials and out-of-town reporters. These reporters are likely to be less sensitive about preserving the "image" of the local community.

Still, local officials serve their city badly when they ignore or impede national media representatives instead of informing them about the city, and cooperating with their attempts to cover the story. City and police officials should designate liaison officers and distribute names and telephone numbers of police and other relevant officials, the place they can be found if trouble develops, and other information likely to be useful.

National and other news organizations, in turn, could help matters by selecting a responsible home office official to act as liaison in these cases and to be accessible by phone to local officials who encounter difficulty with on-the-spot representatives of an organization. . . .

# REPORTING RACIAL PROBLEMS IN THE UNITED STATES

## A FAILURE TO COMMUNICATE

The Commission's major concern with the news media is not in riot reporting as such, but in the failure to report adequately on race relations and ghetto problems and to bring more Negroes into journalism. Concern about this was expressed by a number of participants in our Poughkeepsie conference. Disorders are only one aspect of the dilemmas and difficulties of race relations in America. In defining, explaining, and reporting this broader, more complex and ultimately far more fundamental subject, the communications media, ironically, have failed to communicate.

They have not communicated to the majority of their audience—which is white—a sense of the degradation, misery, and hopelessness of living in the ghetto. They have not communicated to whites a feeling for the difficulties and frustrations of being a Negro in the United States. They have not shown understanding or appreciation of—and thus have not communicated—a sense of Negro culture, thought, or history.

Equally important, most newspaper articles and most television programing ignore the fact [that] an appreciable part of their audience is black. The world that television and newspapers offer to their black audience is almost totally white, in both appearance and attitude. As we have said, our evidence shows that the so-called "white press" is at best mistrusted and at worst held in contempt by many black Americans. Far too often, the press acts and talks about Negroes as if Negroes do not read the newspapers or watch television, give birth, marry, die, and go to PTA meetings. Some newspapers and stations are beginning to make efforts to fill this void, but they have still a long way to go.

The absence of Negro faces and activities from the media has an effect on white audiences as well as black. If what the white American reads in the newspapers or sees on television conditions his expectation of what is ordinary and normal in the larger society, he will neither understand nor accept the black American. By failing to portray the Negro as a matter of routine and in the context of the total society, the news media have, we believe, contributed to the black-white schism in this country.

When the white press does refer to Negroes and Negro problems it frequently does so as if Negroes were not a part of the audience. This is perhaps understandable in a system where whites edit and, to a large extent, write news. But such attitudes, in an area as sensitive and inflammatory as this, feed Negro alienation and intensify white prejudices.

We suggest that a top editor or news director monitor his news production for a period of several weeks, taking note of how certain stories and language will affect black readers or viewers. A Negro staff member could do this easily. Then the staff should be informed about the problems involved.

The problems of race relations coverage go beyond incidents of white bias. Many editors and news directors, plagued by shortages of staff and lack of reliable contacts and sources of information in the city, have failed to recognize the significance of the urban story and to develop resources to cover it adequately.

We believe that most news organizations do not have direct access to diversified news sources in the ghetto. Seldom do they have a total sense of what is going on there. Some of the blame rests on Negro leaders who do not trust the media and will not deal candidly with representatives of the white press. But the real failure rests with the news organizations themselves. They—like other elements of the white community—have ignored the ghettos for decades. Now they seek instant acceptance and cooperation.

The development of good contacts, reliable information, and understanding requires more effort and time than an occasional visit by a team of reporters to do a feature on a newly-discovered ghetto problem. It requires reporters permanently assigned to this beat. They must be adequately trained and supported to dig out and tell the story of a major social upheaval—among the most complicated, portentous and explosive our society has known. We believe, also, that the Negro press—manned largely by people who live and work in the ghetto—could be a particularly useful source of information and guidance about activities in the black community. Reporters and editors from Negro newspapers and radio stations should be included in any conference between media and police-city representatives, and we suggest that large news organizations would do well to establish better lines of communication to their counterparts in the Negro press.*

---

* We have not, in this report, examined the Negro press in detail. The thrust of our studies was directed at daily mass circulation, mass audience media which are aimed at the community as a whole.

In short, the news media must find ways of exploring the problems of the Negro and the ghetto more deeply and more meaningfully. To editors who say "we have run thousands of inches on the ghetto which nobody reads" and to television executives who bemoan scores of underwatched documentaries, we say: find more ways of telling this story, for it is a story you, as journalists, must tell—honestly, realistically, and imaginatively. It is the responsibility of the news media to tell the story of race relations in America, and with notable exceptions, the media have not yet turned to the task with the wisdom, sensitivity, and expertise it demands.

## NEGROES IN JOURNALISM

The journalistic profession has been shockingly backward in seeking out, hiring, training, and promoting Negroes. Fewer than 5 percent of the people employed by the news business in editorial jobs in the United States today are Negroes. Fewer than 1 percent of editors and supervisors are Negroes, and most of them work for Negro-owned organizations. The lines of various news organizations to the militant blacks are, by admission of the newsmen themselves, almost nonexistent. The plaint is, "we can't find qualified Negroes." But this rings hollow from an industry where, only yesterday, jobs were scarce and promotion unthinkable for a man whose skin was black. Even today, there are virtually no Negroes in positions of editorial or executive responsibility and there is only one Negro newsman with a nationally syndicated column.

News organizations must employ enough Negroes in positions of significant responsibility to establish an effective link to Negro actions and ideas and to meet legitimate employment expectations. Tokenism—the hiring of one Negro reporter, or even two or three—is no longer enough. Negro reporters are essential, but so are Negro editors, writers and commentators. Newspaper and television policies are, generally speaking, not set by reporters. Editorial decisions about which stories to cover and which to use are made by editors. Yet, very few Negroes in this country are involved in making these decisions, because very few, if any, supervisory editorial jobs are held by Negroes. We urge the news media to do everything possible to train and promote their Negro reporters to positions where those who are qualified can contribute to and have an effect on policy decisions.

It is not enough, though, as many editors have pointed out to the Commission, to search for Negro journalists. Journalism is not very popular as a career for aspiring young Negroes. The starting pay is comparatively low and it is a business which has, until recently, discouraged and rejected them. The recruitment of Negro reporters must extend beyond established journalists, or those who have already formed ambitions along these lines. It must become a commitment to seek out young Negro men and women, inspire them to become—and then train them as—journalists. Training programs should be started at high schools and intensified at colleges. Summer vacation and part-time editorial jobs, coupled with offers of permanent employment, can awaken career plans.

We believe that the news media themselves, their audiences and the country will profit from these undertakings. For if the media are to comprehend and then to project the Negro community, they must have the help of Negroes. If the media are to report with understanding, wisdom and sympathy on the problems of the cities and the problems of the black man—for the two are increasingly intertwined—they must employ, promote and listen to Negro journalists.

## THE NEGRO IN THE MEDIA

Finally, the news media must publish newspapers and produce programs that recognize the existence and activities of the Negro, both as a Negro and as part of the community. It would be a contribution of inestimable importance to race relations in the United States simply to treat ordinary news about Negroes as news of other groups is now treated.

Specifically, newspapers should integrate Negroes and Negro activities into all parts of the paper, from the news, society and club pages to the comic strips. Television should develop programing which integrates Negroes into all aspects of televised presentations. Television is such a visible medium that some constructive steps are easy and obvious. While some of these steps are being taken, they are still largely neglected. For example, Negro reporters and performers should appear more frequently—and at prime time—in news broadcasts, on weather shows, in documentaries, and in advertisements. Some effort already has been made to use Negroes in television commercials. Any initial surprise at seeing a Negro selling a sponsor's product will eventually fade into routine acceptance, an attitude that white society must ultimately develop toward all Negroes.

In addition to news-related programing, we think that Negroes should appear more frequently in dramatic and comedy series. Moreover, networks and local stations should present plays and other programs whose subjects are rooted in the ghetto and its problems.

# INSTITUTE OF URBAN COMMUNICATIONS

The Commission is aware that in this area, as in all other aspects of race relations, the problems are great and it is much easier to state them than to solve them. Various pressures—competitive, financial, advertising—may impede progress toward more balanced, in-depth coverage and toward the hiring and training of more Negro personnel. Most newspapers and local television and radio stations do not have the resources or the time to keep abreast of all the technical advances, academic theories, and government programs affecting the cities and the lives of their black inhabitants.

During the course of this study, the Commission members and the staff have had many conversations with publishers, editors, broadcasters, and reporters throughout the country. The consensus appears to be that most of them would like to do much more but simply do not have the resources for independent efforts in either training or coverage.

The Commission believes that some of these problems could be resolved if there were a central organization to develop, gather, and distribute talent, resources, and information and to keep the work of the press in this field under review. For this reason, the Commission proposes the establishment of an Institute of Urban Communications on a private, nonprofit basis. The Institute would have neither governmental ties nor governmental authority. Its board would consist in substantial part of professional journalists and, for the rest, of distinguished public figures. The staff would be made up of journalists and students of the profession. Funding would be sought initially from private foundations. Ultimately, it may be hoped, financial support would be forthcoming from within the profession.

The Institute would be charged, in the first instance, with general responsibility for carrying out the media recommendations of the Commission, though as it developed a momentum and life of its own it would also gain its own view of the problems and possibilities. Initial tasks would include:

**1. Training and Education for Journalists in the Field of Urban Affairs.** The Institute should organize and sponsor, on its own and in cooperation with universities and other institutions, a comprehensive range of courses, seminars and workshops designed to give reporters, editors, and publishers the background they need to cover the urban scene. Offerings would vary in duration and intensity from weekend conferences to grants for year-long individual study on the order of the Nieman fellowships.

All levels and all kinds of news outlets should be served. A most important activity might be to assist disc jockeys and commentators on stations that address themselves especially to the Negro community. Particularly important would be sessions of a month or more for seasoned reporters and editors, comparable to middle management seminars or midcareer training in other callings. The press must have all of the intellectual resources and background to give adequate coverage to the city and the ghetto. It should be the first duty of the Institute to see that this is provided.

**2. Recruitment, Training and Placement of Negro Journalists.** The scarcity of Negroes in responsible news jobs intensifies the difficulties of communicating the reality of the contemporary American city to white newspaper and television audiences. The special viewpoint of the Negro who has lived through these problems and bears their marks upon him is, as we have seen, notably absent from what is, on the whole, a white press. But full integration of Negroes into the journalistic profession is imperative in its own right. It is unacceptable that the press, itself the special beneficiary of fundamental constitutional protections, should lag so far behind other fields in giving effect to the fundamental human right to equality of opportunity.

To help correct this situation, the Institute will have to undertake far-ranging activities. Providing educational opportunities for would-be Negro journalists is not enough. There will have to be changes in career outlooks for Negro students and their counselors back to the secondary school level. And changes in these attitudes will come slowly unless there is a change in the reality of employment and advancement opportunities for Negroes in journalism. This requires an aggressive placement program, seeking out newspapers, television and radio stations that discriminate, whether consciously or unconsciously, and mobilizing the pressures, public, private, and legal, necessary to break the pattern. The Institute might also provide assistance to Negro newspapers, which now recruit and train many young journalists.

**3. Police-Press Relations.** The Commission has stressed the failures in this area, and has laid out a set of remedial measures for action at the local level. But if reliance is placed exclusively on local initiative we can predict that in many places—often those that need it most—our recommended steps will not be taken. Pressure from the Federal Government for action along the lines proposed would be suspect, probably, by both press and local officials. But the Institute could undertake the task of stimulating community action in line with the Commission's recommendations without arousing local hostility and suspicion. Moreover, the Institute could serve as a clearinghouse for exchange of experience in this field.

**4. Review of Media Performance on Riots and Racial Issues.** The Institute should review press and television coverage of riot and racial news and publicly award praise and blame. The Commission recognizes that government restraints or guidelines in this field are both unworkable and incompatible with our Constitution and traditions. Internal guidelines or voluntary advance arrangements may be useful, but they tend to be rather general and the standards they prescribe are neither self-applying nor self-enforcing. We believe it would be healthy for reporters and editors who work in this sensitive field to know that others will be viewing their work and will hold them publicly accountable for lapses from accepted standards of good journalism. The Institute should publicize its findings by means of regular and special reports. It might also set a series of awards for especially meritorious work of individuals or news organizations in race relations reporting.

**5. An Urban Affairs Service.** Whatever may be done to improve the quality of reporting on urban affairs, there always will be a great many outlets that are too small to support the specialized investigation, reporting and interpreting needed in this field. To fill this gap, the Institute could organize a comprehensive urban news service, available at a modest fee to any news organization that wanted it. The Institute would have its own specially trained reporters, and it would also cull the national press for news and feature stories of broader interest that could be reprinted or broadcast by subscribers.

**6. Continuing Research.** Our own investigations have shown us that academic work on the impact of the media on race relations, its role in shaping attitudes, and the effects of the choices it makes on people's behavior, is in a rudimentary stage. The Commission's content analysis is the first study of its type of contemporary riot coverage, and it is extremely limited in scope. A whole range of questions needs intensive, scholarly exploration, and indeed the development of new modes of research and analysis. The Institute should undertake many of these important projects under its own auspices and could stimulate others in the academic community to further research.

Along with the country as a whole, the press has too long basked in a white world, looking out of it, if at all, with white men's eyes and a white perspective. That is no longer good enough. The painful process of readjustment that is required of the American news media must begin now. They must make a reality of integration—in both their product and personnel. They must insist on the highest standards of accuracy—not only reporting single events with care and skepticism, but placing each event into meaningful perspective. They must report the travail of our cities with compassion and in depth.

In all this, the Commission asks for fair and courageous journalism—commitment and coverage that are worthy of one of the crucial domestic stories in America's history.

# CHAPTER 17

# RECOMMENDATIONS FOR NATIONAL ACTION

—

## INTRODUCTION

The Commission has already addressed itself to the need for immediate action at the local level. Because the city is the focus of racial disorder, the immediate responsibility rests on community leaders and local institutions. Without responsive and representative local government, without effective processes of interracial communication within the city, and without alert, well-trained and adequately supported local police, national action—no matter how great its scale—cannot be expected to provide a solution.

Yet the disorders are not simply a problem of the racial ghetto or the city. As we have seen, they are symptoms of social ills that have become endemic in our society and now affect every American—black or white, businessman or factory worker, suburban commuter or slumdweller.

None of us can escape the consequences of the continuing economic and social decay of the central city and the closely related problem of rural poverty. The convergence of these conditions in the racial ghetto and the resulting discontent and disruption threaten democratic values fundamental to our progress as a free society.

The essential fact is that neither existing conditions nor the garrison state offers acceptable alternatives for the future of this country. Only a greatly enlarged commitment to national action—compassionate, massive and sustained, backed by the will and resources of the most powerful and the richest nation on this earth—can shape a future that is compatible with the historic ideals of American society.

It is this conviction that leads us, as a commission on civil disorders, to comment on the shape and dimension of the action that must be taken at the national level.

In this effort we have taken account of the work of scholars and experts on race relations, the urban condition and poverty. We have studied the reports and work of other commissions, of congressional committees, and of many special task forces and groups both within the Government and within the private sector. . . .

[No American—white or black—can escape the consequences of the continuing social and economic decay of our major cities.

Only a commitment to national action on an unprecedented scale can shape a future compatible with the historic ideals of American society.

The great productivity of our economy, and a Federal revenue system which is highly responsive to economic growth, can provide the resources.

The major need is to generate new will—the will to tax ourselves to the extent necessary to meet the vital needs of the Nation.

We have set forth goals and proposed strategies to reach those goals. We discuss and recommend programs not to commit each of us to specific parts of such programs, but to illustrate the type and dimension of action needed.

The major goal is the] creation of a true union—a single society and a single American identity. . . . Toward that goal, we propose the following objectives for national action:

- Opening up opportunities to those who are restricted by racial segregation and discrimination, and eliminating all barriers to their choice of jobs, education, and housing.
- Removing the frustration of powerlessness among the disadvantaged by providing the means for them to deal with

the problems that affect their own lives and by increasing the capacity of our public and private institutions to respond to these problems.

- Increasing communication across racial lines to destroy stereotypes, halt polarization, end distrust and hostility, and create common ground for efforts toward common goals of public order and social justice.

... We propose these aims to fulfill our pledge of equality and to meet the fundamental needs of a democratic and civilized society—domestic peace [and] social justice....

## I. EMPLOYMENT

... [Pervasive] unemployment and underemployment are among the most persistent and serious grievances [in minority areas. They are] inextricably linked to the problem of civil disorder.

[Despite growing Federal expenditures for manpower development and training programs, and sustained general economic prosperity and increasing demands for skilled workers, about 2 million—white and non-white—are permanently unemployed. About 10 million are underemployed, of whom 6.5 million work full time for wages below the poverty line.]

... [The] 500,000 "hard-core" unemployed [in] the central cities [who] lack a basic education [and are unable to hold a steady job are made up in large part of Negro males between the ages of] 18 and 25. [In the riot cities which we surveyed, Negroes were three times as likely as whites to hold unskilled jobs, which are often part time, seasonal, low paying and "dead end."]

... Negro males between the ages of 15 and 25 predominated among the rioters. More than 20 percent of the rioters were unemployed; and many of those who were employed worked in intermittent, low status, unskilled jobs—jobs which they regarded as below their level of education and ability....

[The Commission recommends that the Federal Government:

- Undertake joint efforts with cities and states to consolidate existing manpower programs to avoid fragmentation and duplication.
- Take immediate action to create 2 million new jobs over the next 3 years—1 million in the public sector and 1 million in the private sector—to absorb the hard-core unemployed and materially reduce the level of underemployment for all workers, black and white. We propose 250,000 public sector and 300,000 private sector jobs in the first year.
- Provide on-the-job training by both public and private employers with reimbursement to private employers for the extra costs of training the hard-core unemployed, by contract or by tax credits.
- Provide tax and other incentives to investment in rural as well as urban poverty areas in order to offer to the rural poor an alternative to migration to urban centers.
- Take new and vigorous action to remove artificial barriers to employment and promotion, including not only racial discrimination but, in certain cases, arrest records or lack of a high school diploma. Strengthen those agencies such as the Equal Employment Opportunity Commission, charged with eliminating discriminatory practices, and provide full support for Title VI of the 1964 Civil Rights Act allowing Federal grant-in-aid funds to be withheld from activities which discriminate on grounds of color or race.

The Commission commends the recent public commitment of the National Council of the Building and Construction Trades Unions, AFL–CIO, to encourage and recruit Negro membership in apprenticeship programs. This commitment should be intensified and implemented.]

# II. EDUCATION

. . . Education in our democratic society must equip the children of the nation to develop their potential and to participate fully in American life. For the community at large, the schools have discharged this responsibility well. But for many minorities, and particularly for the children of the ghetto, the schools have failed to provide the educational experience which could overcome the effects of discrimination and deprivation.

This failure is one of the persistent sources of grievance and resentment within the Negro community. The hostility of Negro parents and students toward the school system is generating increasing conflict and causing disruption within many city school districts.

But the most dramatic evidence of the relationship between educational practices and civil disorders lies in the high incidence of riot participation by ghetto youth who have not completed high school. . . .

The bleak record of public education for ghetto children is growing worse. In the critical skills—verbal and reading ability—Negro students fall further behind whites with each year of school completed. . . . [The high unemployment and underemployment rate for Negro youth is evidence, in part, of the growing educational crisis.]

We support integration as the priority education strategy because it is essential to the future of American society. We have seen in this last summer's disorders the consequences of racial isolation, at all levels, and of attitudes toward race, on both sides, produced by three centuries of myth, ignorance, and bias. It is indispensable that opportunities for interaction between the races be expanded. . . .

We recognize that the growing dominance of pupils from disadvantaged minorities in city school populations will not soon be reversed. No matter how great the effort toward desegregation, many children of the ghetto will not, within their school careers, attend integrated schools.

If existing disadvantages are not to be perpetuated, we must improve dramatically the quality of ghetto education. Equality of results with all-white schools . . . must be the goal. . . .

[To implement these strategies, the Commission recommends:

- Sharply increased efforts to eliminate de facto segregation in our schools through substantial federal aid to school systems seeking to desegregate either within the system or in cooperation with neighboring school systems.

- Elimination of racial discrimination in Northern as well as Southern schools by vigorous application of Title VI of the Civil Rights Act of 1964.
- Extension of quality early childhood education to every disadvantaged child in the country.
- Efforts to improve dramatically schools serving disadvantaged children through substantial federal funding of year-round quality compensatory education programs, improved teaching, and expanded experimentation and research.
- Elimination of illiteracy through greater Federal support for adult basic education.
- Enlarged opportunities for parent and community participation in the public schools.
- Reoriented vocational education emphasizing work-experience training and the involvement of business and industry.
- Expanded opportunities for higher education through increased federal assistance to disadvantaged students.
- Revision of state aid formulas to assure more per student aid to districts having a high proportion of disadvantaged school age children.]

## III. THE WELFARE SYSTEM

. . . Our present system of public [welfare] ". . . is designed to save money instead of people, and tragically ends up doing neither."

This system is deficient in two critical ways:

First, it excludes large numbers of persons who are in great need, and who, if provided a decent level of support, might be able to become more productive and self-sufficient. [No Federal funds are available for millions of unemployed and underemployed men and women who are needy but neither aged, handicapped nor the parents of minor children.]

Second, for those included, it provides assistance well below the minimum necessary for a decent level of existence, and imposes restrictions that encourage continued dependency on welfare and undermine self-respect. . . .

[A welter of statutory requirements and administrative practices and regulations operate to remind recipients that they are considered untrustworthy, promiscuous, and lazy. Residence requirements prevent assistance to people in need who are newly arrived in the state. Searches of recipients' homes violate privacy. Inadequate social services compound the problems.

The Commission recommends that the Federal Government, acting with state and local governments where necessary, reform the existing welfare system to:

- Establish, for recipients in existing welfare categories, uniform national standards of assistance at least as high as the annual "poverty level" of income, now set by the Social Security Administration at $3,335 per year for an urban family of four.
- Require that all states receiving Federal welfare contributions participate in the Aid to Families with Dependent Children-Unemployed Parents Program (AFDC–UP) that permits assistance to families with both father and mother in the home, thus aiding the family while it is still intact.
- Bear a substantially greater portion of all welfare costs—at least 90 percent of total payments.
- Increase incentives for seeking employment and job training, but remove restrictions recently enacted by the Congress that would compel mothers of young children to work.
- Provide more adequate social services through neighborhood centers and family-planning program.
- Remove the freeze placed by the 1967 welfare amendments on the percentage of children in a State that can be covered by Federal assistance.
- Eliminate residence requirements.

As a long-range goal, the Commission recommends that the Federal Government seek to develop a national system of income supplementation based strictly on need] with two broad and basic purposes:

- To provide, for those who can work or who do work, any necessary supplements in such a way as to develop incentives for fuller employment;

- To provide, for those who cannot work and for mothers who decide to remain with their children, a minimum standard of decent living, and to aid in saving children from the prison of poverty that has held their parents.

. . . A broad system of supplementation would involve substantially greater Federal expenditures than anything now contemplated. The cost will range widely depending on the standard of need accepted as the "basic allowance" to individuals and families, and on the rate at which additional income above this level is taxed. Yet if the deepening cycle of poverty and dependence on welfare can be broken, if the children of the poor can be given the opportunity to scale the wall that now separates them from the rest of society, the return on this investment will be great indeed. . . .

# IV. HOUSING

[After more than three decades of fragmented and grossly underfunded Federal housing programs, nearly 6 million substandard housing units remain occupied in the United States.

The housing problem is particularly acute in the minority ghettos. Nearly two-thirds of all nonwhite families living in the central cities today live in neighborhoods marked by substandard housing and general urban blight. Two major factors are responsible:

First: Many ghetto residents simply cannot pay the rent necessary to support decent housing. In Detroit, for example, over 40 percent of the nonwhite-occupied units in 1960 required rent of over 35 percent of the tenants' income.

Second: Discrimination prevents access to many nonslum areas, particularly the suburbs, where good housing exists. In addition, by creating a "back pressure" in the racial ghettos, it makes it possible for landlords to break up apartments for denser occupancy, and keeps prices and rents of deteriorated ghetto housing higher than they would be in a truly free market.]

To date, Federal building programs have been able to do comparatively little to provide housing for the disadvantaged. In the 31-year history of subsidized Federal housing, only about 800,000 units have been constructed, with recent production averaging about 50,000 units a year. By comparison, over a period only 3 years longer, FHA insurance guarantees have made possible the construction of over 10 million middle and upper income units.

[Two points are fundamental to the Commission's recommendations: First:] Federal housing programs must . . . be given a new thrust aimed at overcoming the prevailing patterns of racial segregation. If this is not done, those programs will continue to concentrate the most impoverished and dependent segments of the population into the central-city ghettos where there is already a critical gap between the needs of the population and the public resources to deal with them.

[Second: The private sector must be brought into the production and financing of low and moderate-rental housing to supply the capabilities and capital necessary to meet the housing needs of the Nation.

The Commission recommends that the Federal Government:

- Enact a comprehensive and enforceable Federal open-housing law to cover the sale or rental of all housing, including single-family homes.
- Reorient Federal housing programs to place more low- and moderate-income housing outside of ghetto areas.
- Bring within the reach of low- and moderate-income families within the next 5 years 6 million new and existing units of decent housing, beginning with 600,000 units in the next year.

To reach this goal we recommend:

- Expansion and modification of the rent supplement program to permit use of supplements for existing housing, thus greatly increasing the reach of the program.
- Expansion and modification of the below-market interest rate program to enlarge the interest subsidy to all sponsors, provide interest-free loans to nonprofit sponsors to cover pre-construction costs, and permit sale of projects to nonprofit corporations, co-operatives, or condominiums.

- Creation of an ownership supplement program similar to present rent supplements, to make home ownership possible for low-income families.
- Federal writedown of interest rates on loans to private builders constructing moderate-rent housing.
- Expansion of the public housing program, with emphasis on small units on scattered sites, and leasing and "turnkey" programs.
- Expansion of the Model Cities program.
- Expansion and reorientation of the urban renewal program to give priority to projects directly assisting low-income households to obtain adequate housing.]

# CONCLUSION

One of the first witnesses to be invited to appear before this Commission was Dr. Kenneth B. Clark, a distinguished and perceptive scholar. Referring to the reports of earlier riot commissions, he said:

> I read that report * * * of the 1919 riot in Chicago, and it is as if I were reading the report of the investigating committee on the Harlem riot of 1935, the report of the investigating committee on the Harlem riot of 1943, the report of the McCone Commission on the Watts riot.
>
> I must again in candor say to you members of this Commission—it is a kind of Alice in Wonderland with the same moving picture reshown over and over again, the same analysis, the same recommendations, and the same inaction.

These words come to our minds as we conclude this report.

We have provided an honest beginning. We have learned much. But we have uncovered no startling truths, no unique insights, no simple solutions. The destruction and the bitterness of racial disorder, the harsh polemics of black revolt and white repression have been seen and heard before in this country.

It is time now to end the destruction and the violence, not only in the streets of the ghetto but in the lives of people.

# FREQUENTLY ASKED QUESTIONS

———

*Why didn't Black people just move out of bad neighborhoods?*

A long history of housing discrimination has prevented Black people in cities from moving to better-resourced neighborhoods. Certainly a lot of people tried to move and were met with restrictive covenants, legal agreements that prohibited specific racial groups from purchasing real estate in particular communities—typically predominantly white communities. Black people were often met by angry neighbors and violence to keep them from moving out of depleted neighborhoods. There were also economic factors. The Black middle class was historically much smaller than the white middle class. Racist hiring practices and the refusal to hire Black people in higher-salaried jobs created another hurdle that prevented a large number of people from moving into what was seen as majority-white middle-class neighborhoods. The narrative around white flight is that it happened after cities were burned in the 1960s. But actually it started twenty years earlier. In a lot of ways, the riots were a response to the reality that so many white people had already moved out of those communities. Immediately after World War II, a growing number of suburban communities and middle-class communities were racially restricted. And so services, opportunities, quality education all migrated to these new places, leaving a depleted tax base in their wake and populations that were increasingly desperate, increasingly impoverished, and increasingly angry.

### *The introduction talked a lot about policing but not crime. Are the problems with police relations just a result of Black people committing more crime?*

There's a problem with presuming a relationship between race, crime, and policing. Statistically there is a higher incidence of some crimes among African Americans. But one of the easiest ways to dispel that presumption is to point out that white Americans have phenomenally high homicide rates compared to white people in other Western democracies, but nowhere would we say that the amount of violent crime committed by white people in American society warrants aggressively policing them *as a racial category.* Men are much more likely to commit murder than women, but we don't societally endorse the wholesale profiling and aggressive policing of men as an entire demographic. Nowhere do we presume that men, who are far more likely to commit acts of violence than women, are a problem categorically, for instance. And so we have racial profiling in Black communities in a way that doesn't happen in white communities or with violence in other parts of the population.

Today the vast majority of arrests are for nonviolent offenses—behavior as inoffensive as vandalism or jaywalking. Any neighborhood put under the same level of policing as Black neighborhoods would have a much higher crime rate. But there just aren't enough police to arrest every jaywalker or vandal or nonviolent drug offender in the suburbs as there are in inner cities.

As the *Kerner Report* points out, policing over the course of many years became a proxy for lots of other institutions that were failing. People had difficulty finding quality education for their children or jobs paying reasonable wages, but they didn't have a problem coming into contact with police. The police became the only well-funded and omnipresent state institution in inner-city communities. The result was resentment that built up, and that produced something else that the report talks about: uprisings that became an outlet for that resentment and anger.

## *Why do people burn down their own neighborhoods?*

It's interesting that critics refer to these places as "their own neighborhoods." One of the things that historically motivates people during uprisings is that they don't feel a sense of ownership or that they are stakeholders in their community. They feel that institutions generally do not serve them well. Asking them why someone would have burned down their neighborhood is the kind of question that a stakeholder in a particular community would ask someone who very much feels they are not one. The people who live in the community not only don't feel like stakeholders, but often feel their actions are targeting institutions—and an entire system—that have specifically exploited them. The physical structures that are burned are just symbols of that system that has made progress so difficult in their lives. To use Kerner's word, the "ghetto" is an extractive economy. The people who profit from businesses in the community do not live in the neighborhood. So the neighborhood itself is a symbol of these bigger problems.

## *How come nothing has been done about these problems?*

The *Kerner Report* came out at the exact moment when liberalism, as it was then known, was about to collapse. It came out just months ahead of the 1968 presidential election, in which Richard Nixon famously ran on a law-and-order platform and raised support among many people, most of them white, who felt that the uprisings and riots in American cities were nothing more than the lawlessness of hoodlums and people who lacked the values of American society: hard work, religion, family, etc. In that climate the political possibilities were curtailed; certainly the likelihood of government following up on the many suggestions of the *Kerner Report* was curtailed. Most of the report's suggestions attempted to bring American society's treatment of African Americans closer to the country's professed ideals. After Nixon, a series of administrations, both Democratic and Republican, were more invested in punitive responses to what they saw as failures of African Americans to live up to the standard of American ideals.

*The report says that we have two different societies, one Black,*
*one white, separate and unequal. That was 1967. We've since had*
*a Black president. Do you think the assessment of the report still is*
*the case today?*

It's absolutely still the case today. Just look at one specific example: enfranchisement and voting rights. Through gerrymandering,
through purging of voter rolls in majority-Black neighborhoods, and
through the inability of formerly incarcerated people to vote, we have
two completely different relationships to a right as basic as voting. In
many instances there has been a wholesale attempt to disenfranchise
Black voters in the United States. If voting is one of our key rights
and responsibilities of citizenship, then there are not just two different
societies, but a tiered citizenry. Voting is the most obvious example.
We could also look at the data on life expectancy, infant mortality,
lifetime earnings, wealth, educational attainment, employment status,
and the criminal-justice system and see equally stark disparities that
stubbornly correlate with racial categories. That we have two different
societies is one of the most damning statements in the report, and
unfortunately it remains one of the truest.

*There is much conversation currently about abolishing or defunding*
*the police. Did the* **Kerner Report** *examine this question?*

Surprisingly, yes. The *Kerner Report* talked decades ago about the phenomenon of police being involved in many situations that would be
better handled by other social-service institutions, and it recognized
that this could have the effect of exacerbating tension between the
police and the communities they are supposed to serve. The report
made two suggestions. One is that police departments look at the
overreliance on them as an opportunity to establish connection and
rapport with the communities that they're involved in. The second
suggestion is to use other institutions. The commission doesn't say specifically what these might be, but does say that police can refer these
kinds of non-law-enforcement problems to other social-service institutions so that a person need not have contact with police every time
he or she has a verbal dispute or plays music too loud or is involved

in some other small civic infraction that could be handled better and with less possibility of conflict by another institution. This is the essence of what the Defund the Police movement wants—to offload concerns that have fallen under the rubric of policing, sometimes with disastrous results, to be handled by people better equipped to resolve them nonviolently.

It is ironic that the Defund the Police movement emerged in 2020 as an idea associated with the radical left but was proposed fifty-two years earlier by a commission whose overall outlook is as centrist liberal as one could imagine.

### *Is one political party more responsible for the problems with policing and criminal justice than the other?*

While it is easy in the present moment to assume that this might be true, the answer is really no. From the 1970s onward, both Republicans and Democrats wholeheartedly rejected the building of a robust social safety net and spending on urban infrastructure, and instead prioritized the needs of suburbs to the detriment of inner cities and the people who lived there. See, for example, the bipartisan consensus on criminal justice policy in the 1990s. Much of the disinvestment in inner cities and the turn toward punitive public policy was supported by politicians on both sides of the aisle.

### *Has there been any progress since the* **Kerner Report** *first came out?*

We've seen some progress but it has been piecemeal. And even the biggest changes, at least on the federal level, required another huge uprising—the Rodney King riots in Los Angeles in 1992. The 1994 crime bill made provisions for the Department of Justice to provide oversight for chronically troubled police departments, places where violence had become a habitual and chronic factor in the interactions between police and community. And the tool, called a consent decree, has been used with varying degrees of success in the past quarter century. A few police departments, like the LAPD and Newark, New Jersey, seemed to make significant strides as a result of their consent decrees, but other cities were not nearly as successful. Some people dismiss consent decrees as incrementalism, but they are one of the most significant changes to come out since Kerner.

### Are there any other institutions besides policing that are connected to these issues?

I think the real question is, are there any institutions that are *not* connected to these issues in terms of racial inequality? The Kerner Report takes pains to point out that policing is not simply the problem, but rather the tip of the iceberg of a wider set of bureaucratic concerns and failures. It's unlikely that we would ever have a situation where we have communities with terrible schools, terrible housing, terrible municipal services, and high unemployment but really excellent policing. The problem is not policing. It's the climate of inequality in which policing exists, which warps lots of other institutions too.

One key element here is that police are the only one of these institutions that physically has contact with people, the only one whose representatives place their hands on members of these communities. But by no means should we take that as evidence that other institutions are implicated in the problems we're talking about right now.

### What can we do to not end up back in the same place in terms of civil disorders ten years from now?

The first thing we can do is create ways to limit the number of encounters that armed police have with Black Americans by creating alternate institutions, trained in de-escalation, trained in social work and dealing with mental health crises, who can answer to regular, everyday 911 calls that do not involve violent crimes, be it parking tickets, traffic collisions, people with mental health crisis, or homelessness. Creating such institutions needs adequate funding to achieve a more robust social safety net and urban infrastructure—better healthcare, better education, better housing.

***The* Kerner Report *is very critical of the media. How should the media cover riots, or as they call them, civil disturbances, now?***

I think the *Kerner Report*'s criticism of media goes even deeper than simply the coverage. The report went to the institutional faults in the media that made poor coverage a probability in the first place. It points out that, for instance, in 1967 and 1968 there were very few Black reporters of these stories and it calls for what we would now describe as diversification of the media. It also points out that some media do a better job than others—for instance those that avoid tabloid exaggeration about uprising—but they still don't seem to get the fundamental human dimensions beneath the stories.

These issues are relevant in the context of George Floyd's death, but we are dealing with a very different kind of media, now divided into cable and social media. Newspapers no longer carry the weight they did in 1968. News media are still overwhelmingly white and overwhelmingly male in a country that is rapidly diversifying, but depending upon what you look at, you are more or less likely to encounter the kinds of contextual details and historical frame of reference that made George Floyd's death more legible to the viewer.

And so, more than a half century after Kerner first made the observation, you can still say that there's a great deal of work that needs to be done in diversifying American media.

# ADDITIONAL READING

Michelle Alexander, *The New Jim Crow: Mass Incarceration in the Age of Colorblindness* (New York: New Press, 2012).

Radley Balko, *Rise of the Warrior Cop: The Militarization of America's Police Forces* (New York: PublicAffairs, 2013).

Nathan Connolly, *A World More Concrete: Real Estate and the Remaking of Jim Crow South Florida* (Chicago: University of Chicago Press, 2014).

Ruth Wilson Gilmore, *Golden Gulag: Prisons, Surplus, Crisis, and Opposition in Globalizing California* (Berkeley: University of California Press, 2007).

Elizabeth Hinton, *From the War on Poverty to the War on Crime: The Making of Mass Incarceration in America* (Cambridge, MA: Harvard University Press, 2016).

Kenneth T. Jackson, *Crabgrass Frontier: The Suburbanization of the United States* (New York: Oxford University Press, 1985).

Thomas J. Sugrue, *Origins of the Urban Crisis: Race and Inequality in Postwar Detroit* (Princeton, NJ: Princeton University Press, 2014).

Matt Taibbi, *I Can't Breathe: A Killing on Bay Street* (New York: Spiegel & Grau, 2017.